WATERCOLOR
ARTIST'S INDEX

Natural
Landscape

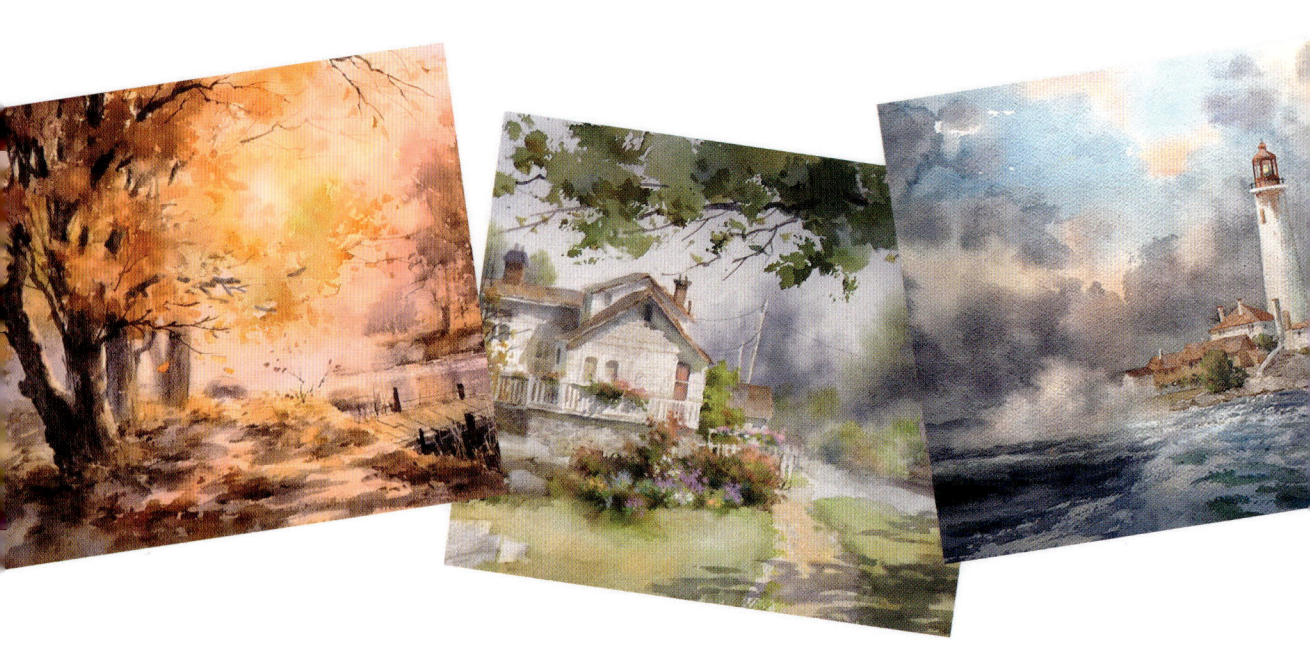

WATERCOLOR ARTIST'S INDEX

Natural Landscape

A Field Trip of Features and How to Paint Them

JOHANNES VLOOTHUIS

DAVID & CHARLES
—PUBLISHING—

www.davidandcharles.com

Contents

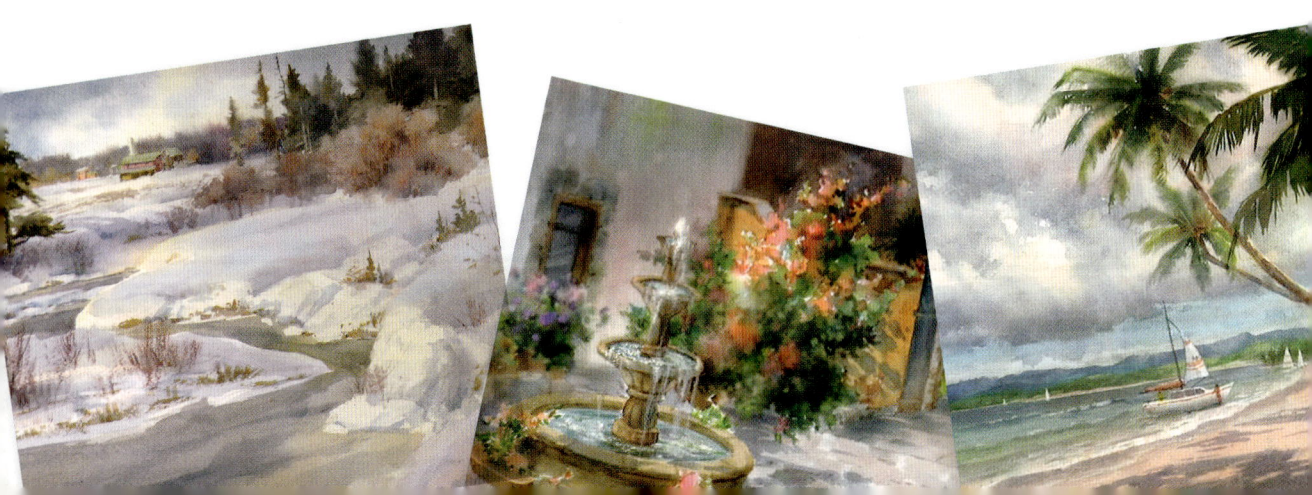

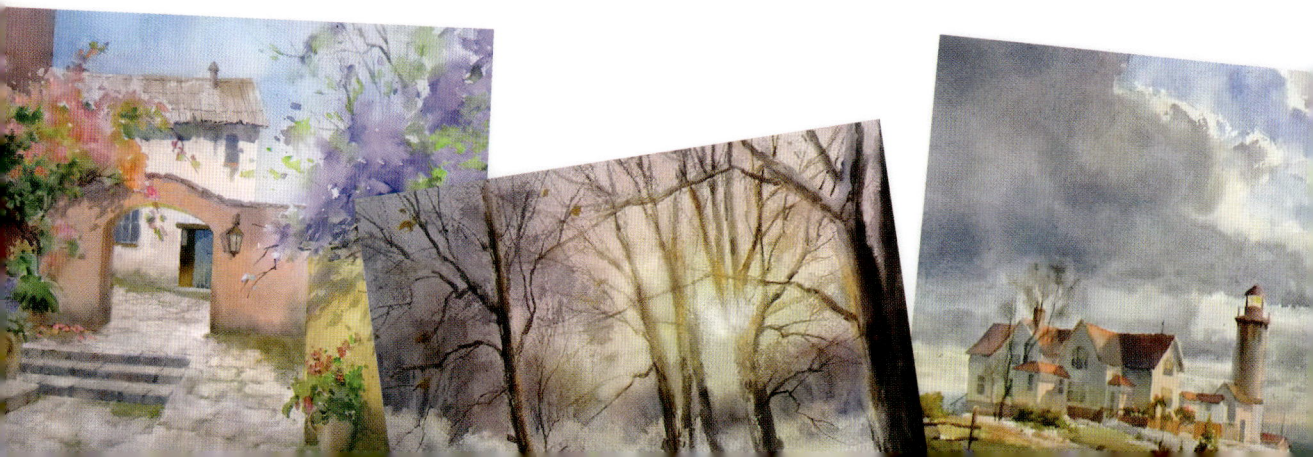

Why Paint with Watercolor?

Watercolor stands apart from other painting mediums because it relies on the white paper to be the equivalent of white paint. The transparency of the medium allows light to pass through the paint and reflect off the white paper. In return, it bounces off the surface layer as it reflects back to the viewer's eyes. This results in a brilliance only achievable in this medium. Think of it like a movie film, where the light passes through the film of paint, reflecting off the paper to reveal vibrant imagery.

I emphasize to my students that the wet-on-wet technique, where a wet medium is applied to wet paper, is vital in landscape painting, particularly for creating soft, ethereal effects in the background. Achieving realistic landscapes in watercolor can be challenging and is not wholly necessary as it often detracts from the medium's poetic qualities, where the abstract and lyrical message should take center stage. The inherent unpredictability of watercolor often leads to delightful, painterly surprises for those with experience, especially when the brush is moved fearlessly. A well-executed watercolor often evokes the sophisticated charm of a storybook illustration, much like those seen in high-quality animated films.

A PHILOSOPHICAL APPROACH TO LANDSCAPE PAINTING

Budding artists often fall into the trap of trying to document exactly what they see. After assessing more than a thousand paintings from students, I've found that the most common flaw in watercolor landscapes is the tendency to nitpick details and attempt to replicate a photo rather than exploit it to convey visual metaphors that substitute nature. These habits often stem from a lack of proper artistic training and the misconception that success in painting lies in accurate representation or in cramming in as many elements as possible—like a visual buffet.

In contrast, the most successful watercolor artists reinterpret real landscape elements as beautifully designed abstract shapes with enhanced colors that excel over nature's boring monochromatic shapes and contour lines.

This book will train you to capture the spirit of a scene rather than replicating the seen details.

Just as reading stimulates the imagination, making the reader an active participant in the story, visual art does the same. A painting's visual cues invite viewers to engage their imagination, mentally expanding the scene rather than simply observing it—sometimes even placing themselves within the narrative. It's human nature to romanticize mental adventures and stories, yet this concept, which I call "The Mind's Vision," is often overlooked in art instruction.

Don't be surprised when admirers of your work say, "I can hear the thunder rumbling in those clouds" or "I want to sit on that rock, dip my feet in the stream, and read a book." These responses are a sign that your painting has sparked their imagination—a welcome reaction.

THE PITFALLS OF WATERCOLOR

Watercolor's charm lies in its unpredictability, but that comes with its challenges. One such challenge is mastering wet-on-wet techniques to prevent the paint from spreading too far, losing a controllable contour, and in some cases causing unwanted backruns or blooms. Despite these challenges, don't shy away from wet-on-wet techniques.

Another major pitfall is how values change as the paint dries—typically lightening by up to 20 percent, especially in darker mixtures. This change can make achieving precise values quite difficult. When the correct value is vital, test your colors on a separate piece of watercolor paper and dry them using a hairdryer before committing to your painting. This simple step ensures greater accuracy and helps you avoid unpleasant surprises in your final work.

Avoid painting shapes too dark if their hue is indistinct from 10ft (3m) away, regardless of what the reference photo shows. Cameras often distort values compared to nature, exaggerating darker tones—even pushing them to black. Conversely, photos can bleach highlights to colorless white as well as fail to capture subtle color transitions, resulting in dull, muddy tones.

Unlike other mediums, watercolor requires you to "negative-paint" the darks into the lights. This skill takes practice to develop. Skill improves with practice and, by applying the techniques in this book, you will soon embrace watercolor's unique charm with confidence. Welcome its quirks, and it will reward you with surprises.

USING THIS BOOK

This book was designed specifically to guide you in developing new, appealing, thoughtfully constructed asymmetrical colorful shapes based on an internal visual language that will substitute real nature elements—helping you move beyond replication to creating art that resonates with beauty and intent.

As a successful art instructor, I encourage you to focus on practicing the step-by-step techniques in this book rather than jumping straight into a full painting. Mastering these baby steps will give you a sense of accomplishment and motivate you to keep going. This approach mirrors how I learned and how I teach my students—by imitating proven, well-designed shapes as fundamental building blocks that eventually will lead to full landscapes.

In the pages that follow you will find information on basic materials and instruction on the fundamental techniques involved in painting with watercolor: painting wet-on-wet and with a "dry brush." Following this are six chapters with step-by-step projects that focus on painting common features of a landscape: Foliage, Water, Sky, Ground, Rocks & Mountains, and Architecture. The two final chapters of the book look more closely at composition and "tricks of the trade" for creating a wide range of special effects from rock textures to sea spray and foliage clusters.

Note: Throughout the book, I reference certain terms that may require clarification. Please consult the glossary for definitions.

Materials

PAPER

Watercolor paper is crafted from cotton fibers, not wood pulp like regular paper. This cotton composition gives it durability, excellent absorbency, and the ability to withstand multiple washes, making it ideal for watercolor techniques.

Cold pressed: This is the paper I use most often because I appreciate its velvety appearance. It is less absorbent than rough paper, making it easier to spray away unwanted paint.

Rough: I often use rough paper for its textured surface, which allows me to achieve convincing loose foliage through dry-brushing. The paper's textured peaks help break up the paint into random-sized clusters, creating a natural, organic look. I primarily turn to rough paper when painting large trees and cumulus clouds. This surface also offers better control over wet paint expanding, as it absorbs water more readily, gripping the paint more effectively compared to cold-pressed paper. However, this increased absorption makes it harder to lift off paint for corrections (see Tricks of the Trade: Making Corrections).

BRUSHES

I prefer to paint using a blend of bright synthetic and sable brushes—sables for their water-holding capacity, and synthetics for their spring and resilience. My favorites are Winsor & Newton's Sceptre Gold brushes in ¾, ½, and ¼in (2, 1, and 0.5cm) sizes, along with several rigger brushes for lines ranging from thin to thick. I also use a chip brush for grasses, round brushes for fine details, and a large brush to wet the paper.

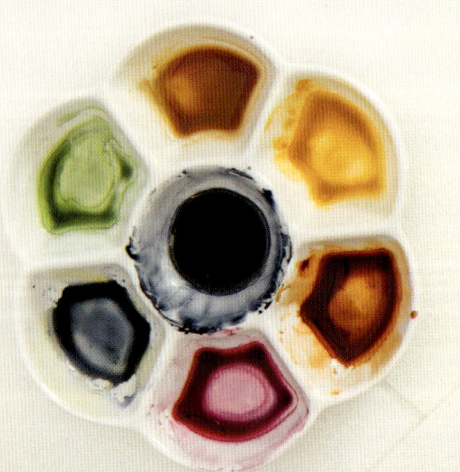

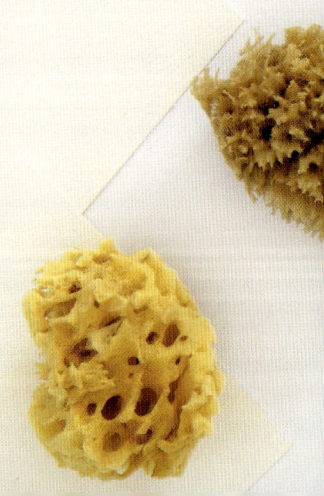

PALETTE

Within my palettes, I completely fill each section from a 1.35fl oz (40ml) tube of watercolor paint, placing the hues according to the color wheel. I then allow the paint to harden. Prior to a painting session, I spray the sections with water and keep the pigment wet so that it may easily be taken out into the mixing area.

For most applications, you only need six essential pigments: ultramarine blue, transparent yellow, permanent rose, raw sienna, Payne's gray, and burnt sienna. These will cover the vast majority of your mixing needs.

Be aware that some lower-cost student-quality pigments contain fillers, which can lead to muddy or dull results. I've used Winsor & Newton Artist's Quality paints throughout my professional career, though other professional-grade brands perform well too.

ADDITIONAL TOOLS AND EQUIPMENT

For more information on the items listed below, and the techniques you can achieve with them, see Tricks of the Trade.

- **Precision knife/jackknife:** For scoring and scraping to regain the white of the paper.

- **Credit card or palette knife:** Scrape paint to create texture, perfect for rocks and bark.

- **Sandpaper:** A range of grit sizes to create shimmers on lakes, water foam, and water spray.

- **Rubber masking fluid:** To block areas from receiving paint and restore the white paper.

- **Paper towel:** For dabbing to lighten values.

- **Sea sponge:** For creating foliage clusters and frosted winter trees.

- **Cotton swabs:** For lifting out color.

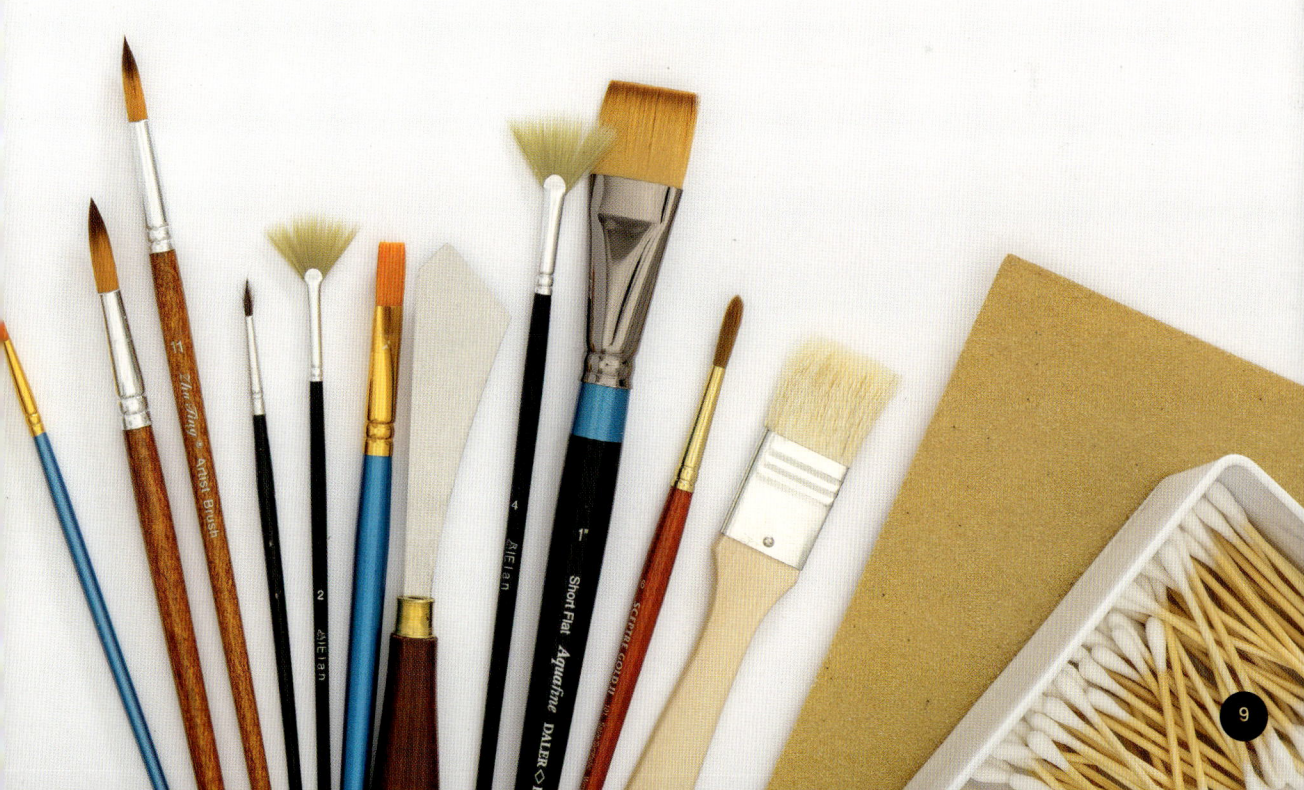

Mixing Paints

This is where the magic happens! A well-executed watercolor painting will display delightful, constant variations of colors, often referred to as a "gradient plane." Mingling colors efficiently on the palette and brush is crucial for a satisfactory outcome. Professional artists minimize disturbing the paint for two main reasons:

1. To maintain the freshness of the paint.

2. By loading the brush with two or three different colors, when the brush strokes the paper, subtle variations appear due to some mixing within the brush bristles caused by the fluidity of the paint.

Nature mostly displays monochromatic colors with little to no shifts. The artist's role is to enhance its forms by exaggerating color shifts for greater impact. In reality, you'll never see as many hue variations (color variegation) as you can create in a painting. Without a doubt, this will add dramatic interest to your work.

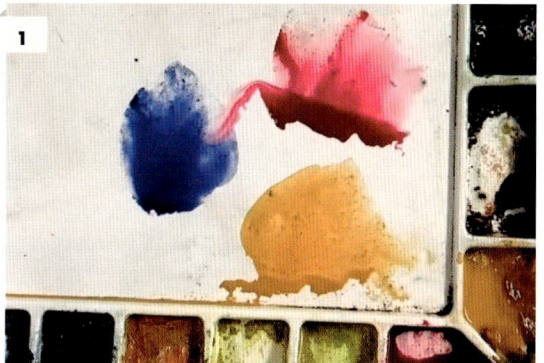

STEP 1 – COLOR PLACEMENT

Dip your wet brush into the pigment well to create a pool of color on the palette. Rinse the brush thoroughly, then bang it against the container to reduce excess water. It should no longer drip. The number of bangs will determine the mixture's value. Water is the equivalent to white in this medium. It may take one, two, or three bangs to get the value and paint consistency just right—the less water, the darker the value. Repeat this process for the next two colors, rinsing in between and adjusting the value with each bang.

STEP 2 – LOADING THE BRUSH

Push your brush forward into each puddle of color, one after the other, with a single stroke and allowing the mixing to happen naturally inside the bristles. In certain cases, you may need to mingle the pigments slightly on the palette, especially to reduce the color saturation, but avoid mixing like cement as much as possible.

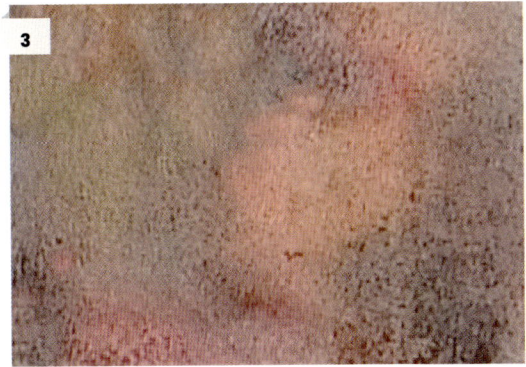

STEP 3 - APPLYING THE PAINT
FOR COLOR VARIEGATION

Apply the loaded brush to the paper. Rotate the brush as you paint to create more varied hue shifts. You should see a pattern where all three hues are noticeable and gradually merge into each other, slightly grayed down from the intermixing. If the separated colors aren't obvious, turn the brush upside down and load it again, dragging it through the second or the third puddle. You can also try double-loading the brush by dragging half of it through one puddle and the other half through another.

Color Variegation

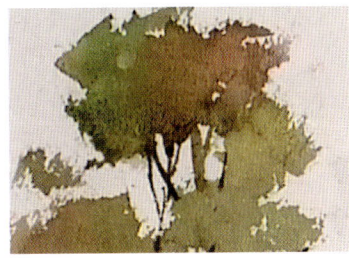

MIXING GREENS

Greens in nature often appear monochromatic, but adding color shifts creates more visual interest. For natural, non-garish greens, load your brush with raw sienna, burnt sienna, ultramarine blue, and transparent yellow. Three hues should be noticeable.

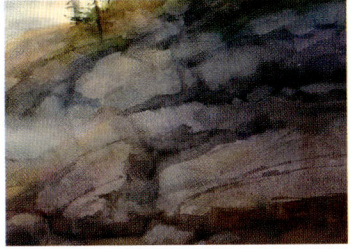

RELOADING THE BRUSH

Make a habit of using a variation of the previous color every time you load more pigment from the palette. This ensures you are constantly variegating the colors. In these rocks the colors shift from warm to cool about every 1.5in (4cm).

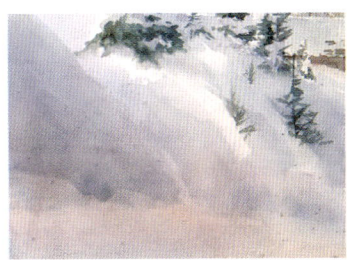

EXAGGERATING COLOR SHIFTS

The shadows in this snow are primarily blue-gray, but they also contain pinks and oranges—colors you wouldn't normally see in nature.

Wet-on-Wet

"Wet-on-wet" is a hallmark technique where pigment is applied to wet paper. The balance between the wetness of the paper, the moisture in the brush, and the timing determines how much the pigment spreads and diffuses, creating varying degrees of softness in the edges. Too much water, and the pigments will spread uncontrollably; too little, and they won't bleed enough. The skill lies in mastering that balance.

In my landscapes, I always incorporate a wet-on-wet effect, typically in the background. This technique adds a soft, atmospheric appeal that enhances the charm of watercolor painting.

EDGES

In watercolor, crisp, defined edges—commonly known as hard edges—create a more rigid, formal appearance. When used unnecessarily, they can make a painting feel "stiff." In some shapes, such as trees, they might not always be desirable, especially when you're trying to create a sense of depth or when areas are located in the periphery of the painting. The softer and more blurred the edge, the farther back an object appears to recede. This is especially useful for creating atmospheric effects such as fog, mist, clouds, smoke, crashing seascape foam, and waterfalls.

TYPES OF EDGES

Totally diffused: The contour is not distinguishable. Applications include very distant foliage and mist.

Soft: The contour is out of focus, yet discernable. Applications include background trees or hills, things that move, such as waterfalls, crashing wave foam, and clouds.

Lost and found: A delightful contour will feature a balance of both soft and hard edges. Hard edges make objects appear closer, while soft edges cause them to recede. The effect is achieved through spot-wetting—that is, wetting just selected areas.

Hard: Hard edges make objects appear closer and in focus. They result from wet paint applied to a dry surface. Watercolor is notorious for overstating hard edges, which can make elements look as though they are cut out from another source and pasted on. It's crucial to discern when to use hard edges and when to apply the three other types of edges mentioned above.

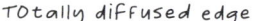
Totally diffused edge

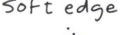
Soft edge

Lost-and-found edges

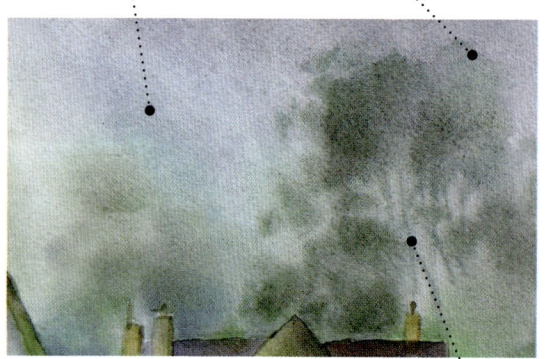

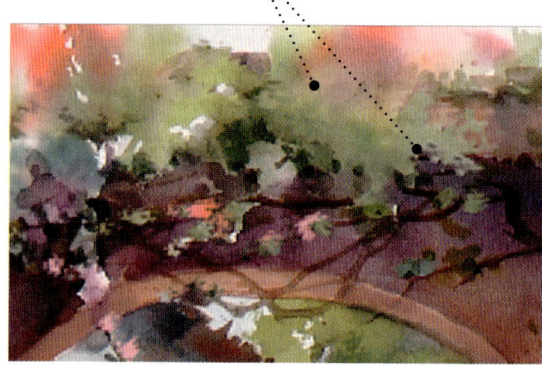

Hard edge

APPLICATION OF WET-ON-WET

The key to controlling wet-on-wet is understanding how much water is on your paper contrasted with how wet your brush is. Here is how you can master the technique:

Soak the paper: To create a bleeding effect, soak your paper thoroughly. This works best for large areas. Wet the paper once and wait about five minutes for the water to penetrate deep into the fibers. To buy more working time, repeat this process up to three times. The repeated soaking allows the water to penetrate deeply, giving you up to 20 minutes until the paper refuses to cooperate.

Lightly dampen the paper: If you're working on a small area and you don't need more than a few minutes, you can lightly dampen the paper instead of soaking it. Do not use a paper towel to remove excess moisture, as this can cause uneven bleeding and unpredictable results. Be patient and allow the water to settle into the paper and wait for the wet sheen to fade before painting.

Paint consistency: Mix a thick swatch of paint on your palette with just enough dampness to load the brush. The brush should have less water than the wet paper to control the pigment as it is released. This ensures the pigment flows but does not spread uncontrollably. The key is to balance the water in the paper with the wetness in the brush.

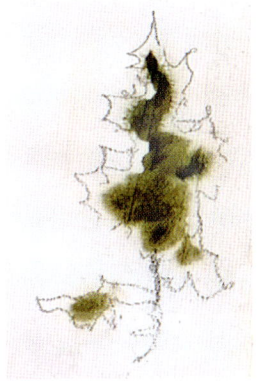

To assess if the paint is likely to expand beyond control, begin well inside the shape. This gives you time to assess the expansion as the water seeps into the cotton fibers. Once you're confident the paint isn't bleeding out of control, work toward the contours so the form becomes softly fuzzy, yet remains recognizable.

Handle excess water in the brush: If you need to pick up excess running paint, prior to applying it, hold your brush upright and squeeze at the ferrule of the brush with a cloth or paper towel to suck out the excess water.

Practice control of the bleeding: One useful exercise to master wet-on-wet is to write your phone number in digits about ¾in (2cm) high with a small round brush. The edges of the numbers should be soft and fuzzy, but not so much that they become too out of focus. Practice with different numbers (such as 4, 8, and 9) to ensure that the gaps don't fill in too much with pigment. This will give you a good sense of how much control you have over the bleeding.

TIP

Rough paper features a more textured surface and is less compressed than cold-pressed paper, making it more absorbent. As a result, it reduces bleeding and offers better control over wet-on-wet techniques. If you prefer better-controlled effects, rough paper can be an excellent choice.

Brushstrokes

Most professional artists use medium-sized round brushes, but I find the brights more versatile, because I use all four sides, plus the corners, constantly rotating and varying the strokes. Push yourself to use a large brush so that you don't fall into the habit of nitpicking. Many professional artists rely on the sleight of the hand to produce spontaneous effects without too much deliberate control. This results in unpredictable outcomes—known as "happy accidents."

DRY-BRUSHING

Dry-brushing reigns supreme among brushstrokes. Its purpose is to create broken clusters of varying sizes. It is a technique that can be used for rendering foliage clusters, conifer tree boughs, crashing waves, and cumulus clouds.

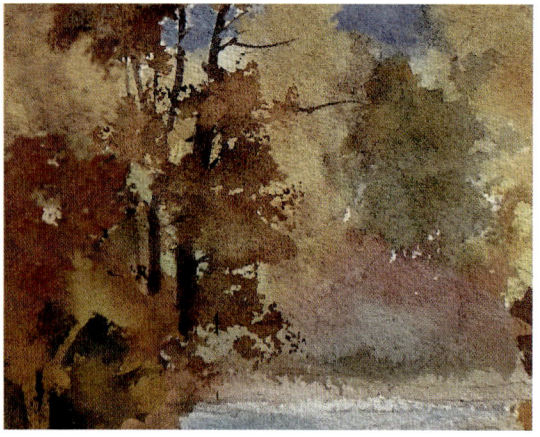

FOLIAGE CLUSTERS

Holding your brush parallel to the paper, apply light pressure as you tap and move it in different directions, primarily forward—similar to shoveling snow. Rotate and use the thin sides, brushing upwards like a car windshield wiper. Let the paint naturally break up into clusters of different sizes, while allowing the paper's texture to further disperse them with a light touch. This works best on dry rough paper, but with experience, cold-pressed paper can also yield good results. The paint should have a creamy consistency. If you get too many specks, the paint is not wet enough.

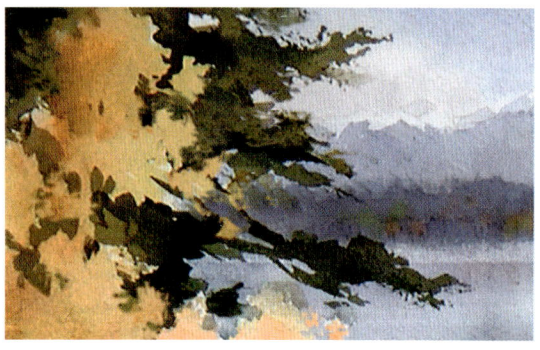

EVERGREEN BOUGHS

Using the thin edge of the brush, jab against the bristles like shoveling snow. This technique creates very effective, unpredictable, and spontaneous effects that capture the irregularity of the boughs of conifer trees.

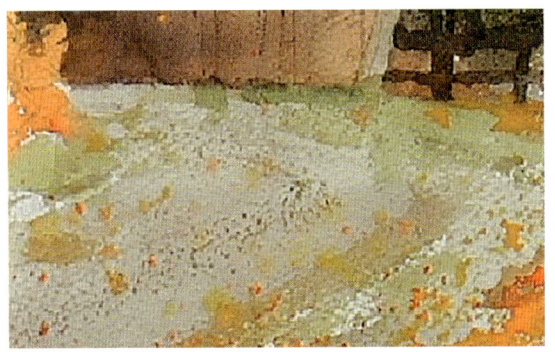

GRAVEL

Gravel on a dirt road emerges from lightly skimming the paper with pasty paint. The technique involves using the flat side of the brush to lightly graze the paper as the moist, not yet wet, paint peels off. Move the brush quickly. By doing so, the paint breaks up into tiny specks thanks to the textured peaks of the paper. If you get large specks, remove excess paint from your brush by dragging it on a separate piece of paper.

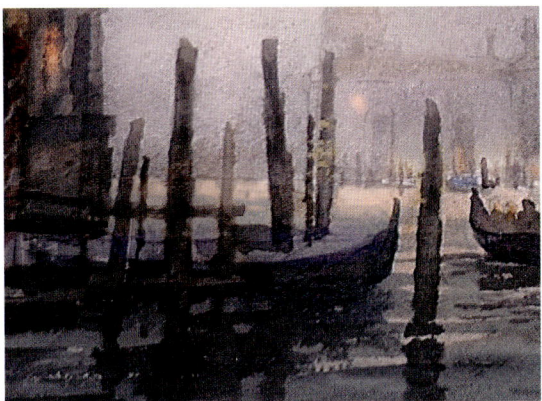

VARIED STROKES

To create irregular lines, use the chisel edge of the brush and pull it from side to side. This technique works well for fence posts and tree limbs. The twist-and-turn application also produces irregular lines, making it ideal for waves.

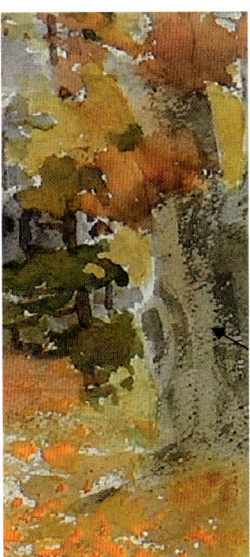

CREATING TREE BARK TEXTURE

This technique creates very effective, unpredictable, and spontaneous effects that capture the irregularity of tree bark, bricks, and shingles.

TIP

You might find that a large round brush is more cooperative than a bright for this technique.

Rub the long convex area of the brush against the paper to break up the paint into random clusters.

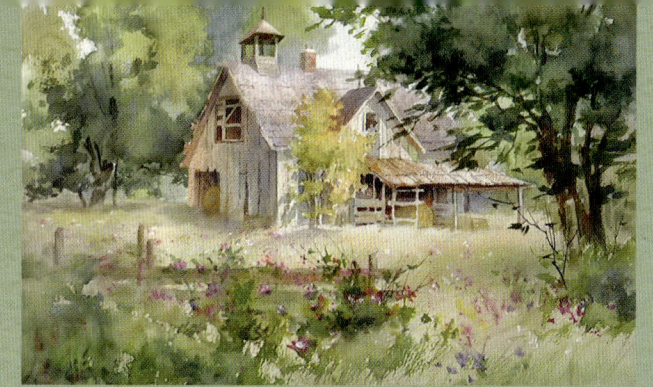

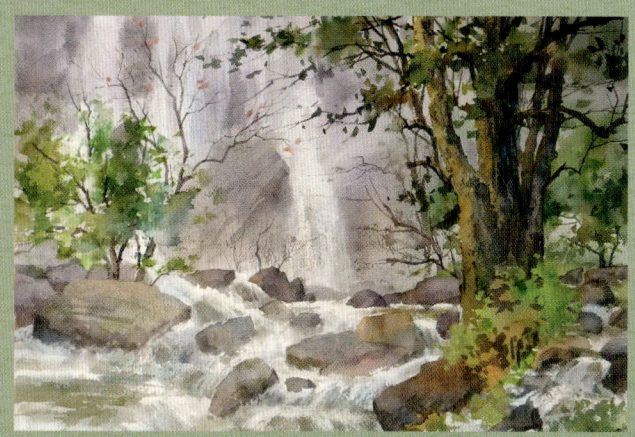

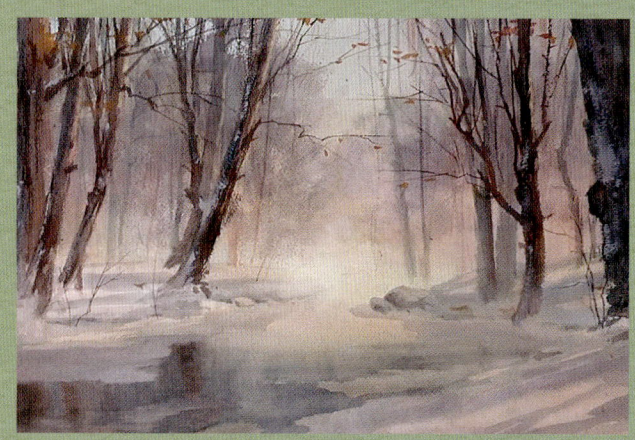

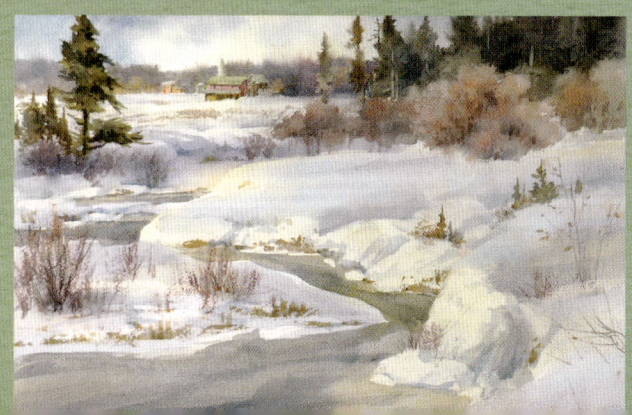

CHAPTER ONE:
Foliage

This chapter gives insight into mastering painterly trees, as foliage appears in all landscapes. Trees vary in size, shape, and subtle color. Focusing too much on individual leaves often leads to over-rendering—building forms leaf by leaf or in small clusters—which can make the painting feel cluttered. Instead, practice creating simple, well-designed symbols for trees, bushes, evergreens, and bare winter forms. Think of portraying them as learning a new language: each shape, texture, and gesture becomes a visual shorthand, capturing the tree's essence. The goal is to suggest rather than replicate, using design, rhythm, and movement to make a landscape feel alive.

Summer Trees

In this composition, warm, golden grass contrasts with the lush green of the trees and bushes, clearly defining the vertical and horizontal planes. Rather than letting bushes run across the entire foreground, I left an open path to invite viewers into the scene. The wildflowers, scattered in a "connect-the-dots" pattern, create a gentle visual path into the field.

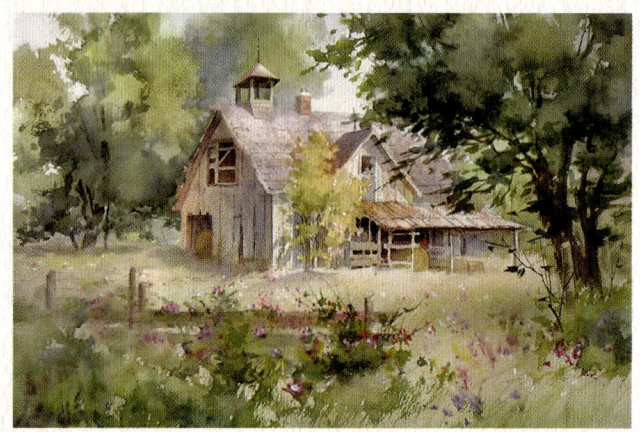

Sun-dappled Memories

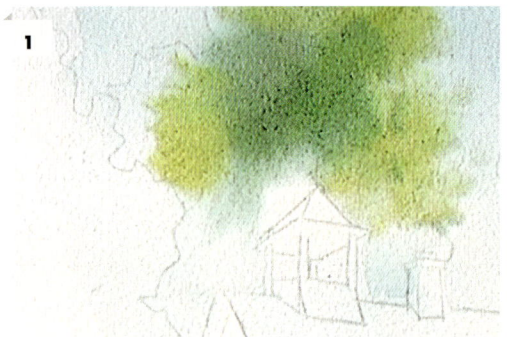

STEP 1 - PAINTING THE DISTANT TREE

For the most distant tree, use the wet-on-wet technique to create a soft, blended appearance. Avoid hard edges, allowing the general form, or contour, to remain definable yet indistinct. This technique helps create atmospheric perspective, making the tree recede naturally into the background.

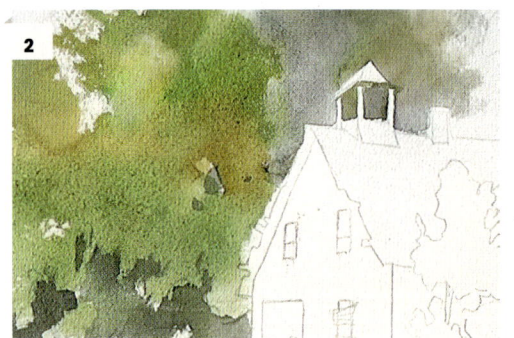

STEP 2 - PAINTING THE MID-DISTANCE TREE

The mid-distance tree will have a combination of hard and soft edges to separate it from the farthest tree, whereas the foreground tree will be all hard-edged to bring it closer. Before painting the mid-distance tree, spot-wet to leave some dry parts inside and around the outer contour (beyond your pencil marks).

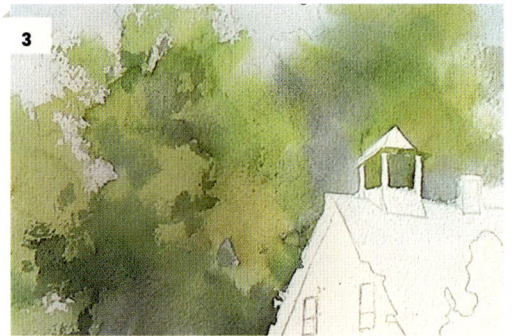

STEP 3 - THE PLAY OF EDGES

Dark areas of foliage are a mix of hard and soft edges, also a result of spot-wetting. When painting shadow areas, be sure to achieve a ratio of one-third light to two-thirds dark, or vice versa. The idea is to avoid equal portions of competing values.

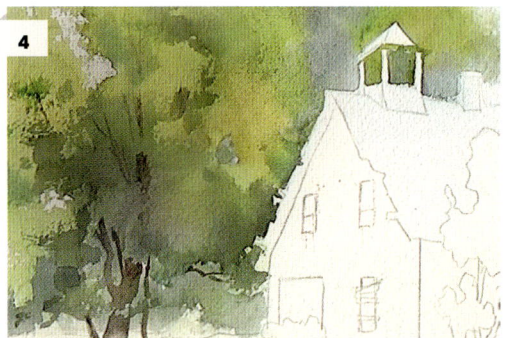

STEP 4 - ADDING BRANCHES

When rendering trees, limit the number of trunks and branches to just a few essential ones. Nature will provide more branches, but mirroring them or overdoing the detail can make them feel cluttered. Only add them into the shadow areas and empty sky gaps. Skip the highlighted portions.

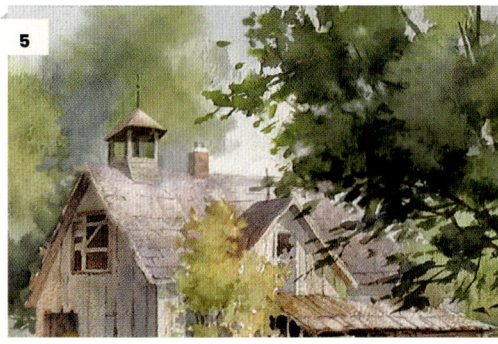

STEP 5 - PAINTING THE FOREGROUND TREE

The hard edges and darker value in the foreground tree, contrasted with the softer background and lighter values in the darks, clearly separate the two planes.

TIP

Making one side of a tree darker than the other side will give it a rounder, more three-dimensional appearance.

Close-Up Leafy Tree

In nature, greens seldom shift dramatically in hue, so I like to introduce ocher-green and green-blue tones to break the monotony. In this composition, the dancing leaves contribute a sense of rhythm to the scene, avoiding a more static appearance or polka-dot effect.

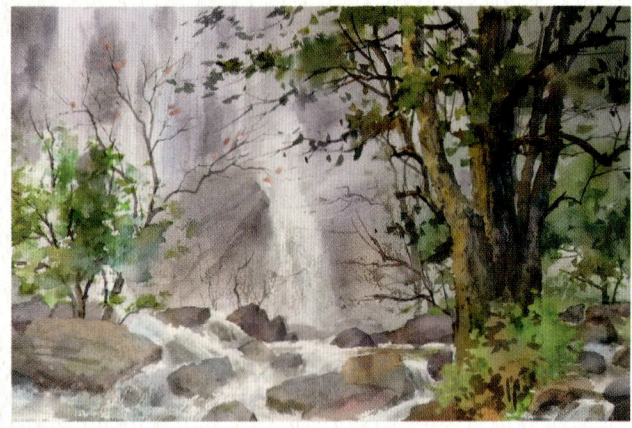

Echoes in the Gorge

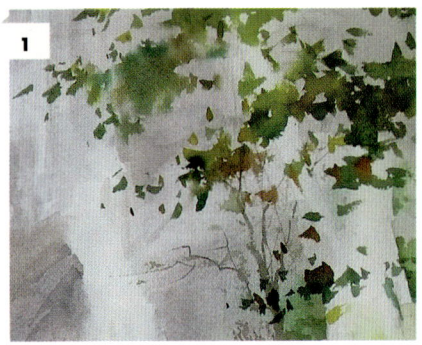

STEP 1 - EXPRESSIVE BRUSHWORK

Using a pointed round brush, gently jab the leaves onto the paper while rocking the brush from left to right to simulate natural growth patterns. Create different size clusters, some of which melt together and others that dangle as individual leaves. The individual leaves should point toward the center to lead the eye. Vary different green hues to add interest. Include some ocher leaves for variation in color and texture.

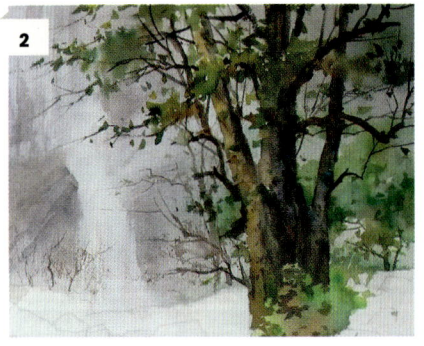

STEP 2 - DEFINE LEAVES AND BRANCHES

Add darks under the leaves to make them appear three-dimensional. Then indicate the branches under those darks.

Autumn Trees

Fall colors offer the perfect chance to showcase the warm, golden hues that viewers seem to love. While summer's greens are popular, they don't resonate as strongly as the rich ochers and oranges of fall.

Since most landscapes feature foliage, how we depict it matters. Nature's grandeur can be impressive, but when scaled down to a painting, the majesty is lost. We can counterbalance this with thoughtful abstract designs and beautiful color transitions.

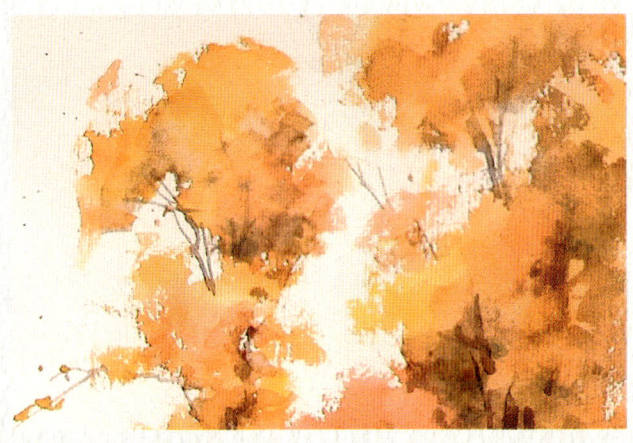

Glowing Cottonwoods

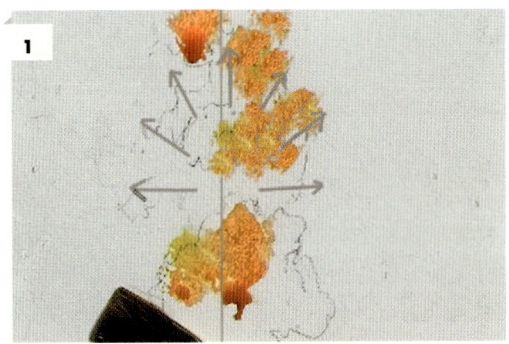

STEP 1 – STARTING FOLIAGE CLUSTERS

Apply the dry-brush technique, following the motion of clock hands. Start at the top and push the brush forward in short bursts, as if shoveling snow. Brush toward the numbers 1, 2, and 3 on one side, and 11, 10, and 9 on the other. Use the flat side and long edge of the brush. Alternate between lifting and caressing the paper. Produce the entire tree with approximately 1-in (2.5-cm) cluster blocks, placing them randomly to avoid producing symmetrical round tree shapes.

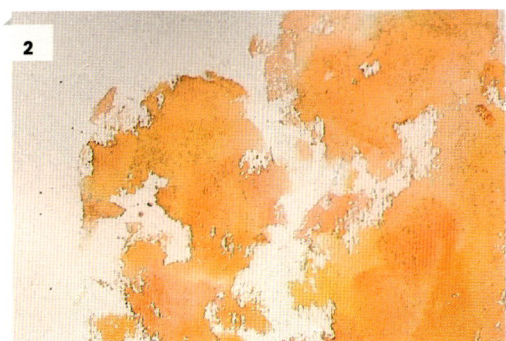

STEP 2 – WORKING ON THE HIGHLIGHTS

Vary the size of the sky gaps—larger, irregular openings are more effective than numerous small ones, which can create a distracting, pixelated look. Think only in clusters compounded with dozens or even hundreds of leaves. Vary the sizes. Barely caress the paper as you dry-brush to break up the clusters near the tree's contour; these don't need to be attached. Gradually transition from yellow-orange to orange, with small touches of pink to add vibrancy and interest.

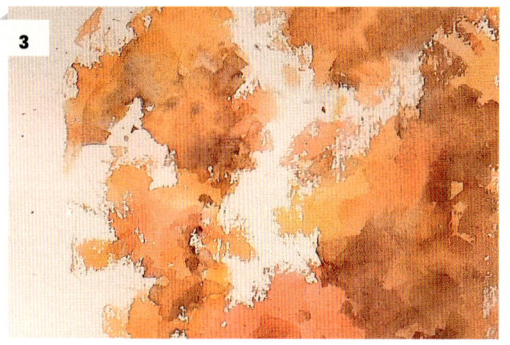

STEP 3 - ROUNDING YOUR TREES

While the paint is still wet, and using a deeper version of the original color, darken the bottom of the clusters and the shadowed sides to give the tree a rounded appearance. A few hard edges here and there bring those areas of the tree into focus. The foliage clusters vary in size to avoid monotonous repetition. To maintain a smooth visual flow, avoid letting the dark areas appear spotty; instead, group them close together or bridge them with adjacent dark clusters.

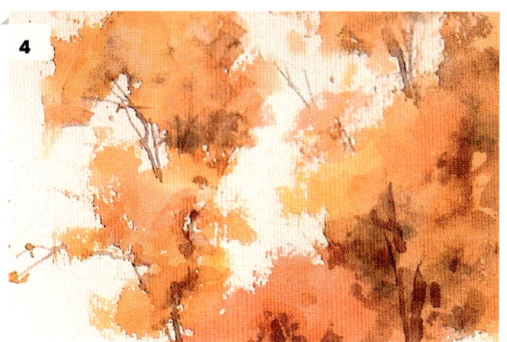

STEP 4 - ADDING BRANCHES

Place the tree trunks and branches in the darker areas only, avoiding the highlights. Keep the trunks shorter than 2in (5cm) to prevent a visual run-off. Take advantage of the large gaps between foliage clusters to fill in with branches. Add a few accents to create an even deeper effect in the foliage.

SPOT-WETTING

When painting trees in the middle ground, follow the same instructions given for Autumn Trees, but use spot-wetting on the contours and inside the form. Watercolor tends to produce hard edges when applied to dry paper, so allowing some areas to bleed helps prevent a "cut-out, pasted-on" effect. Trees in the background will recede further if all edges are soft.

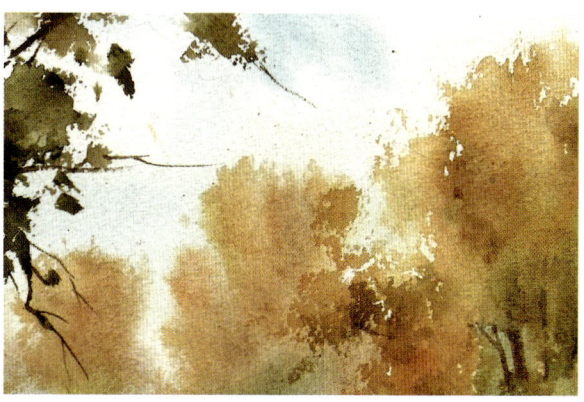

Fallen Leaves

The sun peeking through leaves is a powerful element for award-winning paintings. Leaves can partially block the sun's intense brightness, allowing its warmth to gently seep through—enough to be felt without making you want to turn away, while still comfortably enjoying the sun's glow.

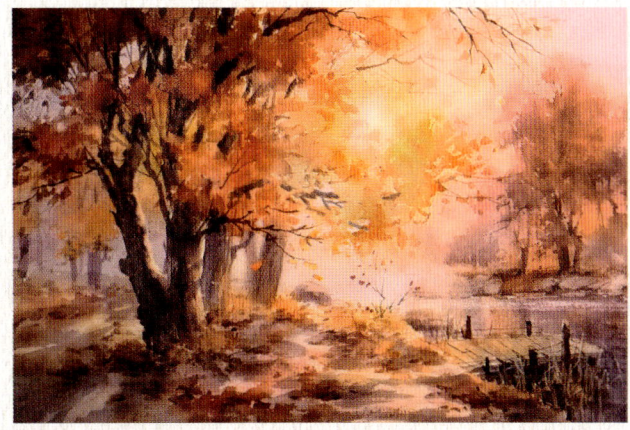

Golden Whisper of Dawn

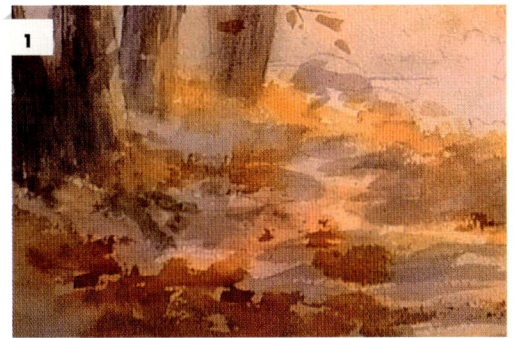

STEP 1 – CREATING LEAF CLUSTERS

Group most leaves in clusters of varying sizes for a natural appearance. To add variety and contrast, include a few individual leaves breaking away from the clusters. The leaves catching sunlight are warmer and lighter in color than those in the shadows.

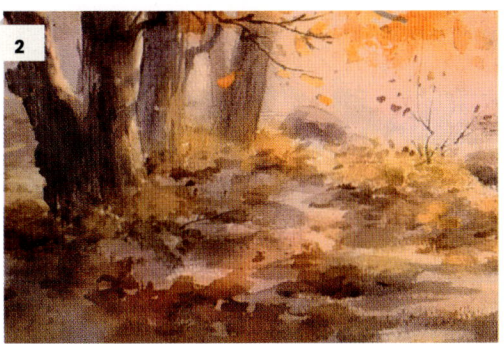

STEP 2 – DARKENING UNDERNEATH

Indicate shadow areas by painting underneath the leaf clumps, as if placing your hand under them to scoop them up. There's no need to add shadows under every cluster—the mind's vision will fill in the untouched gaps, creating a cohesive and believable effect.

Evergreens

Mid–dark evergreen trees are valuable in landscape paintings because they often form the darkest mass, creating strong contrast. It is preferable that your landscapes have a value range from mid-light to mid to mid-dark, somewhat like the music scale. The subject of this painting has a great visual lead-in due to the icy stream. It creates an "S" shape, which is the most effective way to guide viewers in. The farm, in a discordant red color, acts as the focal point.

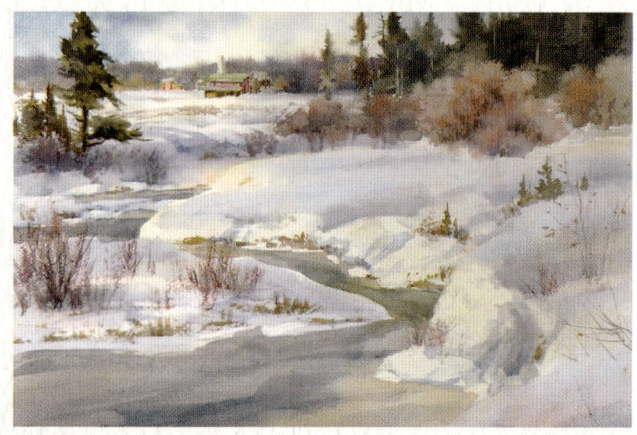

First Thaw Near the Farmhouse

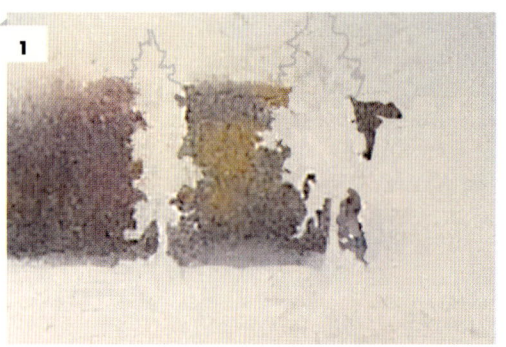

STEP 1 – STARTING WITH THE BACKGROUND

Paint the background hill wet-on-wet, leaving white silhouettes where the upcoming evergreens will stand in the middle ground.

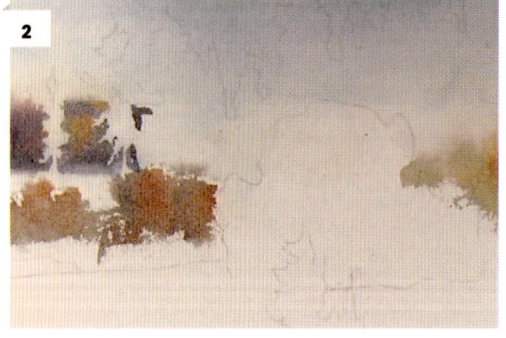

STEP 2 – ADDING BUSHES

Paint the bushes in front of the evergreens first. This allows you to carve out the shape of the evergreens later, using negative painting.

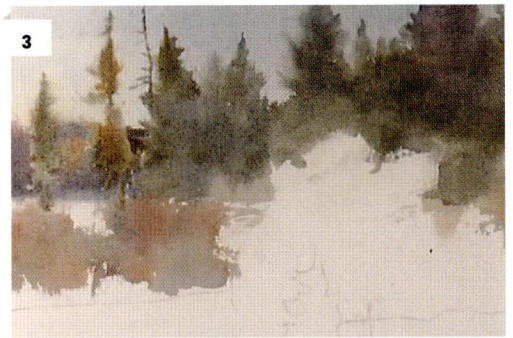

STEP 3 – USING LOST-AND-FOUND EDGES

Spot-wet for both soft and hard edges. Paint the entire mass of trees as one unit. They will read as individual trees once you extend them to the top third of their heights. Vary their heights and widths, allowing some to extend beyond the top to avoid a repetitive "missile tip" look. Cropping trees anchors them, preventing them from looking as if they fit into a confined space. Incorporate some burnt sienna for added variety. Certain parts of these trees shift to an orange hue.

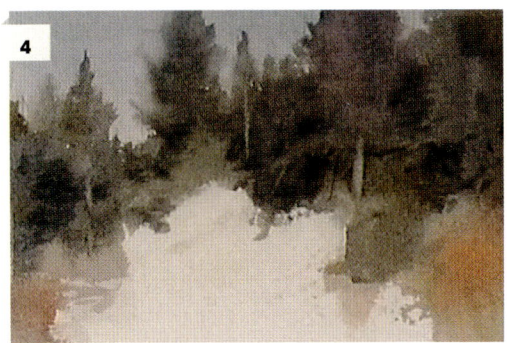

STEP 4 – CREATING THREE-DIMENSIONAL FORMS

To depict the trees as three-dimensional forms, negative-paint the darks starting heavier at the bottom, growing gradually lighter as you move up. Use a thirsty brush to lift out the tree trunks (see Tricks of the Trade: Lightening Value with a Thirsty Brush). The foliage-stripped trunks add a nice touch, breaking the monotony of the triangular forms. This feature adds more to the story.

NEGATIVE PAINTING

With opaque paints, we can layer lighter values over darker ones. Purist watercolor doesn't allow for that approach. In this medium, darker values must be built into lighter washes. This is where negative painting comes in—since the lighter areas are considered the positive shapes, we define them by painting around them. Think of it as sculpting the highlights.

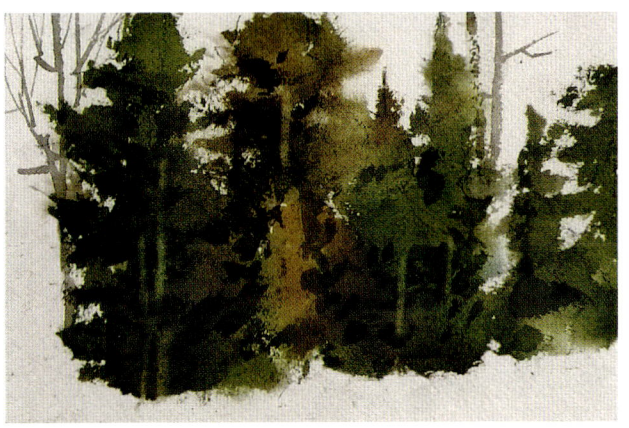

Close-Up Evergreen

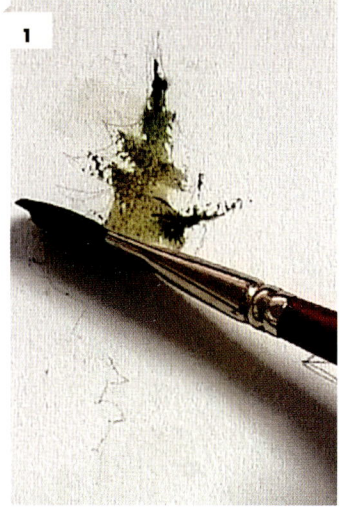

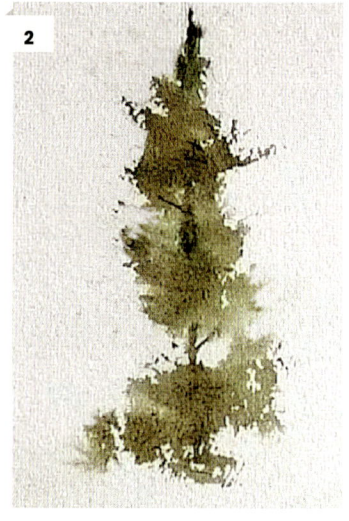

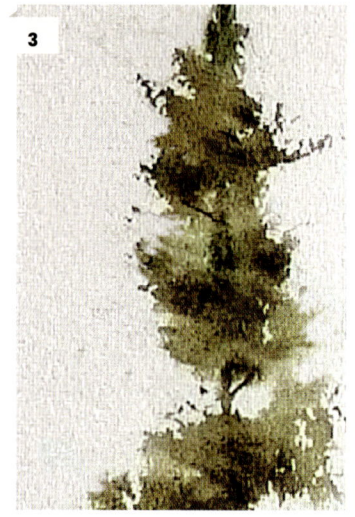

STEP 1 – BRUSHWORK

Spot-wet your paper. Apply the dry-brush technique, using the skinny side edge of your ¾-in (2-cm) brush like a chisel to jab the brush forward against the bristles. Vary the pressure, mostly just caressing the paper and letting its texture naturally produce the broken boughs.

STEP 2 – ADDING A TRUNK

Add the tree trunk as short lines in a slightly darker version of the same color mix.

STEP 3 – PAINTING DARKS

Negative-paint the dark areas under the boughs (see Evergreens). The darker areas should fall under a one-third dark or two-thirds ratio of lights and darks. This avoids competing values.

TIP

Vary the height and width of each evergreen in a group to avoid a repetitive, cloned appearance.

Evergreens in Snow

In this composition, the orange of the building at the heart of the scene creates a focal point below the peaks of the mountains. The monochromatic blue shadows of snow can be made alive by adding pinks, violets, and oranges. The negative-painting technique is crucial for depicting snow on the evergreens.

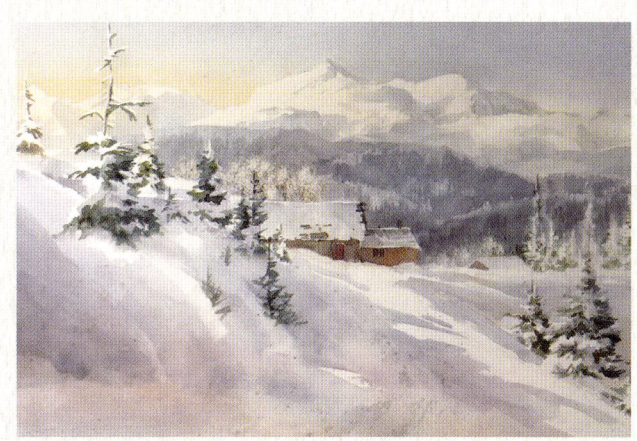

High Country Solitude

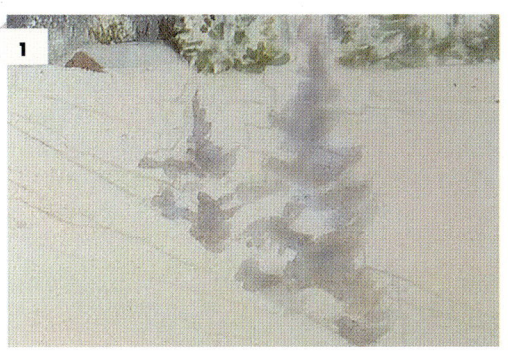

STEP 1 – WARMING UP THE WHITE PAPER

Lightly glaze the whole paper with raw sienna and touches of permanent rose, keeping them separate rather than mixing them. This creates subtle color variation for added interest. Leave some whites for the sunlit portion of the evergreens on the left side. The shadowed side of snow on the evergreens will be primarily blue, with subtle pink and orange touches for richness. Vary the sizes and widths of light and shadow areas to avoid uniformity.

TIP

Watercolor paper often appears too cool to convey sunlight. Tinting the blank sheet with raw sienna will warm it up.

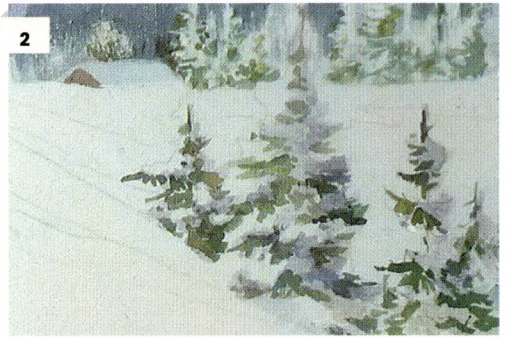

STEP 2 – ADDING THE BOUGHS

Add in a few boughs, peeking out from under the snow using negative painting (see Evergreens). To avoid an unpleasant and repetitive zigzag contour, make them irregular. Evergreens are better designs when there are variations in size of the snow clumps and the boughs. A touch of burnt sienna here and there in the greenery adds warmth.

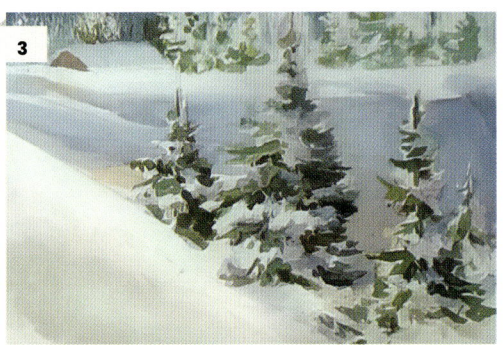

STEP 3 – CREATING A THREE-DIMENSIONAL EFFECT

Using more negative painting, add a darker version of the green to the trees. Place these darks under the boughs. This will create a three-dimensional effect, making the boughs seem to be protruding.

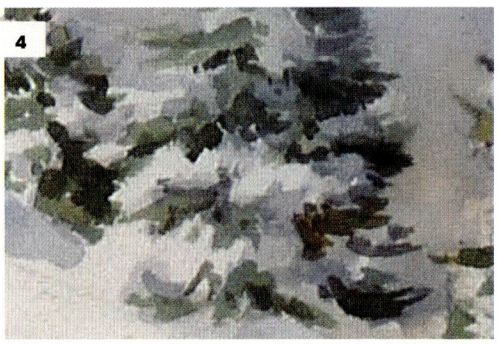

STEP 4 – ADDING ACCENTS

Once the paint dries, add dark green accents at the very bottom of the boughs. Round off the snow clumps by adding a blue shadow under some of them.

Bare Winter Trees

For this piece, I decided to depict a late-afternoon sky with its pleasing gradient. The buildings are well placed, while the overhanging trees create a captivating C-shaped composition that keeps the viewer's eye engaged. Adding light to the windows introduces a cozy ambience, with their reflections serving as a delightful final detail. Winter scenes become more appealing when warm colors are introduced. Additionally, blankets of snow provide natural rest areas within the composition.

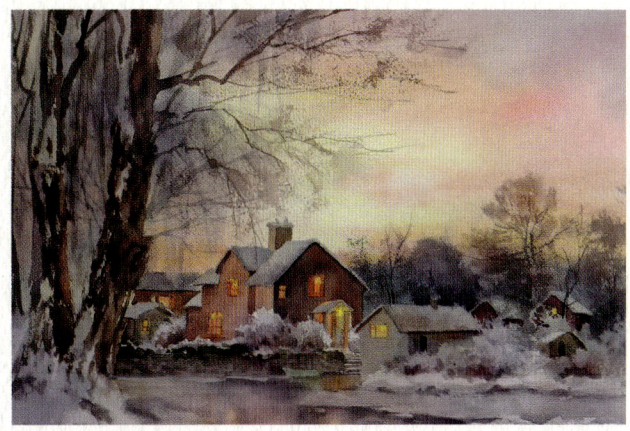

Frozen Serenity, Flickering Warmth

STEP 1 - PAINTING THE BACKGROUND

Use the wet-on-wet technique to paint the distant hills. The rising, fuzzy texture that creeps up in the wet paper will give the appearance of a distant evergreen forest.

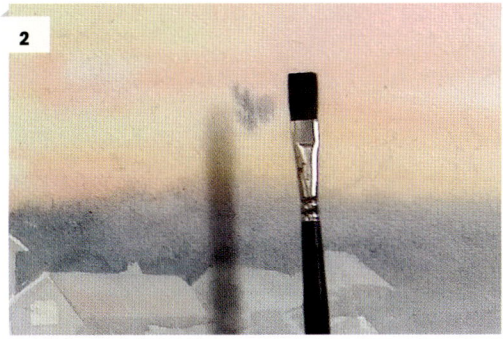

STEP 2 - DEFINING DISTANT TREES

Spot-wet your paper and use the dry-brush technique by pushing upwards, like a shovel, while angling the strokes toward positions on a clock face (see Autumn Trees). This approach creates a pleasing mix of soft and hard edges. The trees have more sense of belonging when there are see-through sky gaps. Allow open areas to reveal glimpses of the background hill to give a sense of belonging.

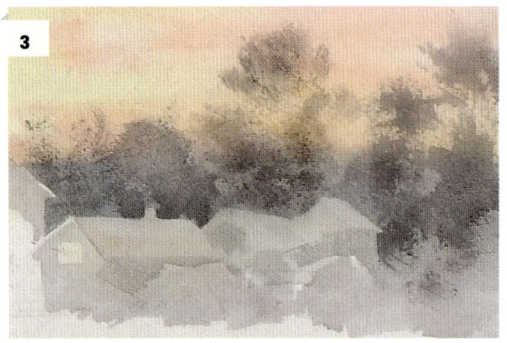

STEP 3 – PAINTING THE MID-RANGE TREES

The closer row of trees should be darker—this pushes the distant plane back. Avoid symmetrical, round-contour tree shapes. Always strive for asymmetrical tree images (see Sunset: Abstract Shapes).

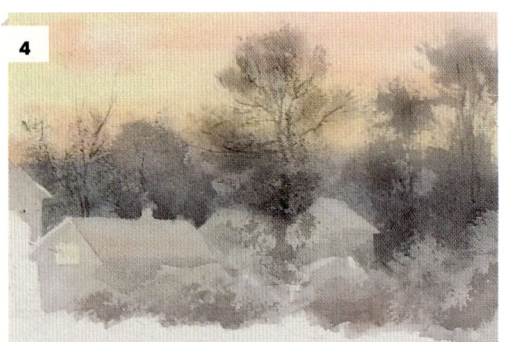

STEP 4 – ADDING TREE TRUNKS AND BRANCHES

Add trunks and supporting branches that match the tree's body in both value and color. You don't need to paint as many branches as you see in nature—just a few will make the trees appear complete and convincing to the viewer.

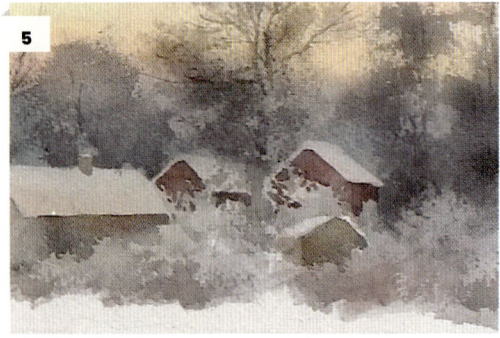

STEP 5 – WORKING ON THE BUSHES

The bushes accumulate snow, making them lighter toward the top surface. The snowy sides of the bushes are darker. Echo some of the sky colors for harmony. Negative-paint to define their round forms (see Evergreens).

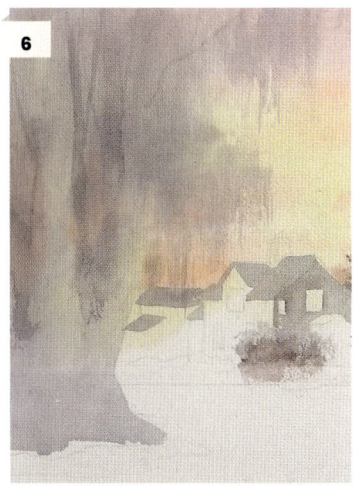

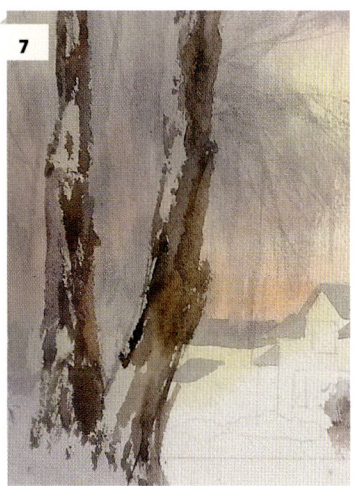

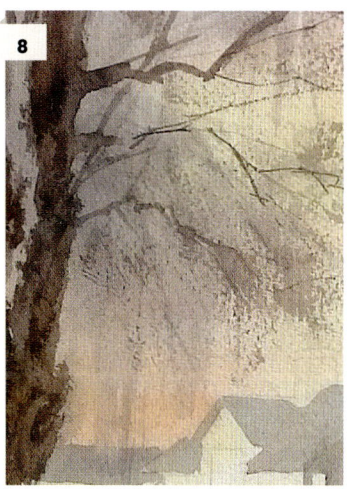

STEP 6 – PAINTING SNOW ON TRUNKS

The snow is a mid-value added to fill in the entire foreground tree. It will be painted over with a darker color. The overhanging wispy areas represent icicles weighing down the overhanging branches. Echo the warm sky colors in the snow for harmony.

STEP 7 – BRINGING OUT THE BARK

Negative-paint the tree bark, leaving random spots of snow. Avoid isolated spots that are too far apart to maintain unity. Bridge areas of snow closely so the eye flows smoothly across the form, preventing viewers from struggling to visually connect disconnected areas of light and dark.

STEP 8 – GIVING BRANCHES CHARACTER

Gnarled branches with pronounced angles (I call them elbows), add character to trees and are much more visually appealing than branches that resemble snakes.

> **TIP**
>
> You can add as many twigs to bare trees as you like, as long as they are light in value and very thin.

Close-Up Bare Tree

The branches of bare trees become thinner as they grow out from the trunk. The thickness of the trunk, limbs, and twigs is key. You'll need a #6 brush and three sizes of rigger brushes to capture these variations in bare trees. Viewers appreciate the addition of single dangling leaves, as they create a sense of the eye connecting the dots.

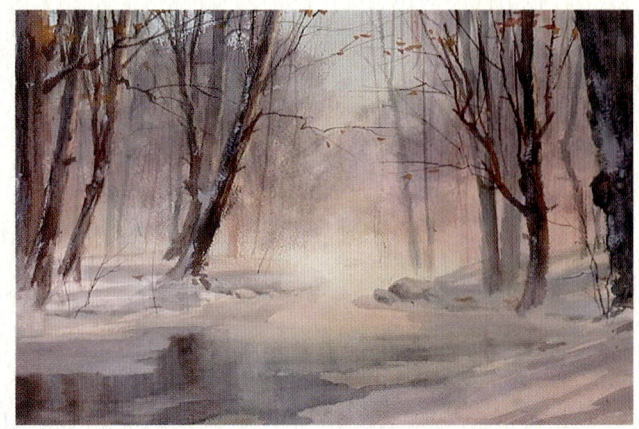

Through the Winter Haze

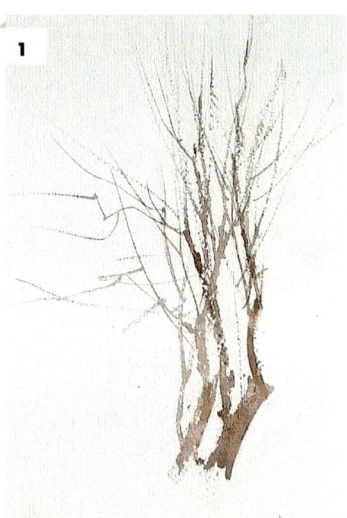

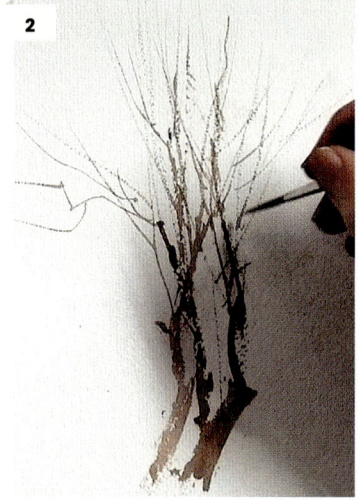

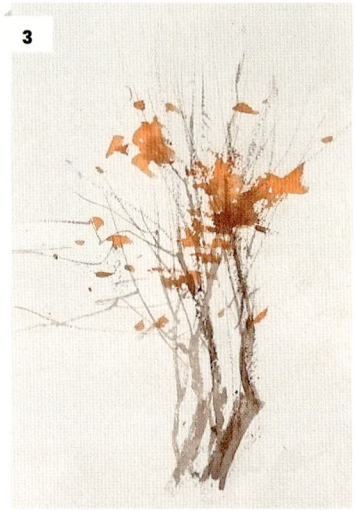

STEP 1 – BRUSH RANGE

A #6 round brush is suitable for the main supporting tree trunks. As a trunk starts to fork out, switch to your widest rigger brush. As you move toward the top, migrate to the medium-size rigger, and then the thinnest. This main trunk becomes the axis of the tree.

STEP 2 – BRANCH DIRECTION

Stemming from the axis, all branches on the right side are directed toward the numbers on a clock (1, 2, 3), while all branches on the left aim toward 11, 10, 9 o'clock.

STEP 3 – MINIMAL FOLIAGE

The figure is also enhanced with leaf clusters, perfect for a mid-fall season. Vary the sizes of the foliage clusters for a less manufactured look.

Populated Bare Trees

Bare trees with long, flowing branches invite the viewer's eye to follow their elegant lines, creating visual movement through your painting. Varying these trees—some lush and full from rich soil, with abundant twigs filling much of the space, others sparse and aging—adds diversity and character, much like the variety found in people.

TIP

Placing more weight on the side closer to the center of your painting avoids an equal balance.

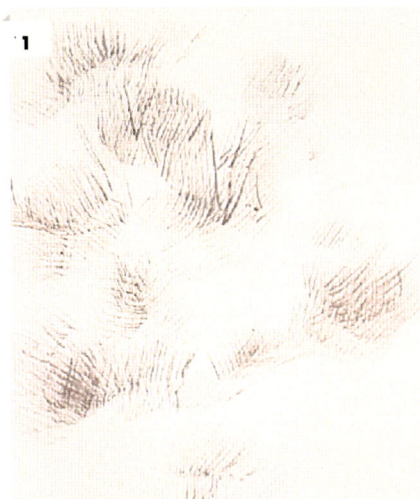

STEP 1 – CAPTURING THE BASIC SHAPE

Use a fan brush to create twigs that crisscross by alternating the brush's direction and varying the sizes of the strokes. In each cluster, guide the brush as if pointing toward different numbers on a clock face. In this case, do not spot-wet because the lines you are adding are so thin.

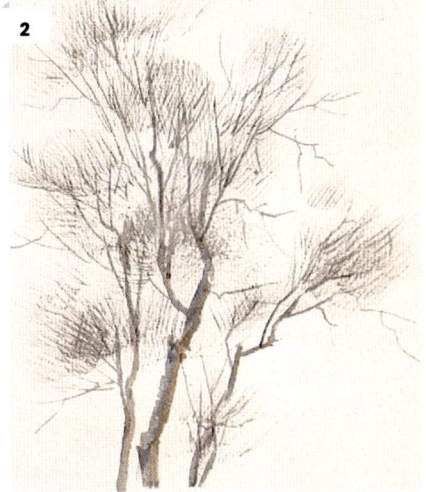

STEP 2 – ADDING TRUNKS AND BRANCHES

Using a #6 round brush, begin the main, heaviest tree trunk at the 6 o'clock position and extend it upward to the 12 o'clock position, tapering into a small twig. Use broken, textured strokes to mimic bark and add color variations on the heavier trunks to avoid a parallel appearance. Direct the branches on the right side toward the numbers past 12, and direct branches on the left side to the numbers before 12. Gradually lighten and thin out the branches as they extend outward. Use all three riggers to vary the widths of the limbs.

Floral Scenes

Paintings of buildings with flowers are commercially popular. Adding flowers to architectural scenes softens the rigid lines and geometric shapes of buildings, creating a pleasing contrast. The vibrant explosions of color add visual interest and delight to the viewer's eye. In this composition, the blue door, which is a discordant color, is an eye-catching element. Leaving it open makes viewers feel welcome to step in, allowing them to finish the painting with their imagination.

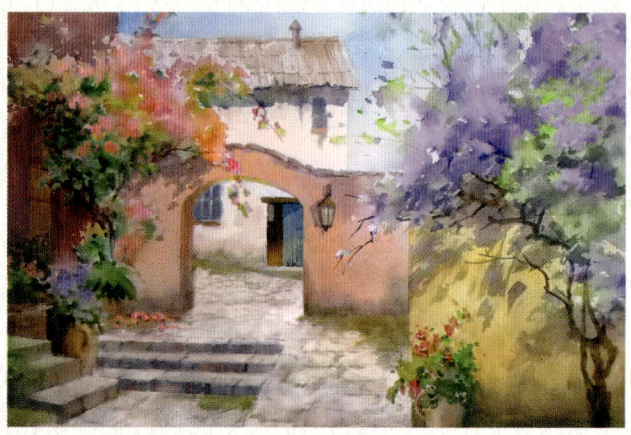

Courtyard Blooms

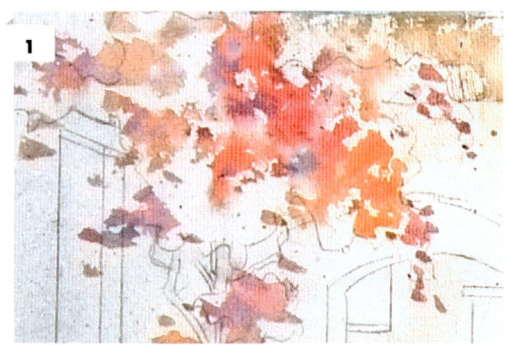

STEP 1 – PLAY OF EDGES

Spot-wet the plant area, leaving some dry parts to create a delightful contrast of edges. Hard edges allow the eye to find focus. Start by dropping in the pink and orange flower colors, in different sizes. The top of the form will feature more flowers than greenery. Touches of blue and purple on the shadow side compensate for the intense warm colors. The hanging branches point toward the center, guiding the viewer's eye.

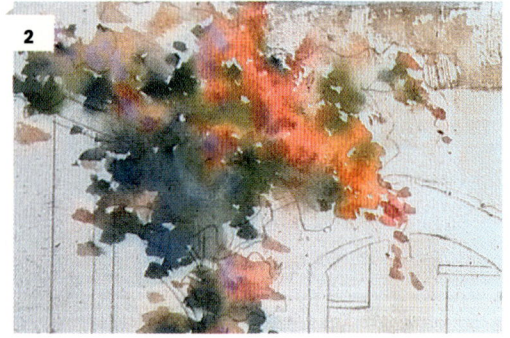

STEP 2 – ADDING GREENERY

While the area is still moist, drop in the greenery, varying from yellow-green, to green, and then to blue-green, the last in the shadow areas. Allow the greens to merge seamlessly with the flowers in some areas. Again, leave a few hard edges for the eye to focus on.

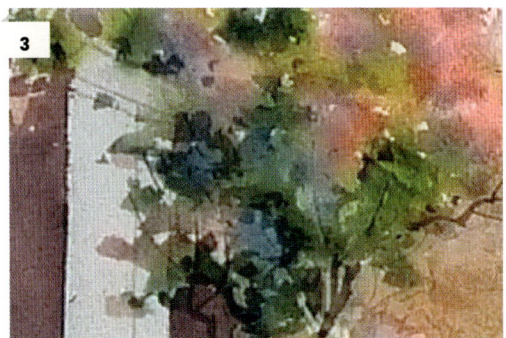

STEP 3 - ADDING ACCENTS

The accents, which are the darkest indentations, give the illusion of three-dimensionality by shaping the bulk of foliage. Start from the base and work your way up. Only add a few darks to the flowers. Avoid a spotty look. Soft edges create a colorful burst effect, enhancing the overall vibrancy.

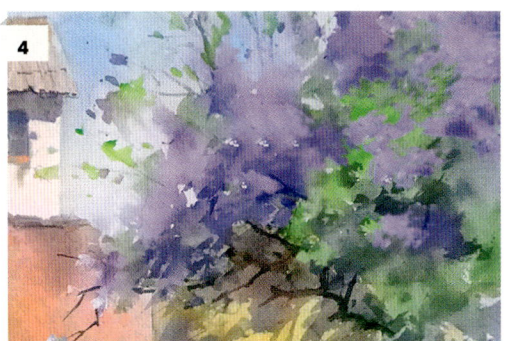

STEP 4 - WORKING OTHER FLORAL GROUPS

Repeat Steps 1 to 3 to paint the lavender-flowered tree and the potted plants in the courtyard. The bleeding edges of the purple tree showcase a colorful burst against the ocher wall. Complementary colors enhance each other.

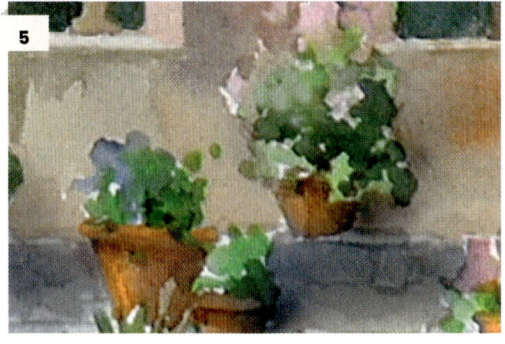

STEP 5 - FINISHING THE FLOWERS

Negative-paint by carving out the lighter foliage forms. Think in clusters—only a few singled-out leaves are necessary. Merge the rest into clumps of varying sizes.

Palm Trees

Palm trees form symmetrical shapes, with both sides and fronds equally balanced. Their elongated trunks have fast-paced lines, making them a challenge to portray. Palm trees have wonderful personalities. They evoke nostalgia, reminding viewers of past trips. You can make them appear to sway by softening their fronds, creating the illusion of an ocean breeze.

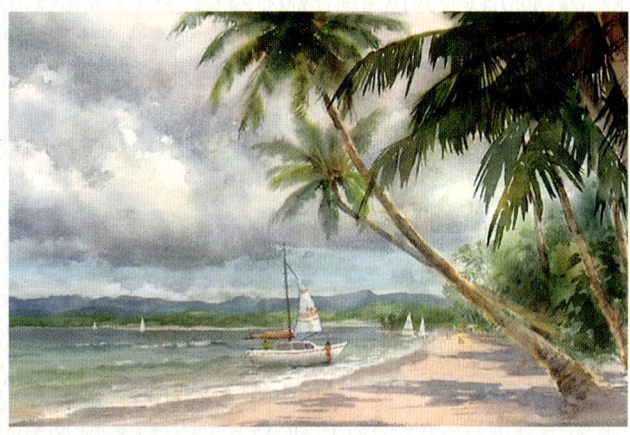

Setting Sail From Paradise

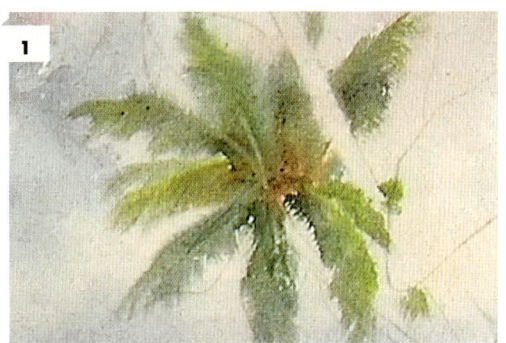

STEP 1 - PAINTING THE FARTHEST TREE

Paint the farthest palm tree entirely wet-on-wet. This will create a soft, blended look that helps it to recede into the background. Wet the entire area and wait until the glisten fades. Use a fan brush to depict the fronds, applying short combing strokes. Allow some bleeding, but maintain the general shapes of the fronds. Drop in some burnt sienna in the center to represent coconuts. Use a thirsty brush to lift out the rachises (see Tricks of the Trade: Lightening Value with a Thirsty Brush).

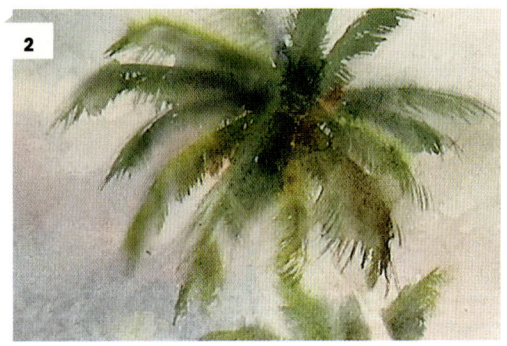

STEP 2 - PAINTING THE MID-DISTANCE TREE

Spot-wet the area and use a fan brush with short combing strokes to define some of the fronds. Make them slightly darker in value so this tree comes forward compared to the farthest palm tree. Again, drop some burnt sienna in the center to represent coconuts. Slightly darken the fronds closer to the center.

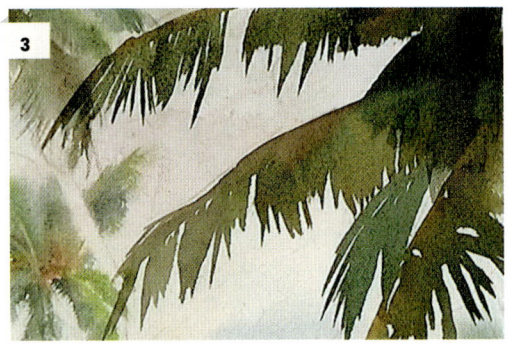

STEP 3 - PAINTING THE FOREGROUND TREE

Using a slightly darker value, paint on dry paper using the chisel edge of a bright brush to form the fronds in irregular patterns. Leave a few open gaps to break the repetition and symmetry.

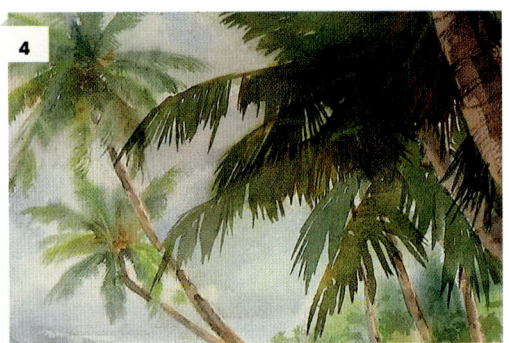

STEP 4 - PAINTING THE NEAREST FRONDS

Make the fronds that are closest to the viewer the darkest ones.

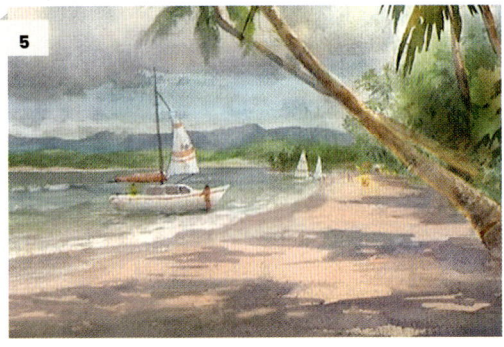

STEP 5 - PAINTING THE SHADOWS

Paint the beach first and allow it to dry. To depict the shadows, mix ultramarine blue with a touch of permanent rose. Glaze over the beach, skipping over some sunlit spots. In general, shadows should have a grayed-down violet tinge. Discretely echo touches of green for color harmony.

Bushes

For Western artists, sagebrush is a valued companion. Its cool gray-green color offers relief and variety, breaking up the monotony of flat grass. Wildlife artists often use these bushes to cover animals' hooves to prevent animals from appearing as though they're floating. Sagebrush can also be used to add beautiful flowers, creating a vibrant punch to a composition. By arranging them thoughtfully, you can guide the viewer's eye through a scene following a "connect-the-dots" sequence.

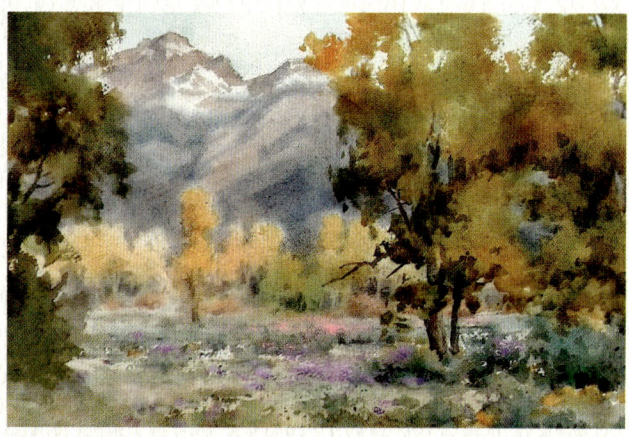

Gros Ventre, Grand Teton National Park

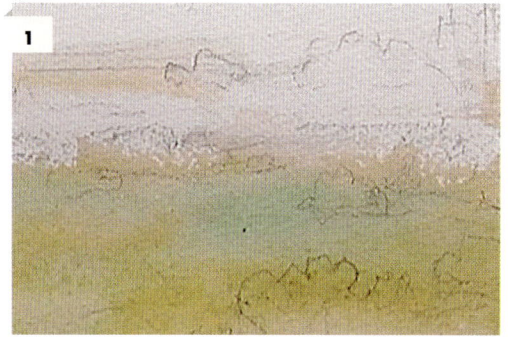

STEP 1 – APPLYING THE FIRST WASH

Working wet-on-wet, subtly vary the colors in the grass field every 1in (2.5cm) or so. Be generous with raw sienna. This golden color is very pleasing in paintings and should be given priority. Add some green to harmonize with surrounding hues.

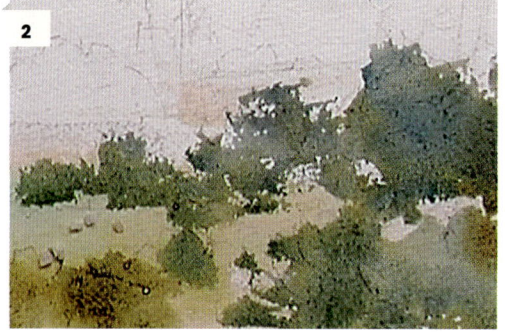

STEP 2 – BUILDING THE SAGEBRUSH FORMS

The color for the sagebrush can be a mix of Payne's gray and raw sienna. Create a graceful, varied line over the top contours of the plants, incorporating different heights to add visual interest. Vary the sizes of the sagebrush forms to create non-repetitive shapes. Use the dry-brush technique to break up the paint to indicate leaf clusters.

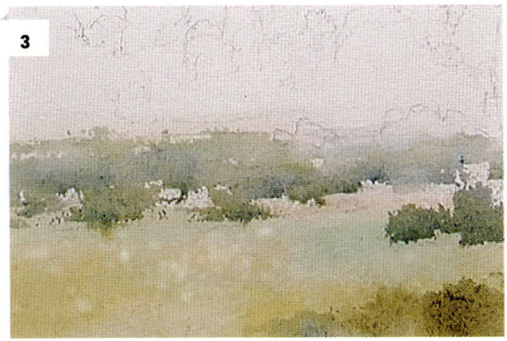

STEP 3 – DISTANT BUSHES

Comply with size perspective, making sure the sagebrush forms become smaller as they recede, and their separate units start to merge together with less definition. A melodic line at the bottom—that is, one without obvious repetition—will guarantee a pleasant, slow eye flow.

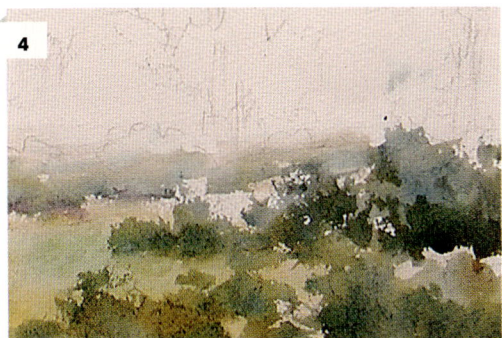

STEP 4 – CREATING THREE-DIMENSIONAL FORMS

Use negative painting to create a three-dimensional effect. Limit the darks to one-third of the form, leaving the remaining two-thirds as lighter values. Apply this principle to any trees in the painting as well.

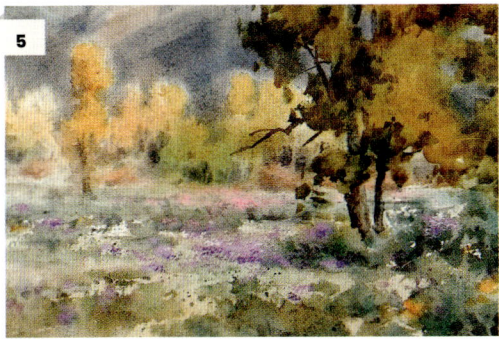

STEP 5 – ADDING FLOWERS

As an option, sprinkle wildflowers onto wet paper to help them blend into the field. Leave some open areas of plain grass for variety.

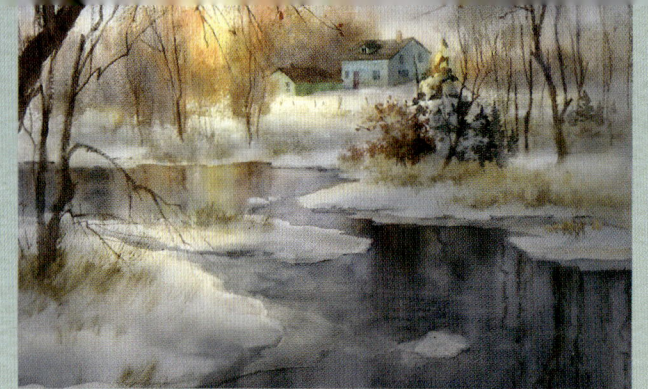

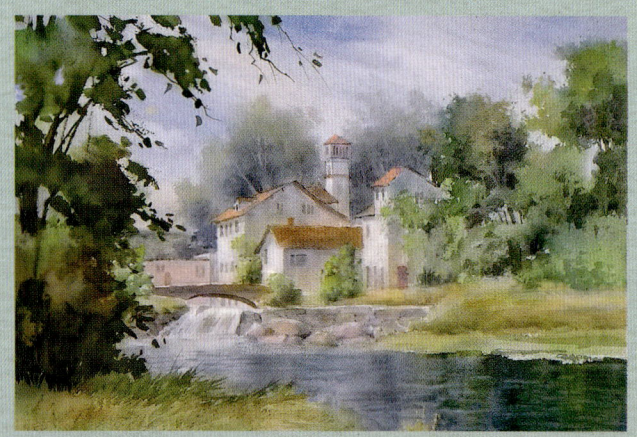

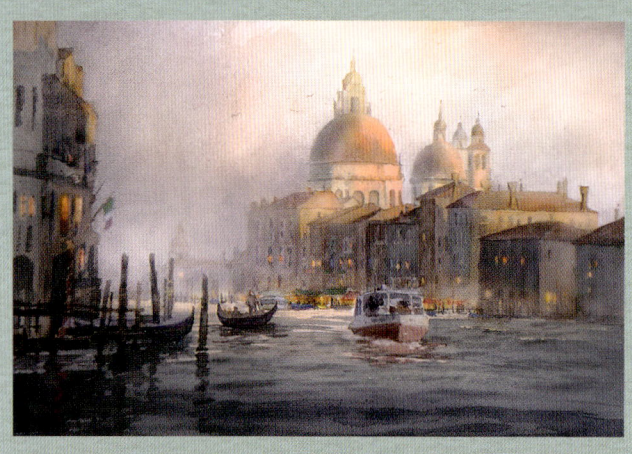

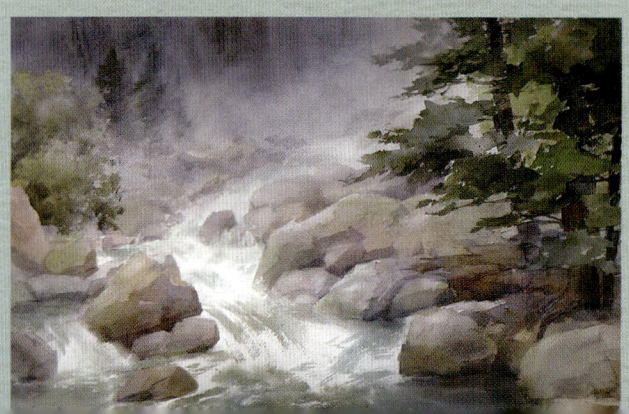

CHAPTER TWO

Water

This chapter teaches you how to successfully portray water in all its forms—the rush of tumbling waterfalls, the roar of crashing waves, or the gentle trickle of a lazy stream—all brought to life through the viewer's imagination, evoked by the efficiency of your depiction. Making water appear as though it is moving is a challenge, but you will acquire techniques to achieve that effect. By understanding and applying a few key principles of reflections, your water will appear believable.

Water Reflections

Water is one of the most popular themes in painting, celebrated in all its diverse forms. Reflections greatly enhance its natural, glassy appearance, making the scene feel convincing. Ideally, your viewers should think, "I could dip my hand in that water." When the water invites a tactile response, you've truly captured its essence.

To make water look wet, reflections are your most effective tool. Introducing playful elements—like ripples or subtle shifts in color—can bring life to otherwise flat, expansive surfaces. Four main types of water reflections are demonstrated below.

TIP

Visualize how the values would translate in a black-and-white version. To add variety and richness, let your reflections reveal subtle tonal shifts.

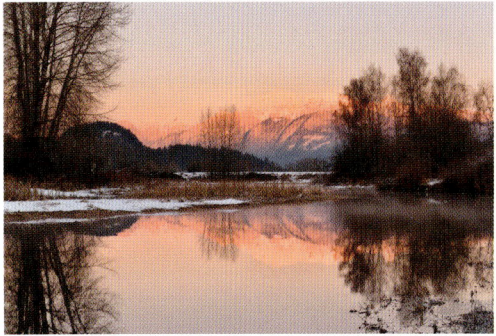

STILL WATER

Reflections like these are typical in small bodies of water, such as ponds, often appearing as slightly blurred mirror images of objects on dry land. However, overly mirrored reflections can lack fresh visual interest. To avoid this repetitive or "cloned" effect, introduce elements like water lilies, algae, or subtle wind shimmers to break up the uniformity and add dynamic variety to the scene.

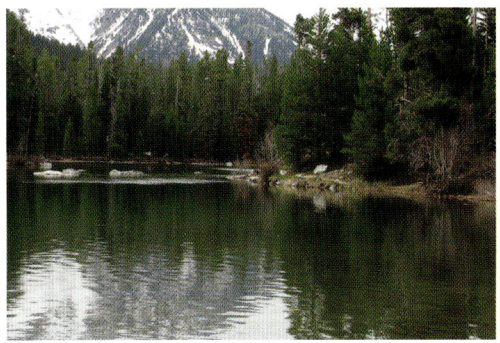

LAZY MOVING REFLECTIONS

These are the most ideal types of reflections, found in lakes with a gentle breeze or rivers with a mild current. They typically appear when the wind is calm but strong enough to create ripples, especially farther from the shore. These reflections add movement and depth, making the water look convincingly wet and lifelike. There is no longer a cloned effect.

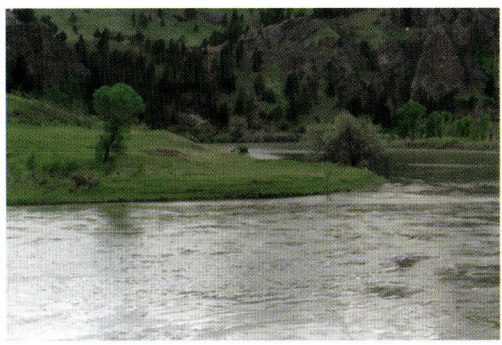

DISTURBED REFLECTIONS

These occur in lakes on windy days or in rivers with strong currents. Reflections are barely visible, making them less effective for creating visual interest in a painting. They often result in large areas lacking nuances, which can make a scene appear flat or monotonous. For this reason, they are not ideal when aiming to highlight reflective surfaces. However, these kinds of reflections are usable with a small portion of a body of water.

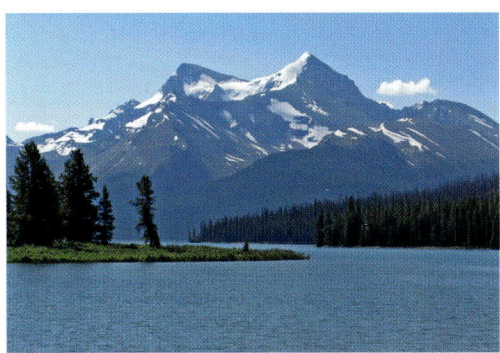

SOLID WATER

This is common in large bodies of water, including seascapes. Unless the water occupies only a narrow strip of your composition, it's best to avoid this type of water. Solid water can lead to large, repetitive areas lacking variety in color or value, resulting in a dull and unengaging section of the painting.

PRINCIPLES OF PAINTING WATER REFLECTIONS

- Dark objects appear lighter in water, while light objects appear darker. In other words, values are closer together.

- Colors in reflections are generally less saturated; reflections from white sources should be muted.

- Reflections should never have hard edges.

- Reflections are typically more elongated than the objects on land. However, feel free to adjust their length and shape to better suit the composition.

Still Water Reflections

Bare trees in winter are ideal for reflections. Their squiggly lines suggest gentle movement in the water, adding visual rhythm. Water is usually darker than the sky—an effect that should always be included to maintain realism in your landscapes.

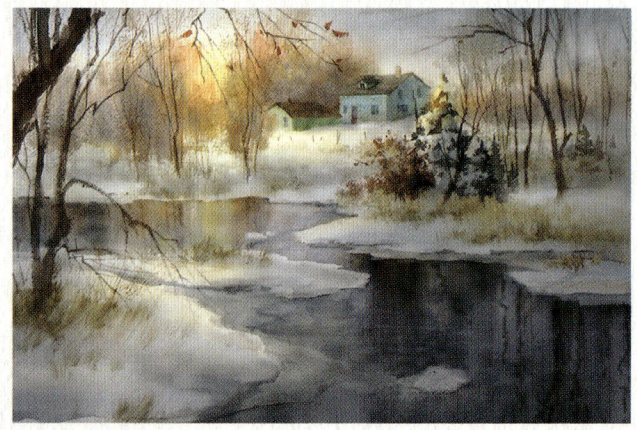

First Light on the Ice

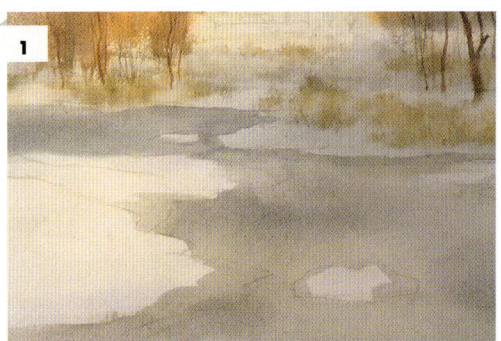

STEP 1 – STARTING WITH THE ICE

Wet the entire pond area with clear water, then apply a warm, dirty, gray wash with touches of raw sienna over the surface. This base layer will provide the tone for the color of ice.

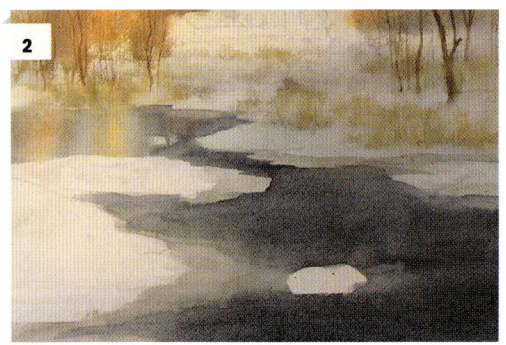

STEP 2 – PAINTING THE MELTED WATER

Rewet the surface, keeping the areas where the ice is dry. Reflect the golden trees and grasses in the pond with vertical strokes to capture their soft, gentle reflections. Next, fill the pond with a blue-gray mixture, using negative painting to carve out areas of ice near the shore. Keeping the ice lighter in color than the water but darker than the snow on land will ensure a smooth transition and add depth to the composition.

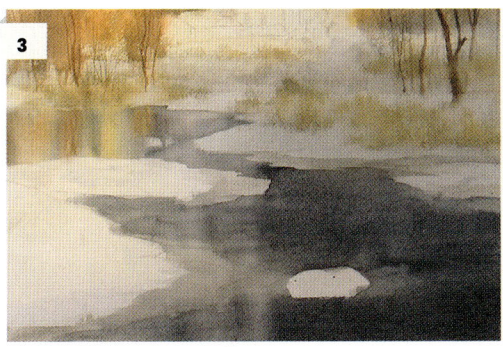

STEP 3 – CREATING MOVEMENT

While the paint is still wet, lift out some streaks of light (see Tricks of the Trade: Blotting with a Paper Towel). This is to avoid a flat area with no variations. This area reflects the sky and will create a pleasing gradient plane with variations of values.

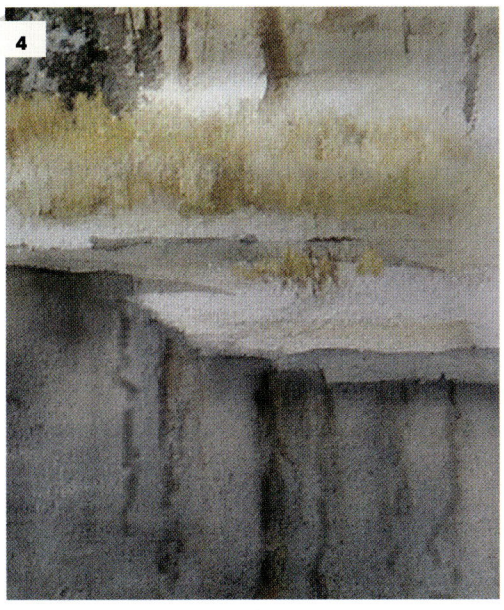

STEP 4 – ADDING REFLECTIONS

A rigger brush is perfect for creating the delicate squiggly lines that represent reflections of bare trees. Start at the snowbank and use the brush to dance along the water's surface, forming these lines. As you reach the bottom third of the pond, break up the reflections into smaller segments to mimic the natural disruption of the water's surface.

TIP

The areas of ice that appear soft edged are gradually submerging into the water, blending seamlessly. To convey the ice as being just above the surface, use a "broken glass" effect—jagged, fragmented edges—to create the illusion of ice cracking and floating.

Lazy Water Reflections

Here, I was drawn to the angle of the buildings, the bridge, and the waterfall of the village. Their strong, intersecting lines and the way they framed the landscape sparked the desire to paint the scene. The reflections are ghostly, identifiable replicas of the landforms. Typically, reflections should be longer than the objects on land.

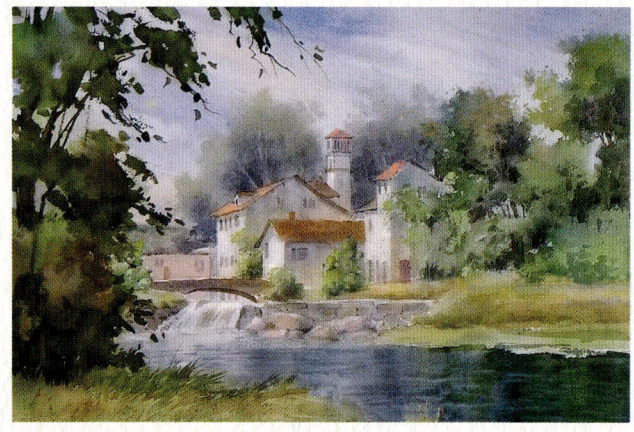

The Village of Whispering Waters

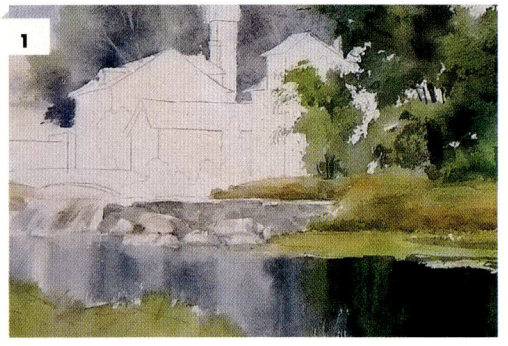

STEP 1 – APPLYING VERTICAL STROKES

Lightly wet the entire body of water—just enough to stop the paint spreading uncontrollably. Use vertical strokes, gently squiggling the brush, to create the reflections of the landforms. If they appear too mirrored, use a clean, moist brush to sweep horizontally across the water to distort the images. Create bands of light and dark, resembling a piano keyboard, to add variation of values.

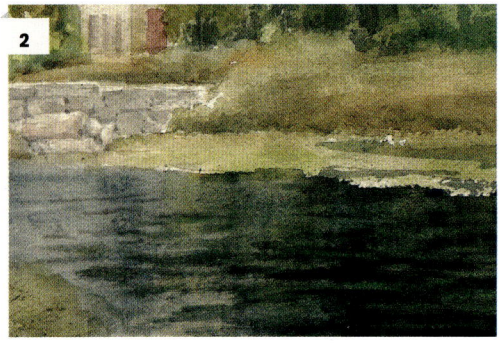

STEP 2 – CREATING WAVELETS

Using a thirsty brush, lift out some streaks of lighter value with short, quick lines to suggest movement (see Tricks of the Trade: Lightening Value with a Thirsty Brush). Once this is done, add the dark wavelets to enhance the sense of motion. This step brings the water to life, giving it the appearance of gentle movement.

Choppy Water

The Grand Canal in Venice is one of the most famous landmarks in the world. The varied angles at the tops of the buildings create appealing shapes to paint. In this composition, I used the dock area to suggest movement, making the water look choppy. To further enhance the illusion of water, I used the dock poles to render squiggly reflections in lazily moving water.

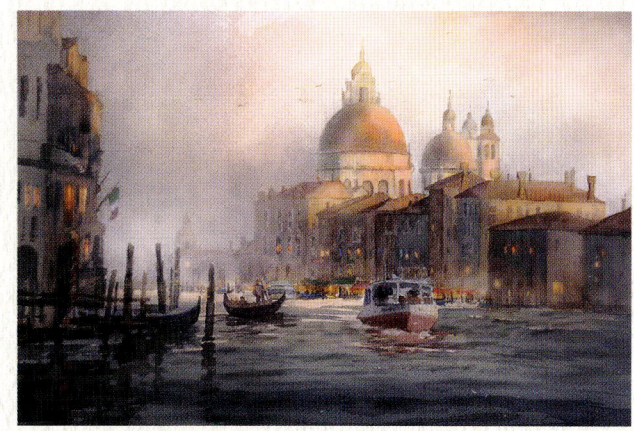

Grand Canal, Venice, Italy

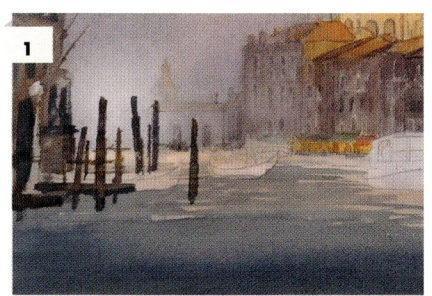

STEP 1 – LAYING AN INITIAL WASH

Working wet-on-wet, lay an initial wash for the canal. The entire area is a muted, grayed-down blue-green. Save white areas around the boats and dock poles to indicate white water due to water disturbance.

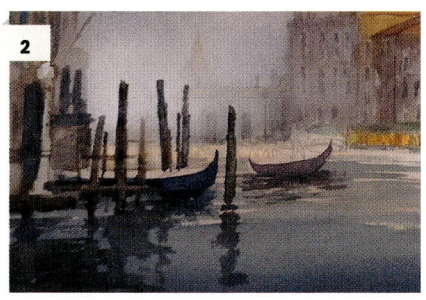

STEP 2 – REFLECTIONS

Rewet the areas where you want to indicate reflections and let the paper absorb the excess water. The right moment to paint is when the glisten just fades. Apply a few squiggly vertical lines to represent lazy movement.

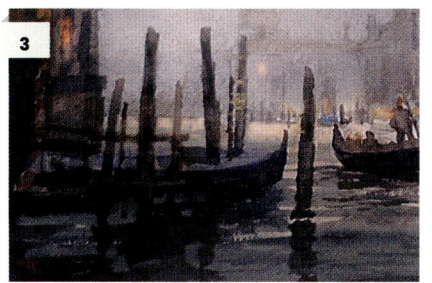

STEP 3 – CREATING WAVELETS

Use a twist-and-turn brush application to create the wavelets with irregular heights. The ones in the foreground are the largest and they gradually diminish in size as they go back.

Bubbling Stream

Slow-moving streams with soft, lazy flowing water and sharp-edged rocks create an appealing and delightful contrast of edges. Fog in the background enhances depth and recession, creating a dreamy atmosphere that softens details and invites viewers to imagine what lies beyond the trees. The stream's "S"-shaped path remains one of the most engaging ways to guide the viewer's eye into the depths.

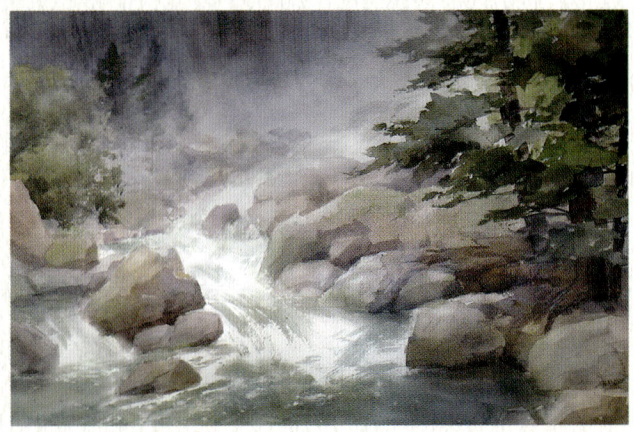

Mountain Runoff, Yosemite National Park

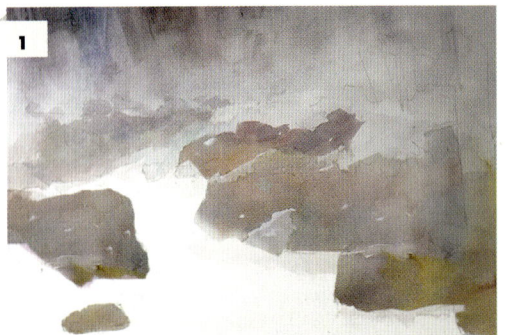

STEP 1 – DEFINING THE SHAPES

Paint the rocks surrounding the stream, leaving the white of the paper untouched. Add water at their base for mist. Vary the colors of the rocks every 1in (2.5cm) or so to create a lively, painterly effect with rich hues. Mix up the sizes of the rocks, leaning toward larger shapes, with smaller ones to avoid monotony and to achieve a more natural look. Focus on designing abstract, irregular shapes to steer clear of symmetry.

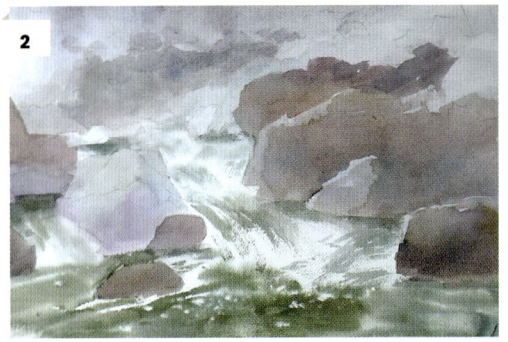

STEP 2 – CAPTURING THE DIRECTION OF THE WATER

Use a fan brush to negative-paint the bubbly white areas, rotating the brush slightly to decrease the size. This will avoid repetitive sweeping patterns. Follow the water's natural flow. If needed, use coarse-grit sandpaper or pastels to add more texture. For added detail, peck out a few floating bubbles with the tip of a precision knife (see Tricks of the Trade).

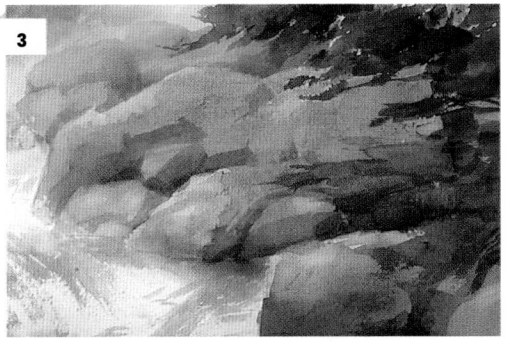

STEP 3 - CREATING ROCK CLUSTERS

Nature provides an abundance of rocks. To simplify, join rocks together to form units of various sizes. Enhance your rocks by adding touches of purple to the shadow sides. This hue is magical to improve the look of rocks. Vary the sizes from large to small and in between.

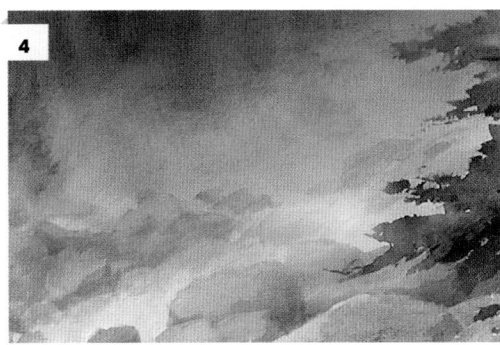

STEP 4 - ADDING ROCKS INTO FOG

Place some rocks in the distant fog as an indicator of the depth of the scene. To produce this effect, add water to that area only. The paint will dilute, producing a lighter value.

TIP

Watercolor is the king of mediums when it comes to depicting fog. Feel free to apply this dreamy effect in a diversity of scenes.

You can use stick pastels effectively to bring out the lively, bubbly textures of waterfalls, rushing streams, crashing waves, and the softness of fluffy clouds.

Waterfall

Painting water is one of the most enjoyable themes, and waterfalls in particular are at the top of the list. The illusory trick is to make the water seem like it is falling, rather than static. Mist isn't always visible around waterfalls, but adding it in a composition like this—along with blurring the edges of the falling water—helps enhance the sense of movement.

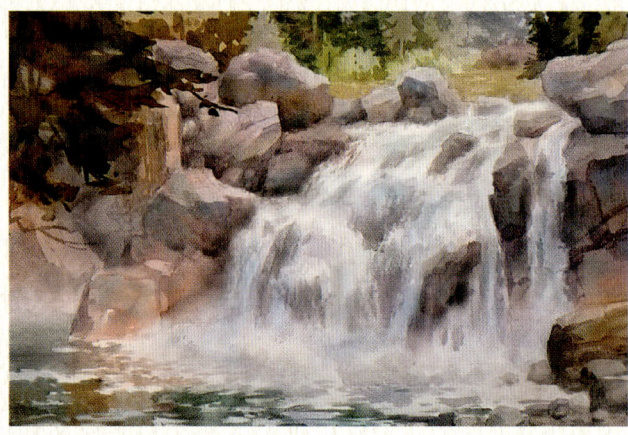

Cool Waters, Ancient Stones

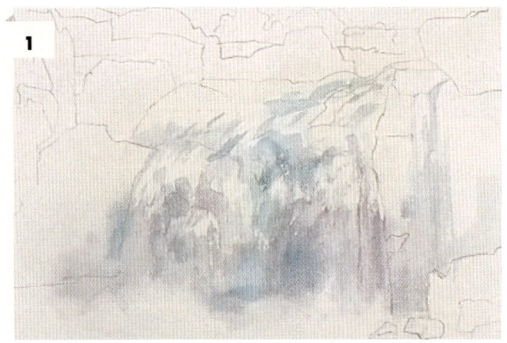

STEP 1 – PAINTING THE RUSHING WATER

Spot-wet inside and outside the contour drawing, but leave dry paper where the water bulges out. The eye will naturally seek out these sharper, drier spots for focus. The shadow areas will be mostly blue, with hints of violet and turquoise placed next to each other. Start brushing from the bottom up to create the effect of white water tumbling over the rocks inside the falls. There should be more shadow than white paper—the more you limit the white foam, the more it will stand out.

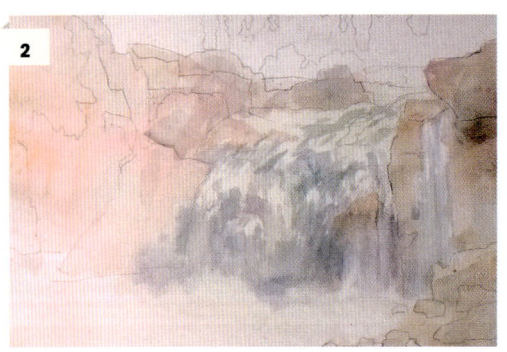

STEP 2 – ADDING THE CLIFF

The highlights of the rocks form your first layer in a mid-light value. Remember, you paint light to dark in watercolor. Vary the colors with yellow-orange, orange, gray, and touches of pink. Each of these similar valued four hues should be identifiable for maximum richness.

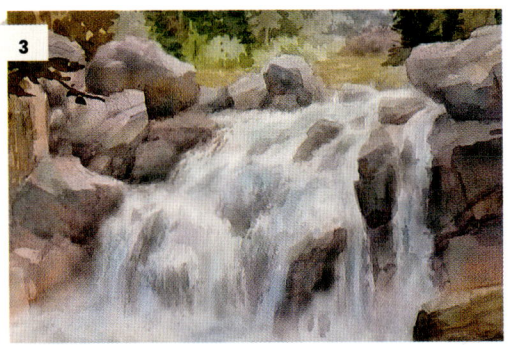

STEP 3 – RENDERING CLIFF FACES

Negative-paint into the water to create melodic lines with the cliff angles. Slightly vary the colors every 1in (2.5cm). Leave some of the initial highlights while rendering abstract forms with the darker color. Introduce orange for reflected light at the base of some sections of cliff.

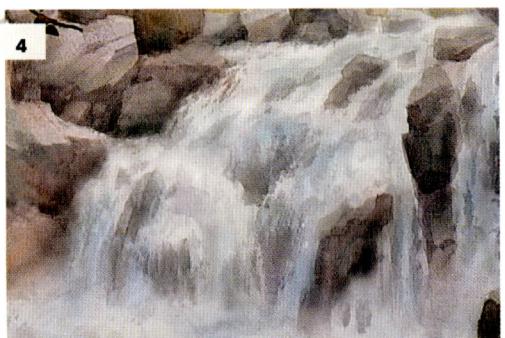

STEP 4 – CREATING SOFT AND HARD EDGES

The water's downpour shows both soft and hard edges. The eye will be able find a way to focus on the hard edges. Include some rocks peeking through the water in a lighter value than the cliffs. Think of a bridal veil to capture the water's natural, transparent quality. Add some mist at the bottom to create a strong contrast with the harder edges of the rocks. Blurred edges convey water movement.

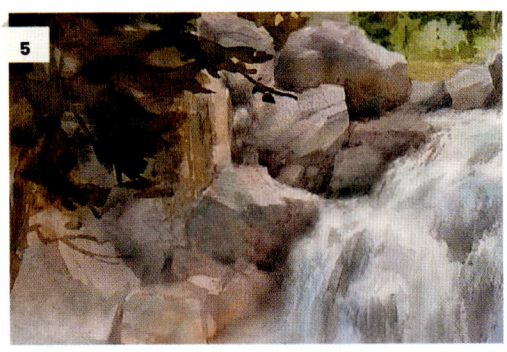

STEP 5 – SCULPTING THREE-DIMENSIONAL FORMS

Focus on creating three-dimensionality. Divide the cliff face into a few abstract shapes to simplify the structure. Define these shapes with crevices. Add dark accents to represent the indentations within these crevices.

TIP

When applying wet-on-wet, to make sure your paper has just the right water absorption to control the paint from spreading too far, simultaneously wet a separate piece of paper and run tests on it first.

Rocks Under Water

Rocks underwater achieve a stunning see-through effect, adding depth to a scene. The technique is a great choice for painting lakes and rivers. It invites viewers to mentally immerse themselves in the scene, imagining the sensation of wading into the water. Such details evoke a mental and emotional reaction, activating the viewer's imagination senses and sparking daydreams.

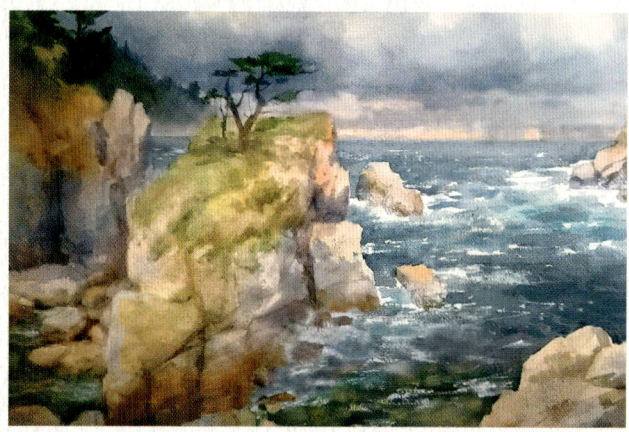

Overlooking 17 Mile Drive, California Coast

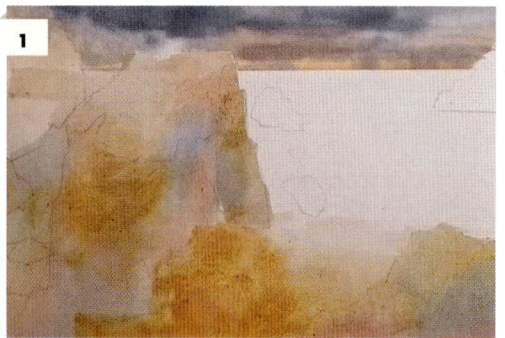

STEP 1 – RENDERING THE CLIFF COLORS

Mix burnt sienna and raw sienna to create a warm, earthy tone for the cliffs. Use this mixture, wet-on-wet, to paint the foreground ocean area where the sunken rocks will be. This will serve as a base for lifting out the darker water later, making the exposed rocks stand out. Allow the layer to dry.

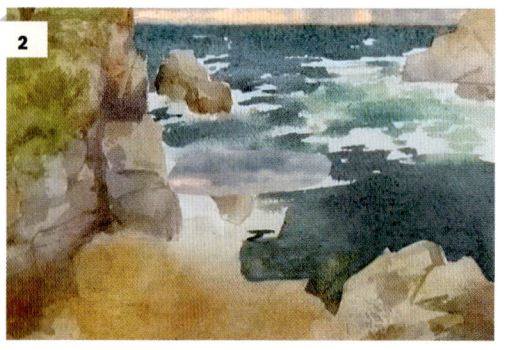

STEP 2 – RENDERING THE OCEAN COLOR

Mix a pool of blue-green, grayed down, in a small container to ensure you have enough for the entire ocean. Test the color on a separate scrap of paper and let it dry to confirm it's the right value. Disturbed water near the rocks is a lighter turquoise-green. Leave pieces of white paper to indicate spumes, but avoid adding them in the far distance where there are no rocks, as this can disrupt the sense of depth.

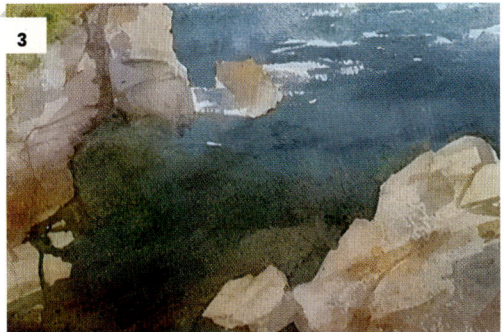

STEP 3 – ADDING A GLAZE

Using the same ocean color, paint on top of the underwater rock color you added in Step 1. When a glaze of watercolor is on top of a preexisting layer, the top layer can be partially removed while it is still wet.

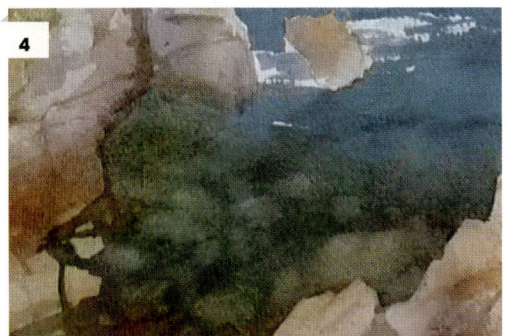

STEP 4 – BRINGING OUT SUNKEN ROCKS

Use cotton swabs and paper towel to lift out areas of the glaze, leaving the underlayer intact (see Tricks of the Trade: Blotting with a Paper Towel). Create natural variations in size and adjust the pressure to control the effect—firmer pressure for subtle highlights to indicate rocks that are closer to the surface, and lighter pressure for darker, more submerged ones. Keep the underwater rocks darker than the dry rocks.

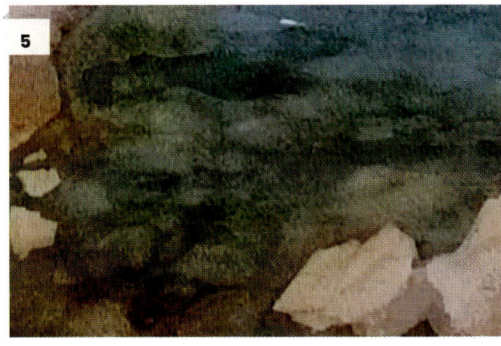

STEP 5 – DEFINING THE ROCKS

Gradually reduce the frequency of the lifted areas as they recede into the distance as the water gets deeper, ensuring a smooth, natural transition. To avoid a flat appearance, darken one side of some lifted shapes, adding depth.

TIP

Place painter's tape at the ocean horizon line to ensure a straight line.

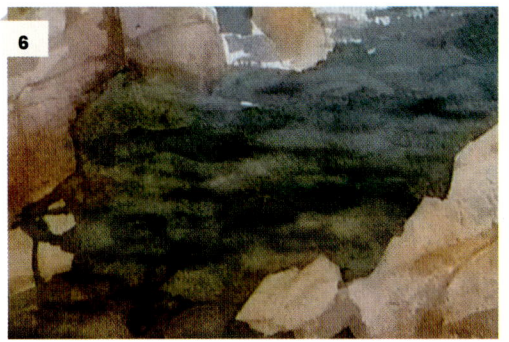

STEP 6 – ADDING WAVELETS

Above the submerged rocks, paint some wavelets on top of the water, making them slightly darker than the first layer of turquoise glaze. This will give the water a sense of movement and enhance the illusion of the submerged rocks.

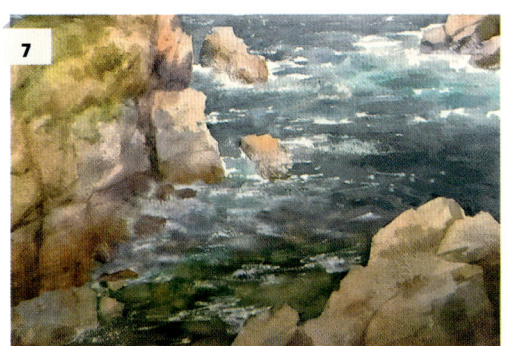

STEP 7 – CREATING SPUMES

Use pastels to create more spumes where water would splash against the rocks and cliff. This will create the illusion of movement in the water. The spumes will naturally appear to float on top, helping to further push the rocks beneath the surface. Make sure enough of the submerged rocks are visible for viewers to recognize what they are.

SEA SPUMES AS A VISUAL PATH

Sea spumes are just one of several elements that can serve as a lead-in to a painting (see Composition: Stage 4). Here, the spumes start at the bottom and gently wend their way toward the lighthouse, intensifying in brightness and activity as they approach the rocks.

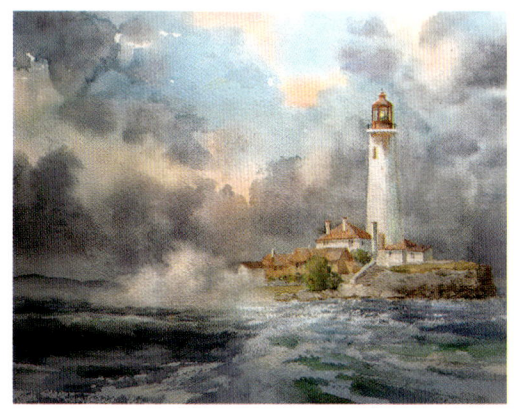

Water Shimmers

The main theme of this painting is the lake, which is why it occupies most of the pictorial surface (see Composition: Stage 1). Adding shimmers to water enhances its glassy appearance and suggests the presence of wind or glistening sunlight. When the sun reflects off the water, shimmers will be white. When wind disturbs the surface and sunlight is absent, the shimmers will be about the same value as the sky.

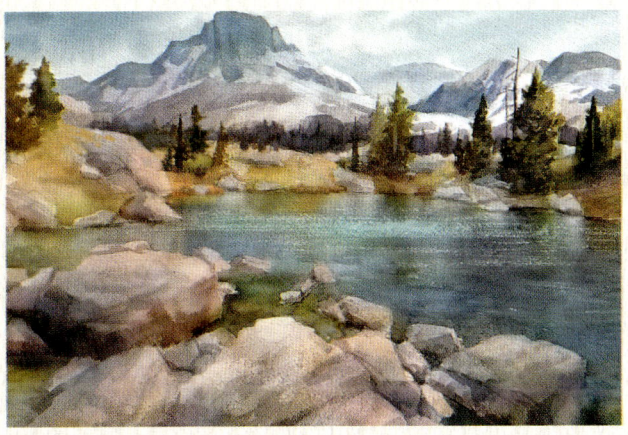

Banner Peak, Sierra Nevada Range

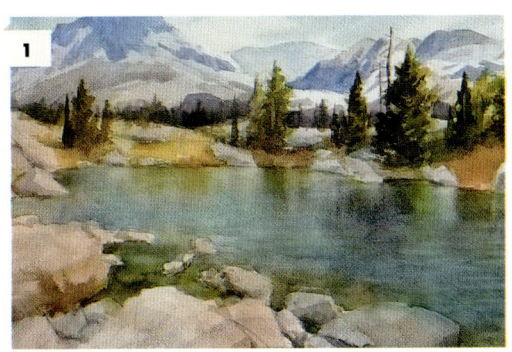

STEP 1 – RENDERING THE LAKE

The entire lake is painted in a blue-green hue. Once the reflections are added, indicate wavelets, starting with larger ones in the foreground and decreasing their size as they regress. You can leave them out when approaching the background. These suggest the effect of wind rippling across the surface.

TIP

There is no end to the special effects you can include in your landscapes. Rain, falling snow, water shimmers, mist and fog, moonlight, smoke coming out of a chimney, and sunbeams.

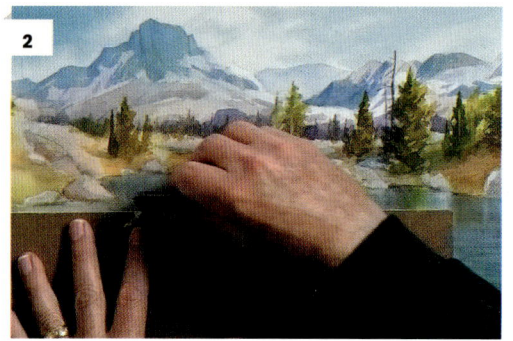

STEP 2 – CREATING THE SHIMMERS

Use a piece of fine-grit sandpaper to create the shimmers by dragging it from side to side with the aid of a ruler (see Tricks of the Trade: Using Sandpaper to Create Shimmers and Water Spray). Keep it perfectly parallel to the canvas border. Leave gaps to reveal parts of the lake beyond the shimmers, extending up to the shoreline. This effect simulates the lovely effect of wind disturbing the water.

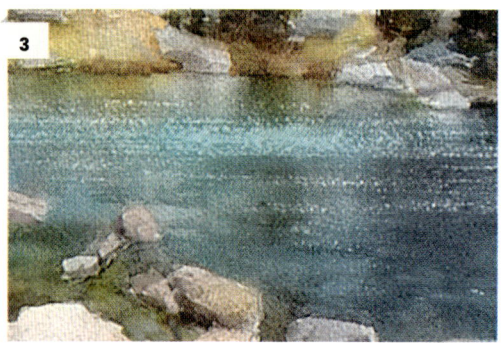

STEP 3 – TAPERING OFF THE SHIMMERS

To avoid an obvious rectangle, gradually taper off the shimmers, reducing them little by little to show a progressive transition. For the illusion of sunlight glistening on the water, sand down all the way to the white paper.

TIP

For subtle wind shimmers, avoid scoring down to the white paper— simply lighten the value or use a sponge to slightly remove some paint.

Ice

Ice serves as a perfect intermediary between snow and water, filling empty spaces in a composition so that bodies of water don't resemble swimming pools and instead take on a pleasing special effect. Shorelines often have too fast-paced leading lines. To slow the visual rush, design ice into graceful, flowing lines. The trees and their reflections act as natural "speed bumps," slowing the pace created by the straight line in the background and the right river bank.

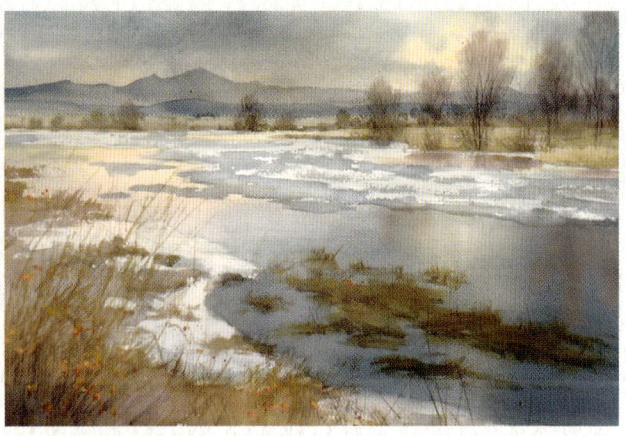

Marshland Melancholy

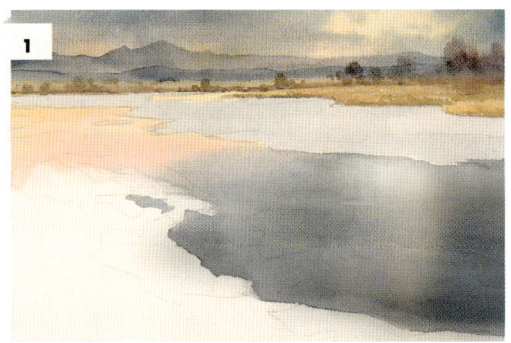

STEP 1 – PAINTING THE RIVER

Paint the river, starting with a dark, cool, gray-blue in the foreground and gradually transitioning to lighter, warmer tones in the distance—reflecting the colors of the late-afternoon sky.

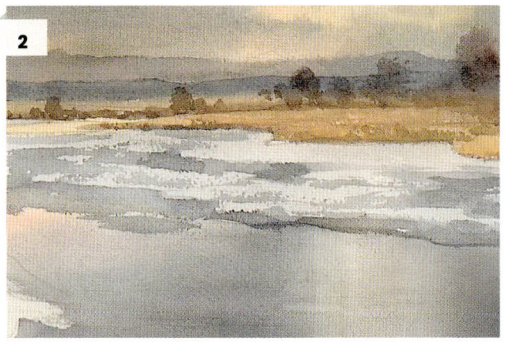

STEP 2 – CREATING AREAS OF ICE

Glaze the white areas of snow and ice with raw sienna to add a touch of warmth. Then, using a lighter value of the water color, paint around the snow mounds to suggest the ice. Ice is usually a middle value—darker than snow, but lighter than the water.

Winding Brook

Slow-moving streams with soft, flowing water paired with jagged ice create a striking and delightful contrast. In this composition, the sunbeam draws attention to the focal point. The brook is intentionally designed with a pendulum-like leading line, guiding the viewer's eye from side to side and into the background. This flowing composition provides a delightful visual tour of the scene.

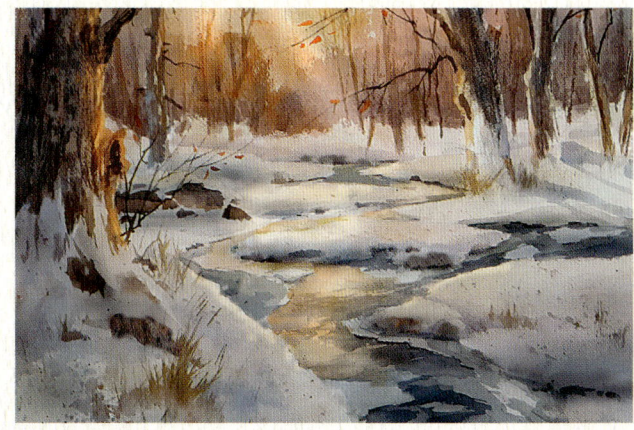

Thaw's First Kiss

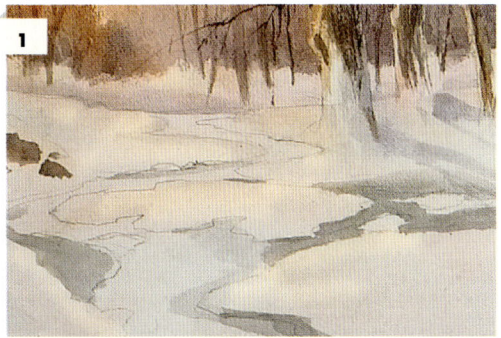

STEP 1 - PAINTING THE ICE

Paint the ice in a mid-value, leaving some white areas of the stream that will be the melting water receiving the sunlight. To maintain a natural look, leave a few blank, isolated, island patches scattered here and there. Ice mostly clings to the snow bank. Make some areas jagged and others smoothly rounded. The brook's center remains mostly free of ice, yet the brook continues its visual path.

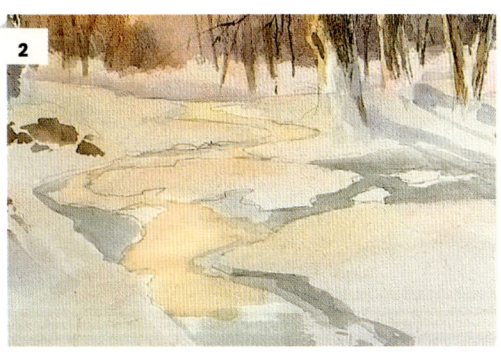

STEP 2 - CREATING THE SUNLIGHT'S GLOW

For the glow of the sunlight, add a yellow-orange tone to the white open spaces that you bypassed within the stream in Step 1.

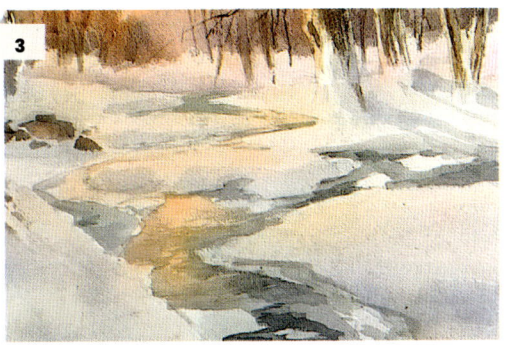

STEP 3 – RENDERING THE MELTING WATER

To depict the water, apply a glaze over some of the sunlit and ice areas using a darker value than the ice. Again, leave variations of jagged, broken-glass-like edges and smooth, round edges.

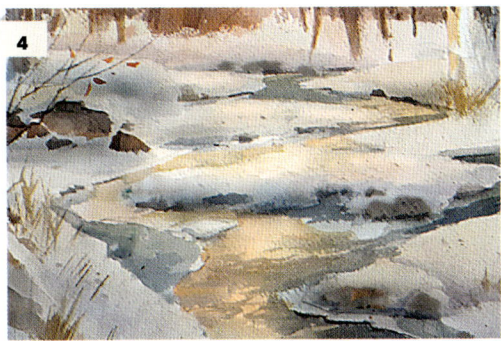

STEP 4 – DEFINING THE BANKS OF THE STREAM

Add thin, dark lines under the snow bank to indicate erosion under the ice.

TIP

A good compositional tool is to make one corner different from the opposite one, both at the top and bottom.

Seascape

Seascapes are relatively easy to paint because they have fewer variables than landscapes. With just a handful of key principles, you can capture the essence of the scene and create compelling paintings. To create the illusion of depth in this composition, think of the cliffs and rocks as chess pieces receding into the distance. Exaggerating atmospheric perspective is a great tool to achieve this.

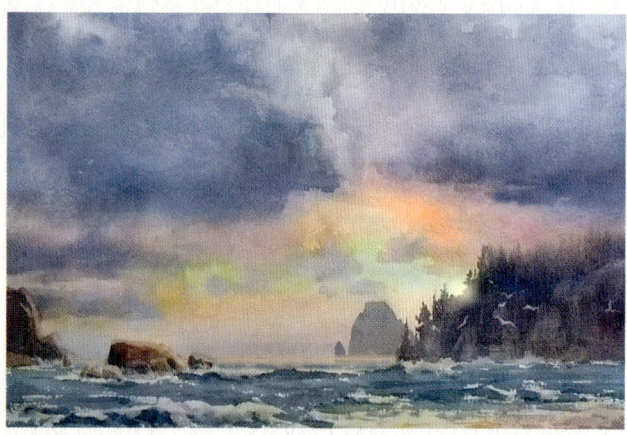

Breaking Through the Tempest

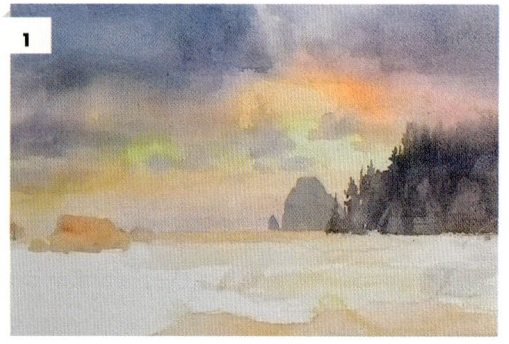

STEP 1 - WARMING THE PAPER

Working wet-on-wet, cover the entire ocean area with a yellow-orange wash. This ensures that the white water will be in sync with the warm sky, creating a harmonious blend between the two planes.

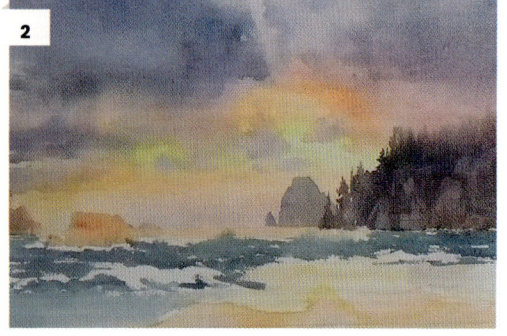

STEP 2 - PAINTING THE OCEAN

The ocean water is a blue-green hue, toned down, with the sky purple for harmony. Negative-paint the crashing foam, leaving the warm white paper untouched. Arrange the waves to create a gentle, rolling eye flow—like a shallow roller coaster—to lead the viewer smoothly across the painting.

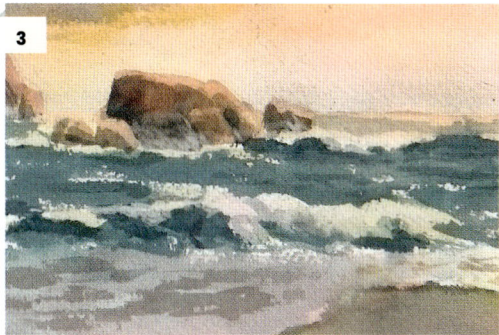

STEP 3 – MAKING WAVES

Darken the rising walls of water and the crashing foam to make the waves look as if they are rolling.

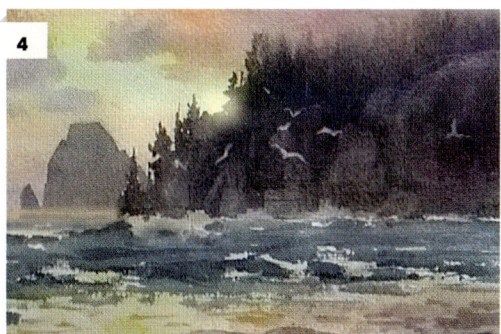

STEP 4 – MAINTAINING A SLOW VISUAL PACE

Avoid creating a single long line of crashing waves, but interrupt them to lead the eye into the scene in slow segments. Painting a wave crest where the water meets the cliffs will also help to slow down the visual pace that would otherwise form a straight line.

TIP

If you cannot distinguish the hue of a shape, that means it is too dark.

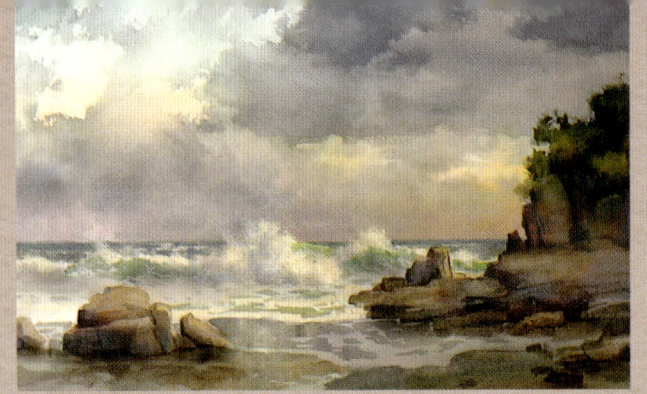

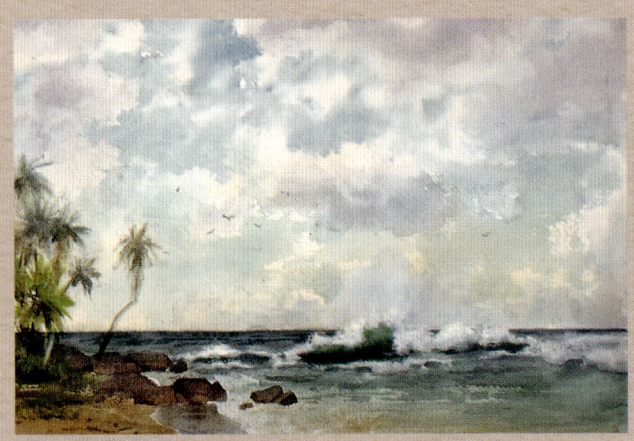

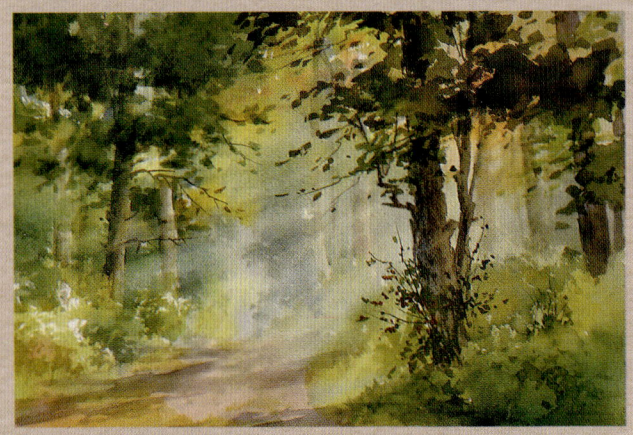

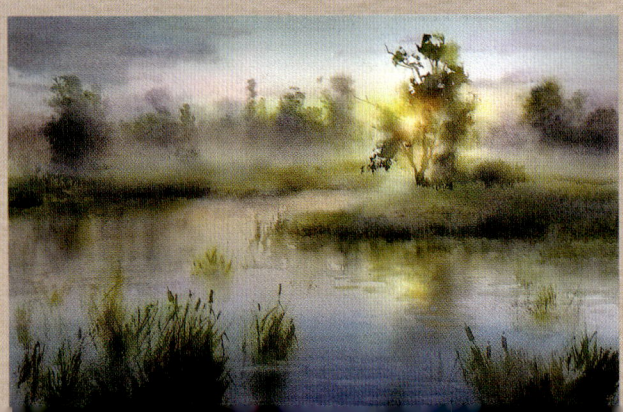

CHAPTER THREE:
Sky

Capturing the vastness of the sky on the limited space of a sheet of watercolor paper is a challenging feat. This chapter guides you through the best compositional techniques to keep viewers engaged in this area for as long as possible as they admire the beauty of a sunset, the impact of a storm, or alluring white cumulus clouds. You will also learn how to arrange clouds to create visual pathways that gracefully lead the eye to the intended focal points, while giving the sky a convincing sense of depth.

Late-Afternoon Sky

Blue skies with white clouds compete with blue seas and white crashing waves. Painting such a scene at sunset can produce visually stunning results. For this composition, I designed the surf foam rolling over the sand in the foreground to guide the viewer's eye in a pleasing "S" movement toward the deep water, following its line as it connects to the rocks. Adding wisps to the crashing wave suggests a strong wind, enhancing the sense of movement. The dark foliage against the bright sky becomes a focal point due to the striking value contrast.

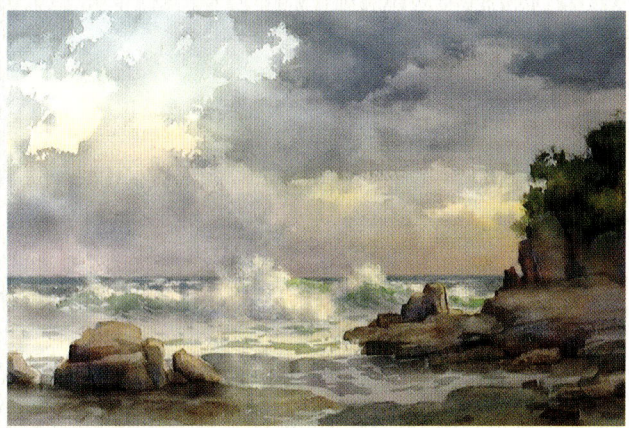

Rhythms of the Breaking Edge

STEP 1 - CREATING A WARM SKY

Begin with a raw sienna wash over the entire painting, gradually subtracting pigment as you approach the zenith. This creates a natural gradient. In the late evening, fluffy clouds directly overhead tend to appear cooler, and gradually become warmer as they approach the horizon.

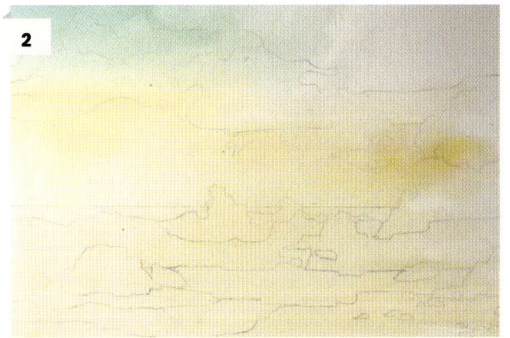

STEP 2 - ADDING TURQUOISE

Create a sky opening with a turquoise green-blue, that will act as a lead-in, guiding the viewer's eye into the composition from the top, which is where we start reading a page of a book. Allow it to gradually blend into the warm tone of raw sienna below. This creates a transition from the cooler sky to the warmer horizon.

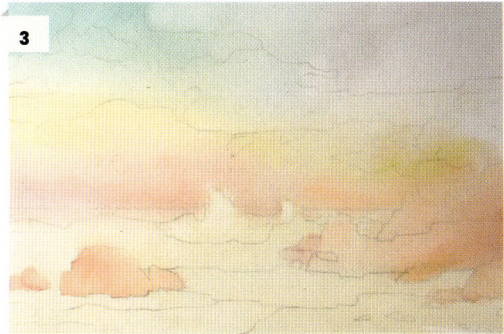

STEP 3 – BUILDING SUNSET COLORS

Intensify the warm colors by adding oranges and pinks near the horizon to fully ignite the sunset. Place the pink farthest from the sun because it is cooler than orange.

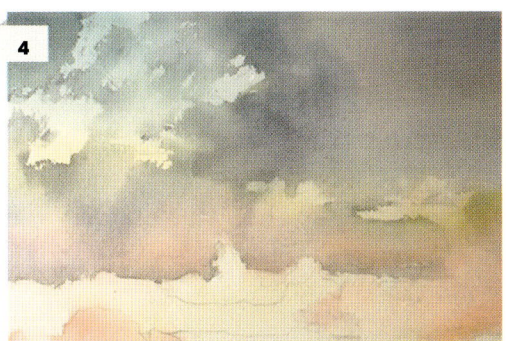

STEP 4 – CREATING THE RAIN CLOUDS

Spot-wet some of the areas where you plan to add rain clouds, while leaving other areas dry to become hard edges for eye focus. This technique ensures soft edges characteristic of natural clouds. Include small cloud fragments breaking away from the main mass to avoid an isolated and artificial effect.

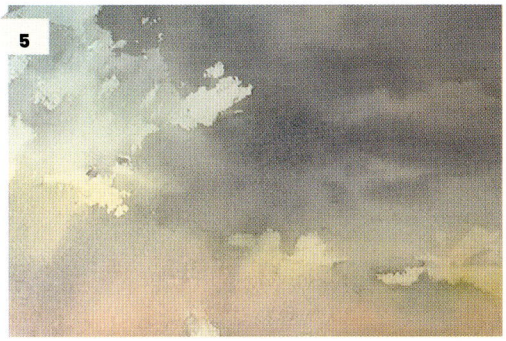

STEP 5 – ENHANCING CLOUD DEPTH

Darken the overhead clouds. These naturally appear darker due to their closer proximity to the zenith. This creates a sense of depth and the illusion of clouds drifting farther into the sky dome.

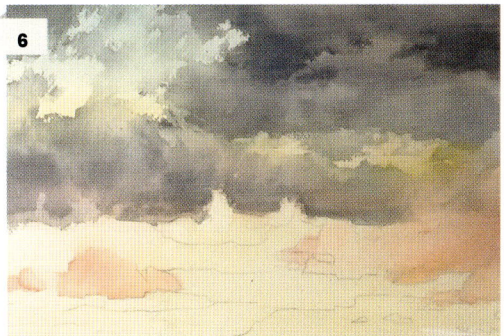

STEP 6 – DARKENING THE BASE

Darken the base of the clouds to give them a more rounded, three-dimensional appearance. To create a fluffy effect, twirl your brush upward in certain areas, allowing the paint to naturally soften and form cloudlike shapes. While they are still wet, add the warm sky colors at the bottom of the dark clouds to reflect the glow underneath.

Cloudy Sky

The sky is admired for its vastness. While we can't fully capture its immense scale in a painting, we can create the best impression by dedicating the largest portion of the canvas to it. To achieve a natural cloudy sky, use the wet-on-wet application. This technique creates soft, blended edges that mimic the fluidity of real cloud formations. By incorporating both the clouds and the blue sky, you can craft a visual path that starts in the top left and gently leads the viewer's eye deeper into the scene, enhancing the sense of depth and movement.

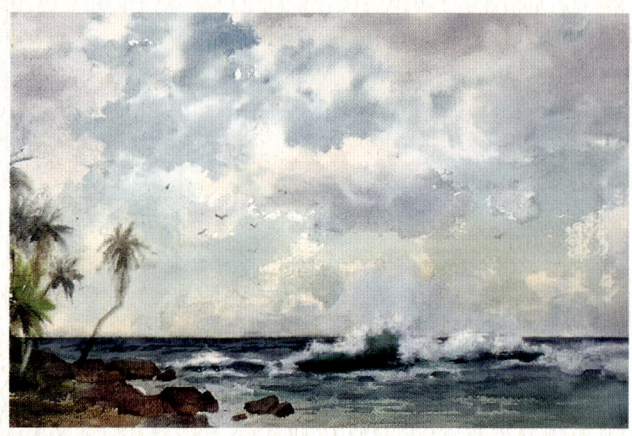

Saltwater Serenade

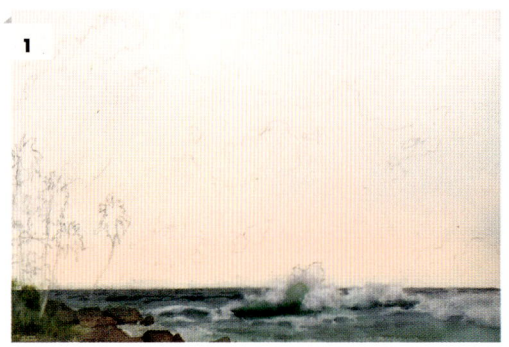

STEP 1 – CREATING A WARM UNDERPAINTING

Begin with a full glaze of raw sienna over the entire painting. Gradually intensify the warmth, transitioning to orange as you approach the horizon because the sun is close. Leave the top portion of the paper intact, allowing its natural warmth to show through. Most papers have a slight tinge of warmth added to them from the manufacturer, becoming an off-white.

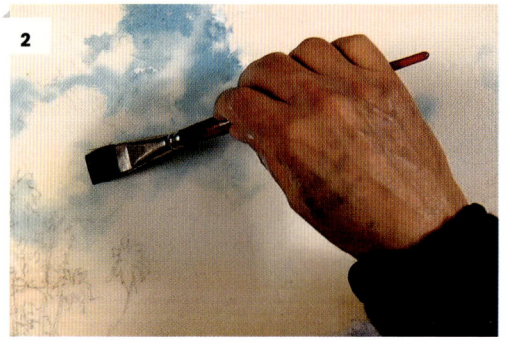

STEP 2 – TAPPING IN THE SKY

Spot-wet certain areas, leaving others dry to achieve both soft and hard edges. Visualize where the blue sky will go as you wet. Use a tap-and-drag technique by rotating the brush while holding it flat in different directions to paint in the blue sky. Start darker at the top, leaving unpainted abstract cloud shapes. This process is carving out the clouds with negative painting. As you progress further down, warm the blue with turquoise.

STEP 3 – ADDING DARKER CLOUDS

Add the shadow portions of the clouds. They should be darker at the top and gradually become cooler (more blue) as they recede toward the horizon. This is where they are denser due to forming rain. Follow the Principles of Painting Cloudy Skies to achieve this.

TIP

Rough paper, with its pronounced texture, is ideal for wet-on-wet techniques. The peaks and valleys in the paper help slow down the water's expansion, preventing it from spreading too quickly. This control allows for better texture and breaks up the paint more effectively—perfect for painting cumulus clouds with hard edges.

Additionally, placing the shadowed part of a cloud in one corner of the painting can encourage the viewer's eye to linger longer in the painting.

PRINCIPLES OF PAINTING CLOUDY SKIES

- White fluffy clouds are cooler closer to the zenith and warmer closer to the horizon.

- The cloud shadows are darker and warmer closer to the zenith, lighter and cooler toward the horizon.

- The blue sky is cooler and darker near the zenith and gradually gets warmer towards the horizon.

- Avoid painting equal amounts of bare sky and clouds.

- For a natural look, create smaller clusters of clouds that represent parts of a main cloud floating away.

Sunbeams

Sunbeams are a stunning effect that can elevate any painting. They work especially well in forest scenes and skies where the filtering light can create a remarkable atmospheric effect. Here, the shadowed foreground draws attention to the hiking trail, adding depth. Sunbeams push the background back, further enhancing the illusion of distance. The rhythmic brushstrokes forming the leaves naturally draw the viewer's focus to the trail, offering an invitation to walk deeper into the forest.

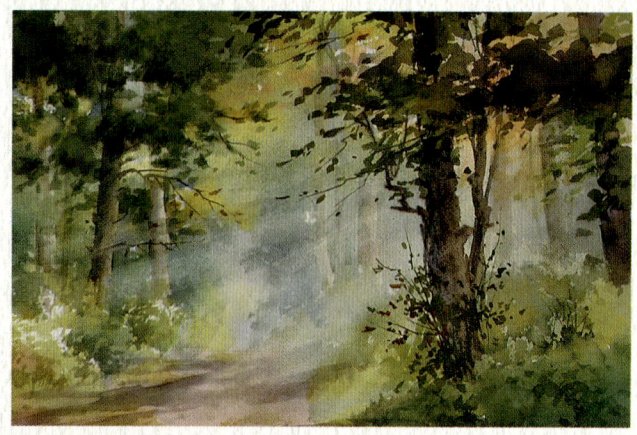

Path of Glimmering Light

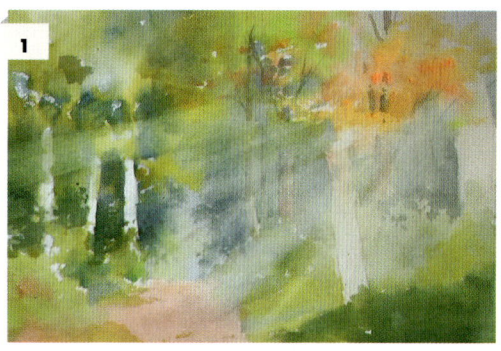

STEP 1 – LIFTING OUT THE SUNBEAMS

After painting the background, lightly spray water over the entire dry painting and allow it to sit for a couple of minutes, letting the water seep into the paper. Next, use dry, folded paper towel to gently lift out the sunbeams. Adjust the size of the paper towel to vary the widths of the beams and the spaces in between, to avoid uniformity. Guide the beams with a ruler.

Each sunbeam should originate from a single point, like hands on a clock, radiating outward. The sunbeams should appear milky and somewhat transparent, to about 50 percent opacity, allowing elements behind them to still be visible. This technique creates a soft, yet dramatic, effect of light filtering through.

TIP

PanPastel's titanium white makes a good alternative to creating sunbeams if lifting out with tissue paper is unsuccessful.

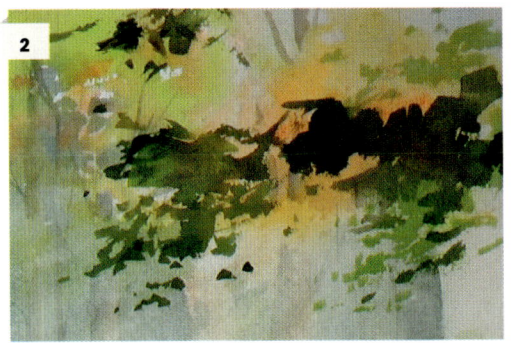

STEP 2 – APPLYING FOLIAGE

The dark tree in the foreground serves to enhance the illumination by providing value contrast, making the light areas pop and emphasizing the light of the sunbeams. To depict the foliage, use jabs and flicking strokes that are "ovalish" with arrowhead points. They should not appear as dots. Use a downward, rhythmic movement and vary the positions and sizes of the leaves to avoid overly repetitive patterns by displaying some in groups.

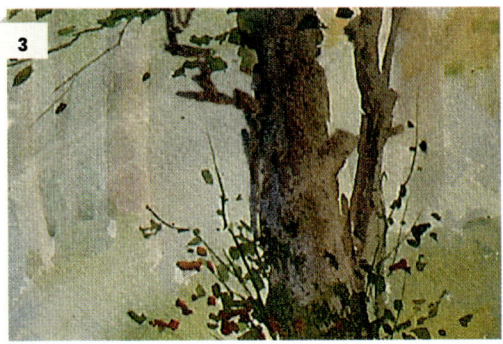

STEP 3 – GIVING TRUNKS CHARACTER

In nature, tree trunks are generally straight and parallel, contributing to a fast-paced visual flow. To soften this, incorporate knotholes, broken branches, and irregular bark textures to break up the straight lines and introduce more organic interest. These details help slow the viewer's eye and add character.

PRINCIPLES OF PAINTING FOREGROUNDS

- The foreground is a vital compositional tool that serves as a walk-in stage, launching a visual path that draws the viewer further into the scene.

- To create depth starting from the foreground, use darker values in that area, where appropriate. This will help establish a gradient plane that transitions smoothly into the scene.

- Avoid elements that could distract from the main composition, such as strong, light–dark value shifts, hard edges, or disjointed colors. These can tug the viewer's focus away from the intended focal areas. An effective composition draws the viewer's eye beyond the foreground, inviting exploration of the middle and background.

Sunset

Sunsets are a powerful theme, drawing viewers in with their golden hues and warm atmosphere. When painting sunlight, it's best to partially conceal the sun behind trees, cliffs, or clouds, allowing its presence to be felt without dominating the scene. In this painting, the trees take on abstract shapes and form graceful lines, while the gradient value in the pond enhances the composition. Landscape elements such as branches, grass blades, and reeds serve as subtle pointers to the focal area, creating a deliberate design flow.

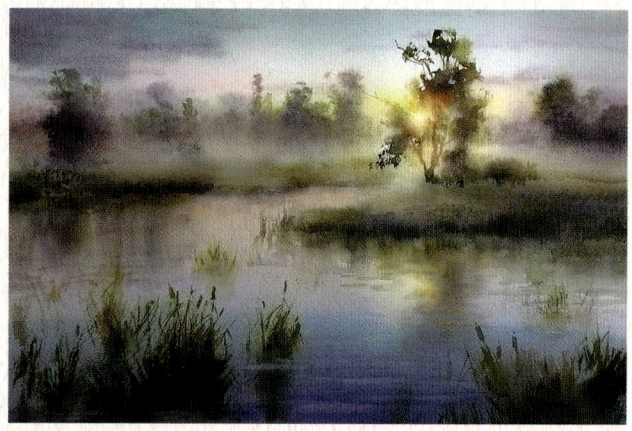

Mist's Soft Awakening

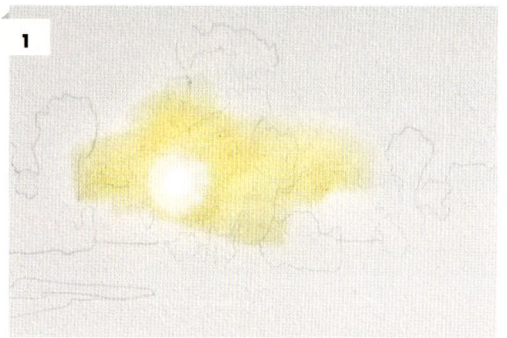

STEP 1 – RENDERING SUNLIGHT

To capture the glow of sunlight, mix yellow with a touch of red to create a warm, radiant hue. After wetting your paper, blot the sun itself with paper towel while spinning it in a circular motion, to avoid paint from filling in the circle. Apply the paint with a whirlpool motion around the sun to convey a radiant effect.

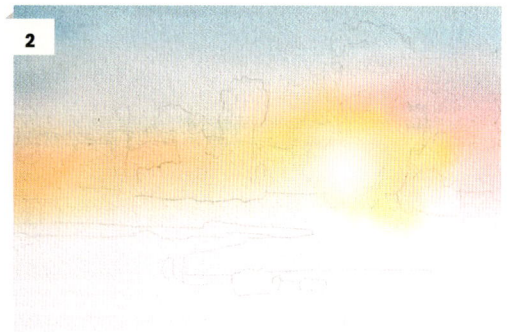

STEP 2 – CREATING SUNSET COLORS

Gradually increase the amount of red in the mixture as you move outward from the sun, transitioning smoothly through yellow-orange, orange, and red-orange, before ending with soft pink. At the zenith, apply turquoise-blue to create a complementary contrast with the warm tones below.

STEP 3 – CAPTURING THE POND COLORS

Mirror the sky's colors in the pond, but ensure they appear slightly desaturated and darker to represent the natural difference between the sky and its reflection.

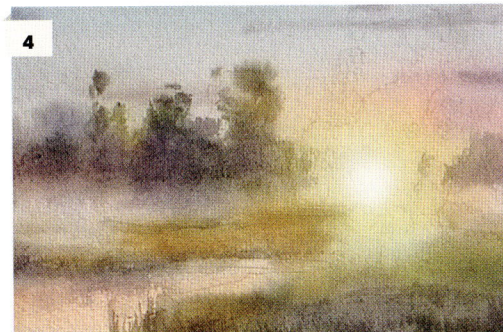

STEP 4 – PAINTING THE DISTANT TREES

The background trees are mid-dark, combining soft edges with just a few hard ones, and featuring a graceful, undulating line along their top contours. Darken the shaded side of the trees with violet to indicate atmospheric perspective. Where there is ground fog, keep that area wetter so the paint can bleed in.

TIP

For background foliage, the wet-on-wet technique creates soft, harmonious transitions, contributing to a classical watercolor feel.

ABSTRACT SHAPES

Abstract shapes are key ingredients to outstanding paintings. A shape divided into two halves with distinctly different sides and an uneven contour is considered asymmetrical, commonly referred to as an abstract shape in art terms. When viewed in a mirror, the flipped orientation should be immediately apparent.

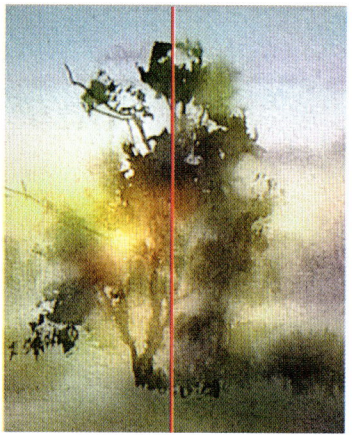 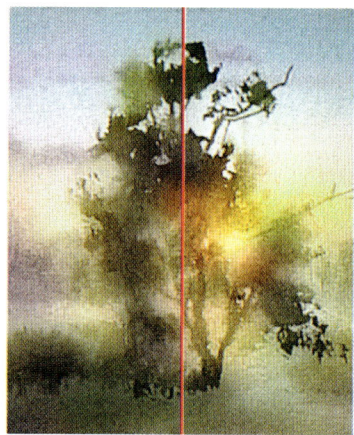

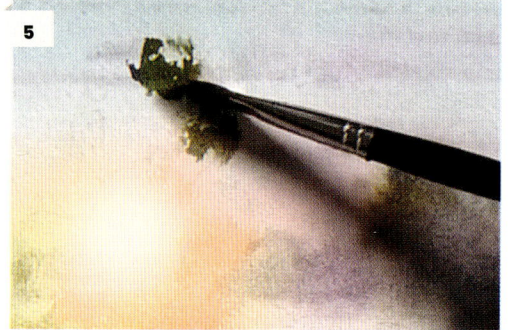

STEP 5 – PAINTING THE LARGE TREE

The foreground tree partially obscures the sun. On the left side of the tree, have the branches lean toward the left; on the right side, have them lean toward the right. This asymmetry mimics the natural direction of branch growth.

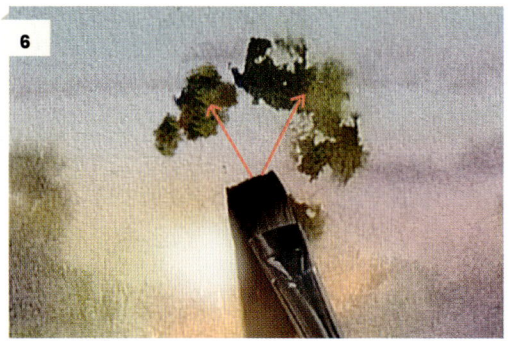

STEP 6 - CREATING FOLIAGE CLUSTERS

Push up with the flat side and the longer, skinny edge of the brush while varying the pressure. Allow the paint to break up (see Brushstrokes). This will create clusters of different sizes for added variety. Heavier pressure will result in solid clusters while light touches will produce tiny specks. This contrast is desirable.

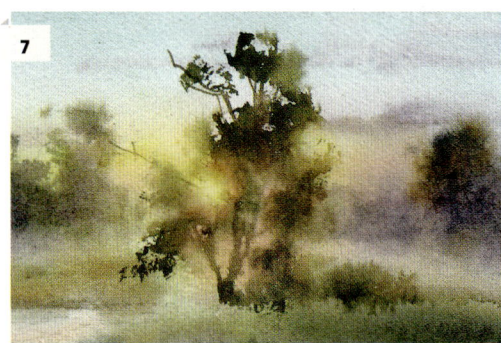

STEP 7 - VARYING THE GREENS

To achieve color variegation, add touches of both warmer and cooler greens, along with ochers, for a more dynamic effect. Permit some of the direct sunlight to shine through the foliage—that's the focal point of your painting.

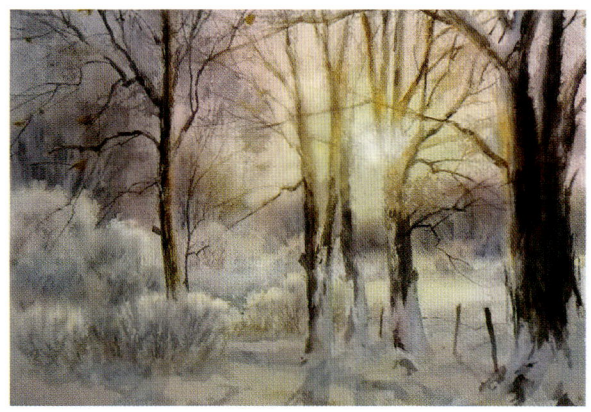

WINTER SUNSETS

When the trees are bare, block most of the sun behind thick trunks.

Thin Clouds

When paintings contain too much visual information, they can become cluttered. Subduing the sky is an option to create a restful area. The structures in this painting have a good variety of angles, with the dome forming a pyramid composition, which is ideal. There's a noticeable sense of recession as details fade—the buildings become cooler and lighter. The thin clouds prompt the eye to "read" the form— an effective compositional technique— standing out just enough to be noticed.

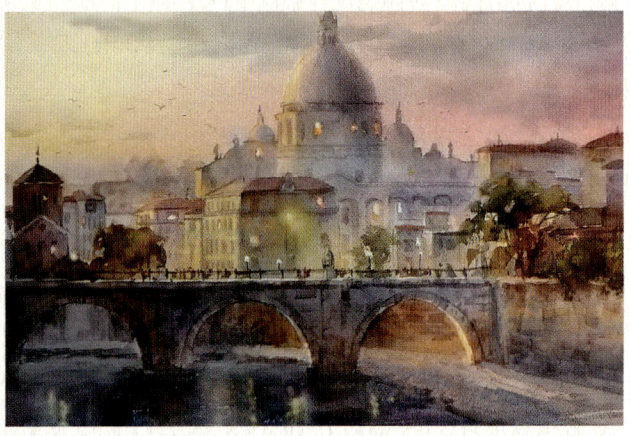

St. Peter's Basilica, Rome, Italy

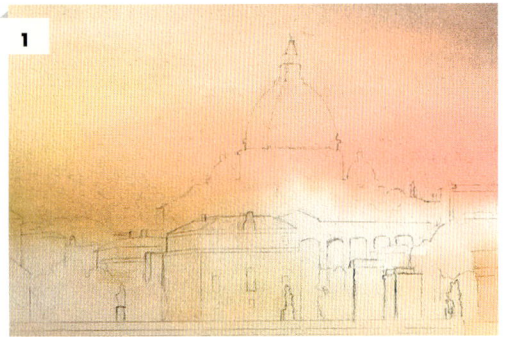

STEP 1 – LAYING DOWN THE SKY COLORS

Begin by wetting the entire sky area. Start with raw sienna, applying it from left to right. As you approach the center, blend in permanent rose to shift the color toward orange. You can paint over any buildings. Gradually reduce the raw sienna in your mixture, so a soft pink glow predominates on the right side. Add a touch of violet at the top right for a gradient color temperature from cool to warm.

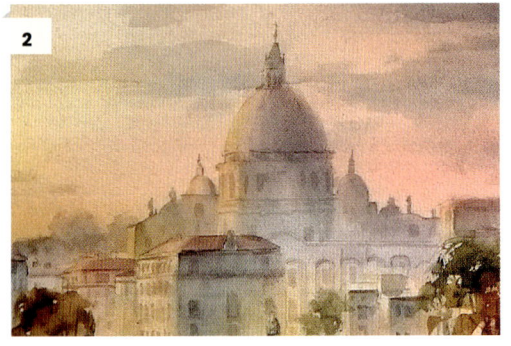

STEP 2 – PAINTING THE CLOUDS

To avoid parallel lines in cloud shapes, gradually rotate your brush starting from the brush's skinny edge to the flat surface to achieve varied strokes. Avoid using the brush as a pen. The value should be slightly darker than the orange sky, but not so dark that it becomes a distraction. To prevent competition between the two halves, add more clouds to one side than the other.

Fog

Adding fog to your landscapes introduces an element of mystery and enhances depth. To create the illusion of distinct planes receding into the distance, fog and mist are invaluable tools. They also soften the harshness of rigid man-made structures, lending them an ethereal quality.

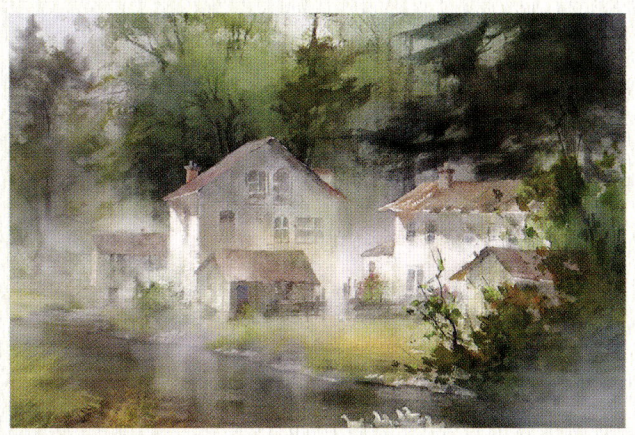

A Dream in Verdant Hues

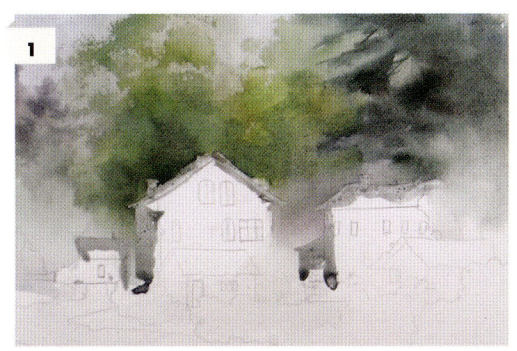

STEP 1 – WETTING THE PAPER

Start by wetting the entire background, then use a paper towel to lift moisture out of random areas. This will result in lost-and-found edges. Allow the water to soak into the paper for about three to five minutes before proceeding.

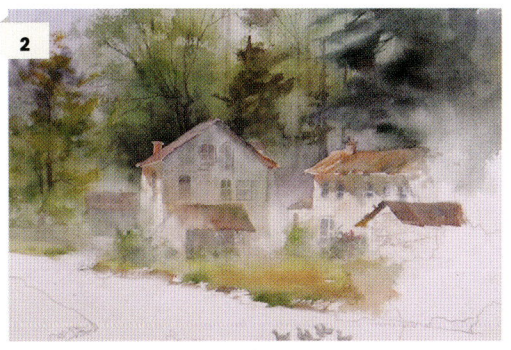

STEP 2 – CREATING FOG

Rewet the bottom third of the background trees. This area should be much wetter than the top two-thirds, allowing the paint to dilute more and creating a lighter value that resembles fog. Repeat the same process for fog in front of the buildings. If necessary you can create convincing fog effects using PanPastel's titanium white.

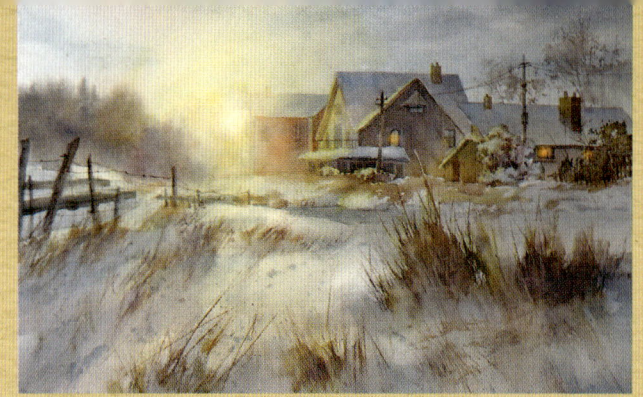

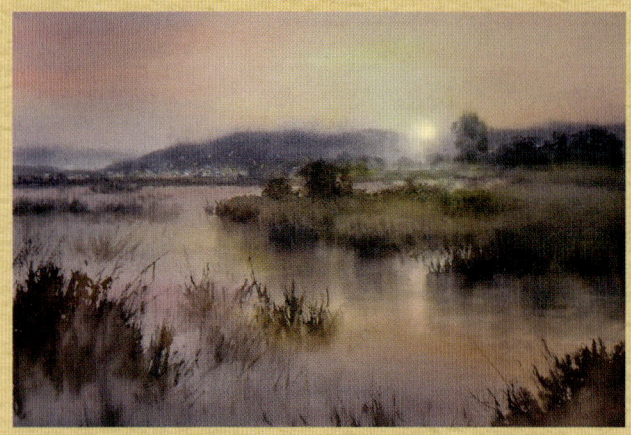

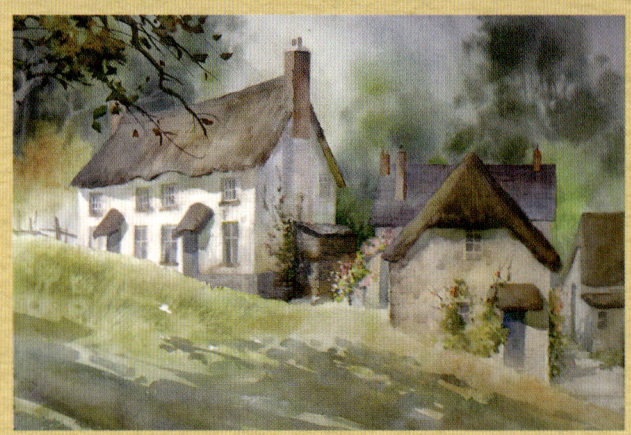

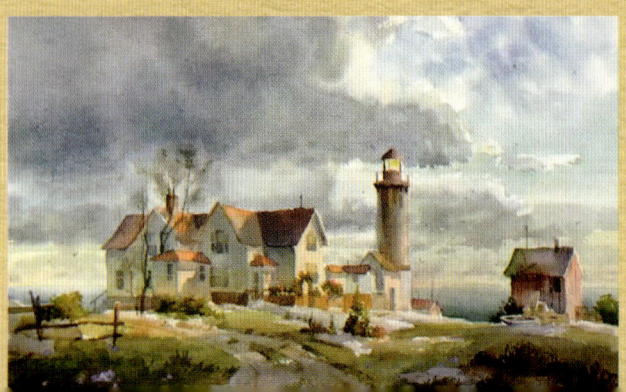

CHAPTER FOUR:
Ground

Unless your painting includes a large body of water in the foreground, it will always feature a ground plane, which offers an almost unlimited range of possibilities. Textures are a top priority in this section. You will learn how to depict various types of grass, roads and streets, patio stones, and a very important element, snow, is explored in depth. This chapter narrows this complex area into series of easy-to-understand guidelines, providing insight into the most common approaches to handle these distinct surfaces.

Tall Grasses

The sunlight, with its long cast shadows, enticed me to paint this scene. The houses in the distance are the focal area. The openings between the tall grasses are arranged in a manner that creates a visual path, guiding the viewer's eye through to the houses.

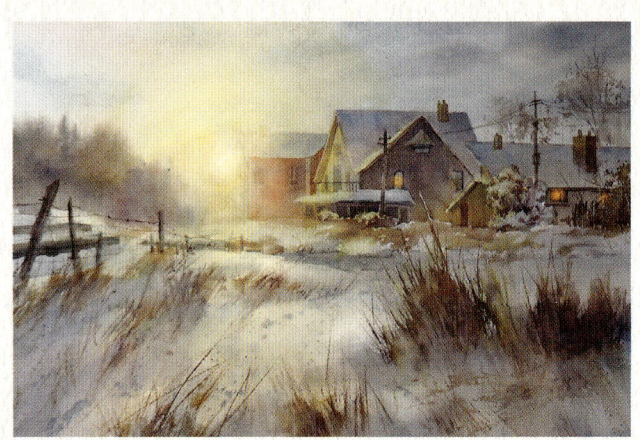

The chill Illuminated

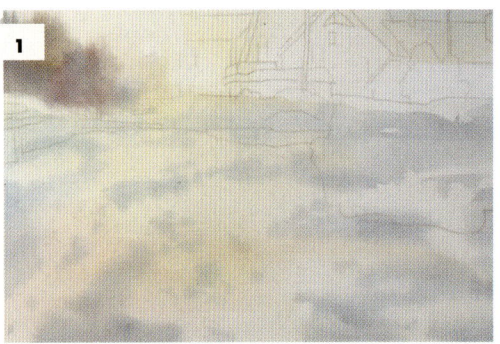

STEP 1 – CREATING SHADOW AREAS IN THE SNOW

Wet the entire ground. Add raw sienna to the sunlit areas and a blue-gray to the parts that don't receive sunlight. Randomly drop in touches of permanent rose to create subtle violet areas.

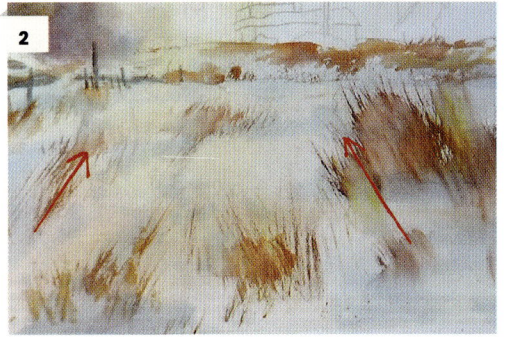

STEP 2 – MERGING THE GRASS

Wet the bottom of the grass clumps so they blend into the snow. On the dry areas, direct the grass strands toward the houses. The strands will act as pointers to direct the eye.

PAINTING GRASSES

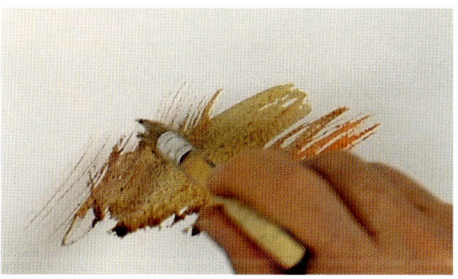

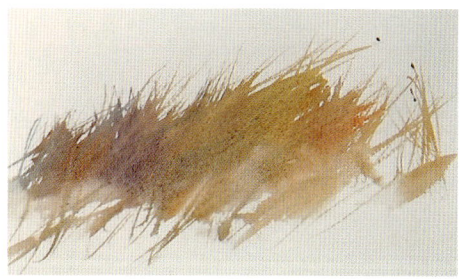

BRUSHSTROKE DIRECTION

Use a chip brush. Position the bristles at a 45-degree angle, slightly varying their directions while maintaining rhythmic patterns. Allow thin strands to stand out. You can add taller strands using a very thin rigger brush.

VARY COLORS

After painting a small area, reload your brush with a different color such as violet. Variegated colors add visual interest due to the shifting of hues.

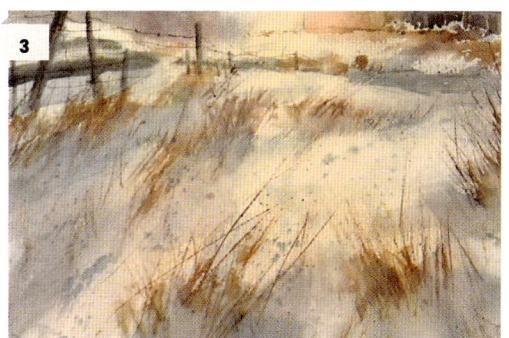

STEP 3 – SPLATTER EFFECTS

The splatter effects represent footprints (see Tricks of the Trade: Splattering). Vigorously tap the brush against your index finger while moving forward.

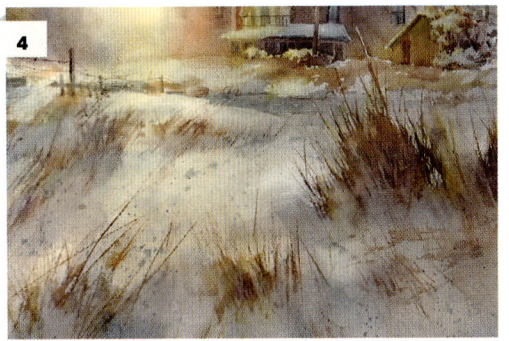

STEP 4 – MAKING THE GRASS THREE-DIMENSIONAL

Go over the grass clumps again, this time darkening the bottom third to bring the lighter strands forward. Apply clear water at the bottom to merge them into the snow.

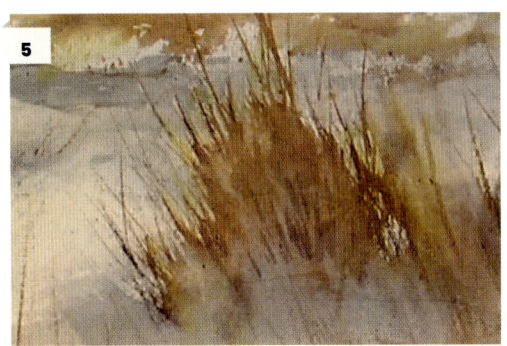

STEP 5 – FOREGROUND GRASS CLUMPS

Only for the foreground clumps, use a thirsty sharp chisel brush to lift out lighter, distinct strands (see Tricks of the Trade: Lightening Value with a Thirsty Brush). Then, refine the indentations using a small round brush, negative-painting with a darker color. This will give your grass dimension.

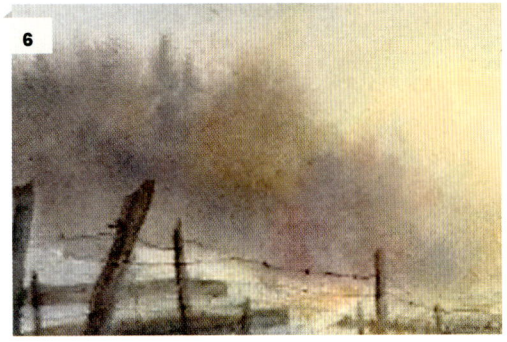

STEP 6 – PAINTING THE BACKGROUND FOLIAGE

Paint the background foliage wet-on-wet, varying the colors. Add a few evergreens for variety. Use yellow ocher to represent the delightful golden willow trees that keep that color in winter.

TIP:

If unsure about an element, practice it on scrap paper first to build confidence and loosen up.

Marsh Grass

Moody paintings featuring sunsets with pastel-colored skies are highly successful. The warm hues are beautifully amplified when reflected in water, enhancing the scene's emotional impact. In this composition, a gracefully curved contour line, formed by marsh grass against the water, guides the eye toward the background in an "S" movement. At the same time, marsh grasses in the pond create a "connect-the-dots" visual path. Using multiple visual paths encourages viewers to explore the composition.

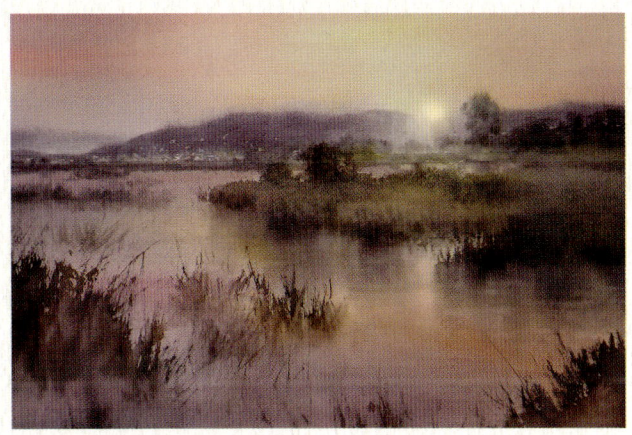

The Horizon's Gentle Sigh

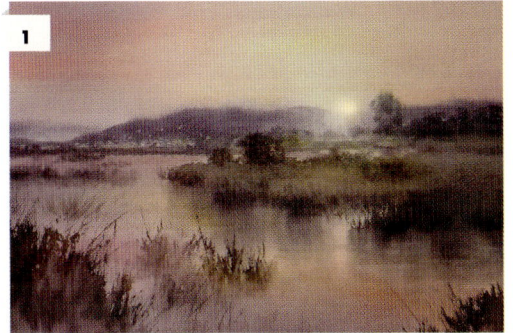

STEP 1 - USING A CHIP BRUSH

This brush with spread-apart bristles is ideal for creating grasses. Rotate it as you pull upward to form reeds in various directions, with most of them angled toward the sunlight—the focal point. The reeds act as visual pointers. You only need a few swoops. Do not paint grass strand by strand at this point. Apply a second layer, selectively, to darken areas and add depth; use these accents sparingly.

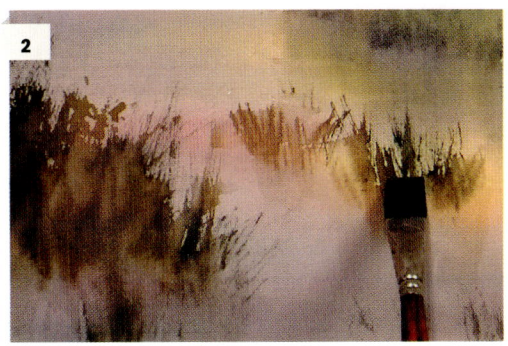

STEP 2 - BLENDING IN

To prevent the forms from appearing as if they are pasted on, wet the bottoms of the grass clumps and blend them seamlessly into the water. Use a thin rigger brush to create longer strands.

Short Grass

Painting grass in watercolor can be challenging. Unlike opaque mediums, it's harder to create individual blades, so it's best to suggest the texture rather than define every detail. Often, just a small, well-rendered patch is enough to imply the whole lawn. Landscapes also benefit from having low-activity zones, which I call "rest areas." A lawn serves this purpose well, offering visual relief from the detailed houses.

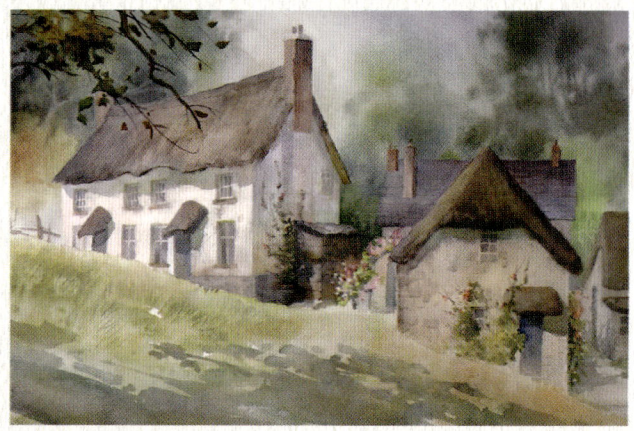

The soul of the countryside

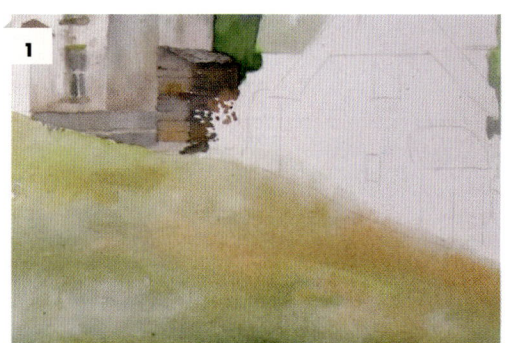

STEP 1 – APPLYING THE FIRST WASH

Start with a flat wash, introducing subtle variations in the greens. Incorporate golden raw sienna to represent dry grass, which will break the monotony of the greens. When an element seems too uniform in color, it gives the appearance that it is spray-painted and amateurish. Color variegation and graying down resolve this.

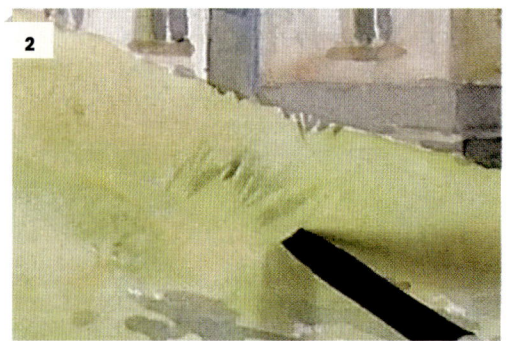

STEP 2 – CREATING BLADES OF GRASS

Use the chisel edge of a ¼-in (0.5cm) brush to negative-paint small clumps of grass. Paint just a few inches at a time, letting viewers fill in the details with their imagination. While lawns have countless blades of grass, there's no need to be explicit—especially in watercolor. Suggesting a limited number of blades helps avoid a flat, carpet-like effect and viewers can easily guess what it is.

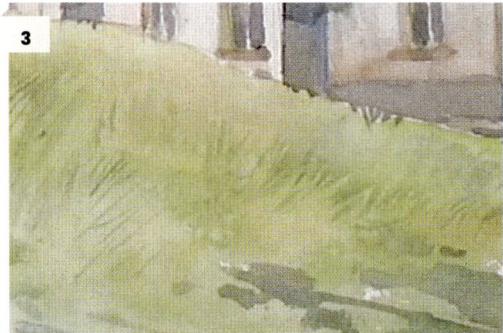

STEP 3 - INTEGRATING THE BLADES

Populate the grass with more hints of grass blades. To integrate them, wet the opposite side of the grass clumps where the dark parts meet the grass above, so they melt softly into the rest of the lawn.

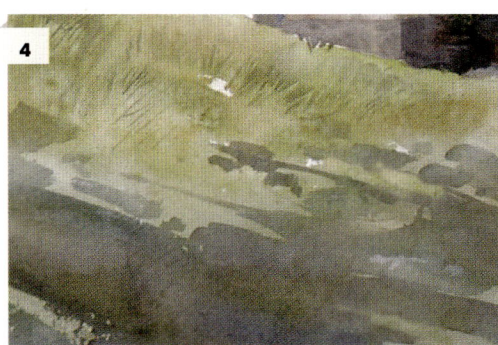

STEP 4 - ADDING SHADOWS

Cast shadows break up the triangular lawn and add variety to the repetitive expanse of grass. Bounce some green in them for color harmony.

GOLDEN GRASS

When painting grass, I tend to prioritize golden ocher grass over green. In this example, the green grass gradually blends into the ocher grass, creating a seamless transition between the two. I always tells my students to "go for the gold."

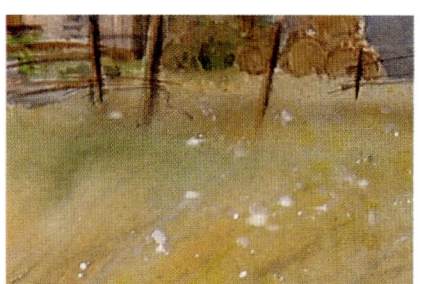

Dirt Road

If a scene you like includes a paved road, consider transforming it into a dirt road. This allows you to incorporate patches of grass to break up parallel lines. Adding puddles can further enhance visual interest and suggest recent rain, adding life to the scene. In this composition, the road serves as a visual path, taking the viewer farther into the scene.

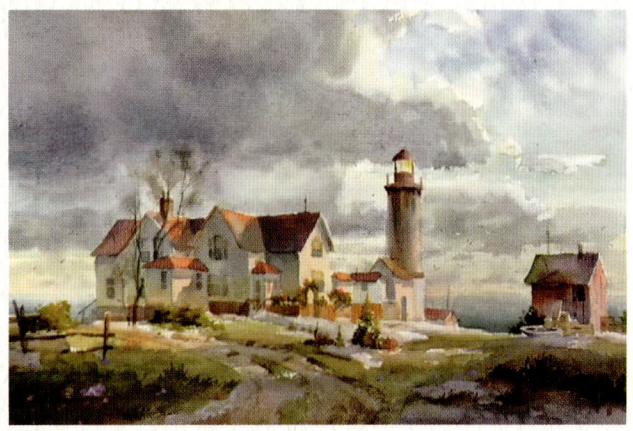

Beneath the Gathering Clouds

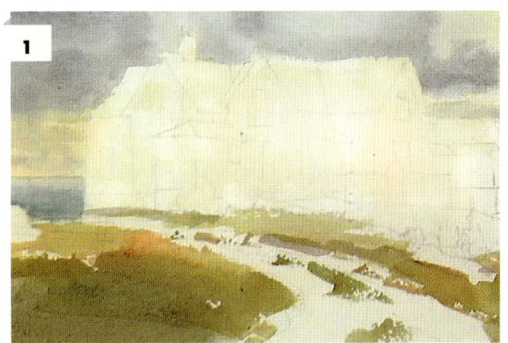

STEP 1 – VARYING THE GRASS COLORS

Paint the surrounding grass, reserving the white paper for the upcoming road. Vary the grass color, introducing touches of raw sienna here and here. An alternative can be to have the golden ocher grass predominate. Add patches of grass inside the dirt road area, designed to lead the viewer's eye into the scene.

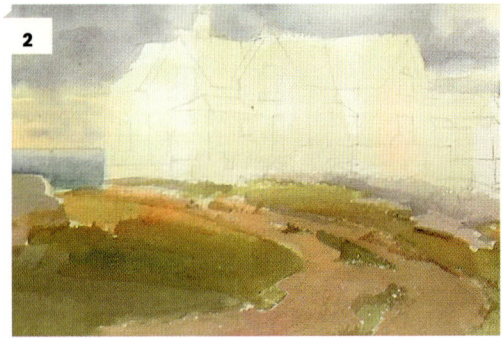

STEP 2 – APPLYING THE DIRT ROAD COLOR

The dirt road is a muted, grayed-down peach color, with neutral gray areas to suggest a gravel texture. Avoid monotony by varying the hues within the road—introduce subtle shifts in peach and gray tones to create interest and to avoid a flat, uniform appearance.

PRINCIPLES OF PAINTING CAST SHADOWS

- Shadows should be darker near the object casting them, becoming lighter as they move away.

- All light gaps should vary in size; the smaller the gap, the darker it should be inside, compared to larger ones.

- Keep your shadow shapes abstract, combining multiple small light gaps into different sizes and shapes.

- Echo surrounding hues in your shadows for color harmony.

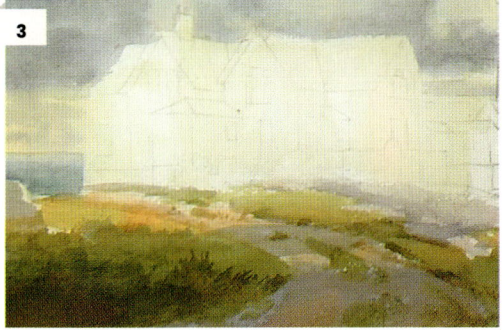

STEP 3 – ADDING CAST SHADOWS

Glaze cast shadows across the road and the lawn, leaving gaps to let sunlight peek through. This avoids the shadow from appearing pasted on and adds a sense of dappled light; it also negates the parallel lines of the road. The glazing technique allows the underlying colors to remain visible, creating a luminous effect, a fantastic attribute of watercolor.

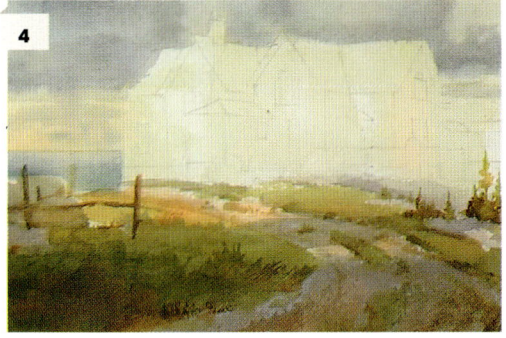

STEP 4 – PERKING UP THE LAWN

Add a few fence posts and small evergreen trees to enhance the ground plane by telling a story.

Patio

Patio stones can become repetitive, with each square inch presenting the same visual information. Introducing cast shadows added much-needed variety in this composition, creating a rhythmic, directional movement towards the arch. The technique encourages viewers to mentally walk through the arch, drawing them deeper into the painting, and adds to the narrative.

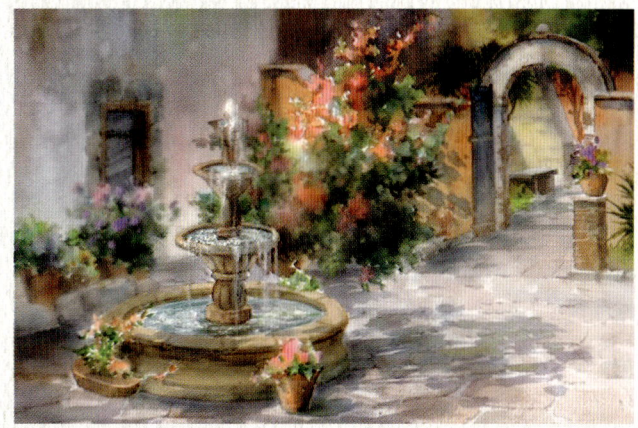

The Echo of Soft Splashes

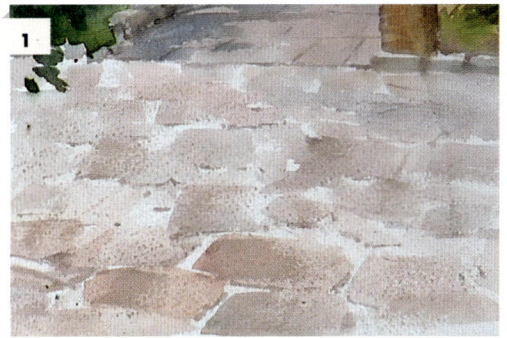

STEP 1 - LAYING THE GROUND WORK

The patio stones are a warm mixture of burnt sienna, Payne's gray, and touches of permanent rose. The three colors should be noticeable. Merge some patio stones together to make them look less spotty and repetitive. Leave portions of the mortar showing in some sections.

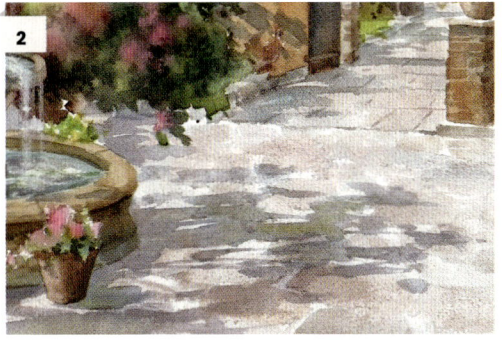

STEP 2 - CAST SHADOWS

Ensure the light spots representing the mortar vary in size to avoid a repetitive, manufactured look. For a cohesive feel, subtly echo surrounding colors into the shadows. While these echoed colors might not be noticeable in real outdoor settings, this is where artistic interpretation can make shadows more vibrant.

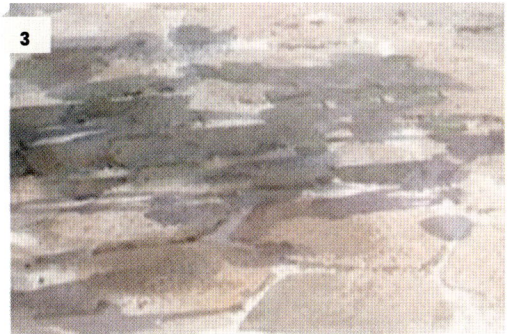

STEP 3 – MAKING THE STONES THREE-DIMENSIONAL

On some of the stones, apply darker tones on the side opposite the light source. This will suggest they are elevated.

Focal Elements

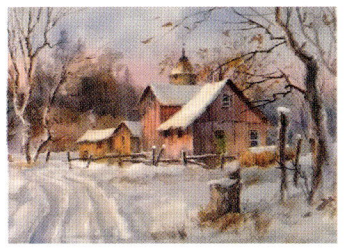

BUILDINGS

Consider light and shade when positioning buildings. This building is at a three-quarter view with the lighter side of the structure facing inward. Note the gradient plane on the shadow side.

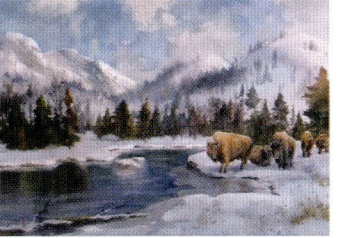

GROUPS OF ANIMALS

When grouping animals in a herd, each position should vary. Avoid obvious even numbers such as two or four. Add shadows under animals to ground them, even on an overcast day, or they will appear like they are hovering.

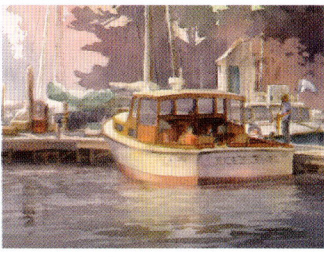

BOATS AND VEHICLES

To avoid a flat, pasted-on appearance, position vehicles and boats at a three-quarter view. Here, the port side and rear are both visible.

Snow on Ground

The star of leading lines is the "pendulum" line, which gently sways viewers from side to side. Viewers naturally follow the contour lines formed by the contrasting values (see Composition: Stage 4). In this composition, the winding stream serves this purpose, with the orange bush becoming the focal point, the "pot of gold" at the end of the rainbow. In winter scenes, adding ice to water enhances interest and rewards viewers for following the visual path.

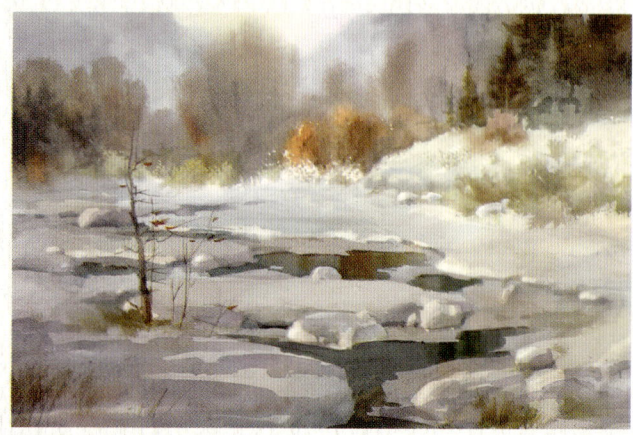

The Stream's Icy Lullaby

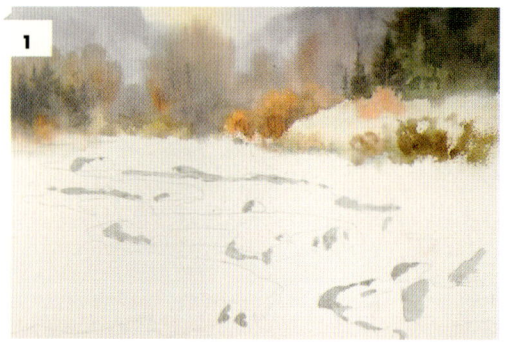

STEP 1 – SAVING THE WHITES

Use masking fluid to protect the white areas struck by sunlight at a 90-degree angle, thus receiving 100 percent direct light (see Tricks of the Trade: Rubber Masking Fluid). These will be the lightest values in the painting, and limiting these white areas makes them stand out more due to fewer competing areas.

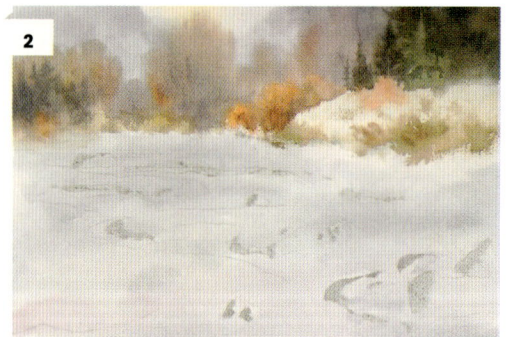

STEP 2 – PAINTING THE SNOW

Paint the top of the snow with a light, grayed-down blue color, keeping it at a mid-light value. Reload your brush several times to subtly introduce pinks and oranges, which will harmonize with the background hues. When the pink mixes with the blue, it will produce an appealing violet.

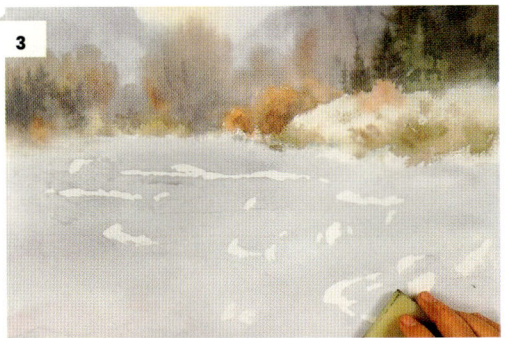

STEP 3 - REMOVING THE MASKING FLUID

Gently remove the masking fluid with the masking fluid eraser (see Tricks of the Trade: Rubber Masking Fluid).

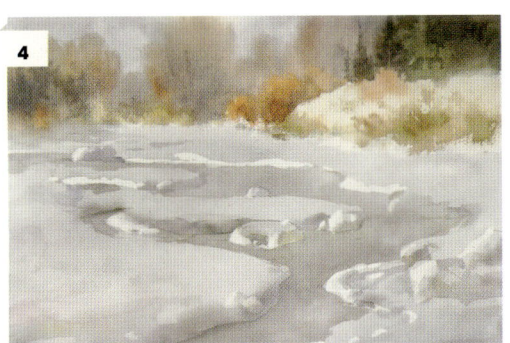

STEP 4 - ROUNDING OFF THE SNOW BANK

Darken the sides of the stream bank and the protruding mounds, which will become snow-covered rocks. This will add dimension to the scene by making the snow look thick. The slanted snow bank on the right will be in light due to the 90-degree angle that receives 100 percent of the sunlight.

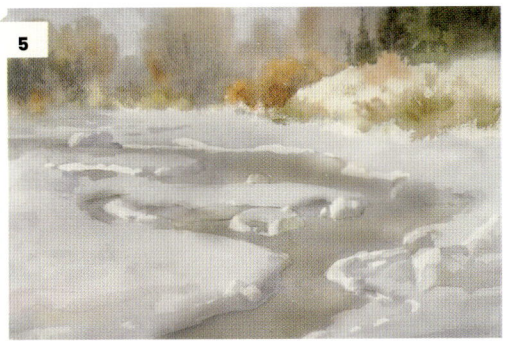

STEP 5 - MAKING THE ICE LOOK CONVINCING

A simple formula to remember is that ice is a mid-value between the snow and the water. While the paint is still wet, drop in some burnt sienna to mimic trapped frozen mud often found in ice.

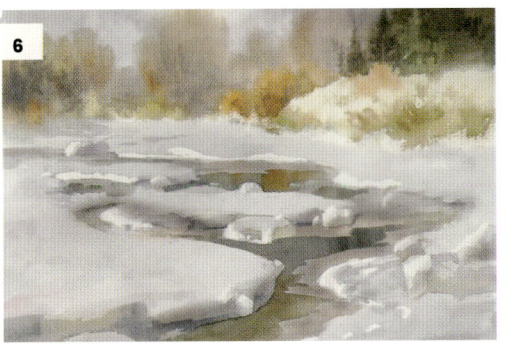

STEP 6 - PAINTING THE MELTING WATER

Portray the stream using a darker value than the ice. Use negative-painting techniques to create the jagged, broken glasslike edges that are typical of ice. The foreground water can be a warm, grayed orange to suggest a shallowness exposing the stream bed. There is no need to connect all the water; leaving gaps will help slow down the viewer's eye. The ice and snow banks will continue to guide the eye through the scene.

Cobblestone

Village scenes are popular painting themes because we can relate and engage more readily to man-made environments rather than to raw nature. A town or village with a street lead-in is very inviting to walk along. Since streets are formed by straight lines, you'll want to slow down the visual pace by softening as many straight lines as possible. Casting shadows over the street helps to reduce a visual rush, while adding grass and flowers can offset the harsh straight lines.

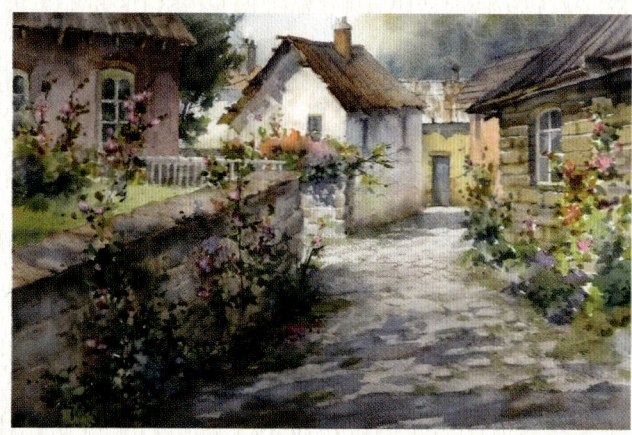

Passage of Time in Rural Mexico

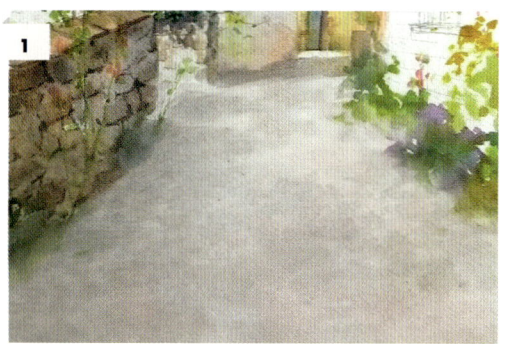

STEP 1 – LAYING THE FOUNDATION

Wash a light warm gray value over the whole street. Inject a few hints of permanent rose and burnt sienna, mostly in the foreground, to add subtle color variation, making sure the additional hues are barely noticeable.

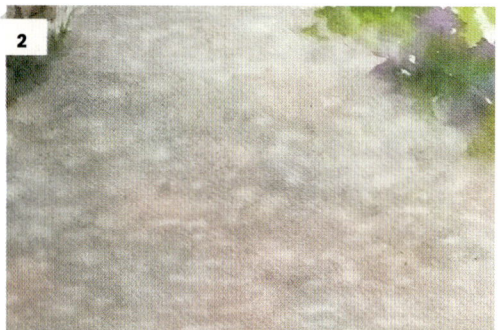

STEP 2 – BRINGING OUT THE COBBLESTONES

While the paint is damp, and as soon as the glisten fades, randomly sprinkle some clear water droplets by banging a brush against your finger. Small, lighter, polka-dot bumps will appear, giving the illusion that they are cobblestones. Use a cotton swab to lift out additional stones if necessary. Vary the sizes, with the drops gradually diminishing in size as they recede. Group some together for variety. Leave blank areas here and there for contrast. Allow to dry.

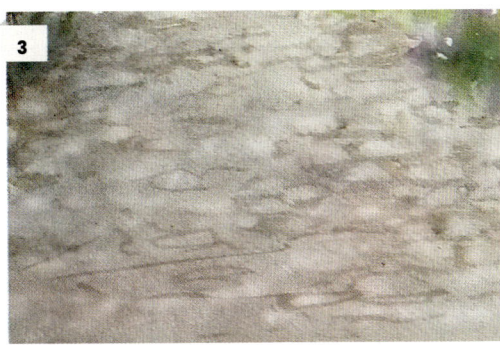

STEP 3 – MAKING THE STONES THREE-DIMENSIONAL

Pick the stones with the lighter protrusions and darken the sides of some (not all) of them to elevate them to three-dimensional forms.

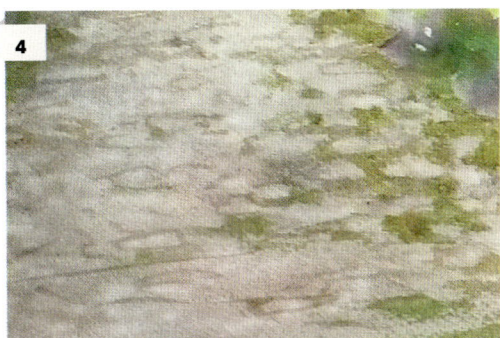

STEP 4 – ADDING GRASS PATCHES

Dry-brush grass patches around some of the stones for variety. Place greenery closer to walls where there would be less trampling from foot traffic.

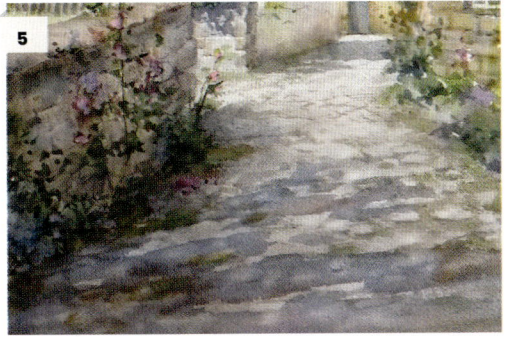

STEP 5 – ADDING CAST SHADOWS

Add cast shadows, directing the sun spots inwards to usher the viewers in. Echo some of the surrounding colors in the shadows to maintain harmony. Use a cotton swab to lift out stones in the shadows so they stand out. This technique enhances texture, grounding the shadows and making them appear to be transparent.

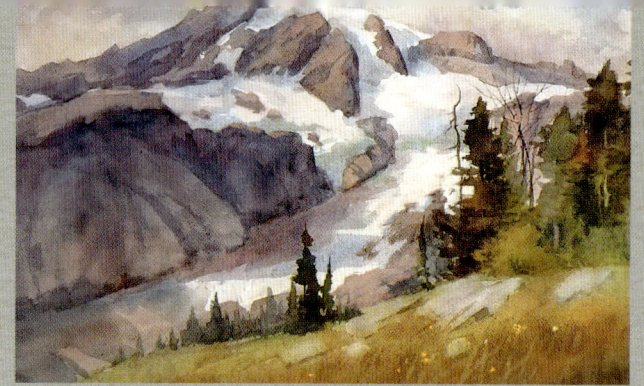

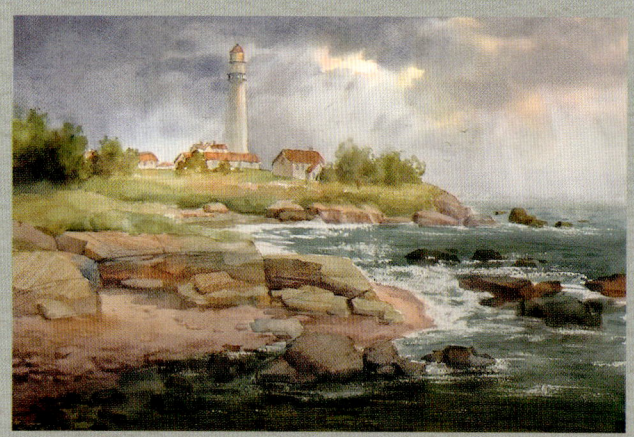

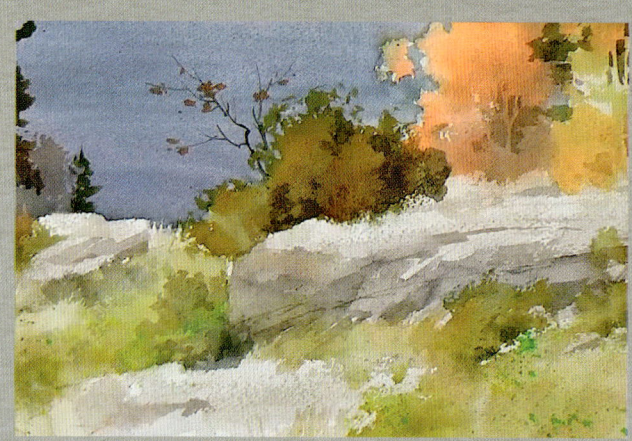

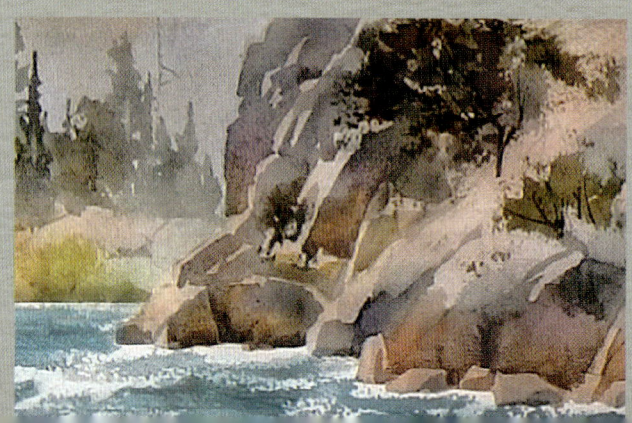

CHAPTER FIVE

Rocks & Mountains

The challenge my students face most often is that of painting rocks. There's a natural tendency to create stiff, overly symmetrical shapes that need a lot of adjustment to feel convincing. Colors copied directly from photos or plein-air studies can make them appear dull, muddy, and lifeless. In this chapter, you will learn how to breathe new life into rocks, giving them a makeover with bold, vibrant colors. You will also explore techniques for painting epic mountains, capturing their immense scale and grandeur to create truly dramatic landscapes.

Rocky Mountain with Glacier

A painting can't fully capture the grandeur of a rocky mountain, but giving it ample space within the confined area of the canvas helps enhance the illusion of its immensity. Surrounding it with smaller elements creates a sense of majesty through comparison. For example, the scale of the trees here acts as a reference point, highlighting the mountain's grandeur.

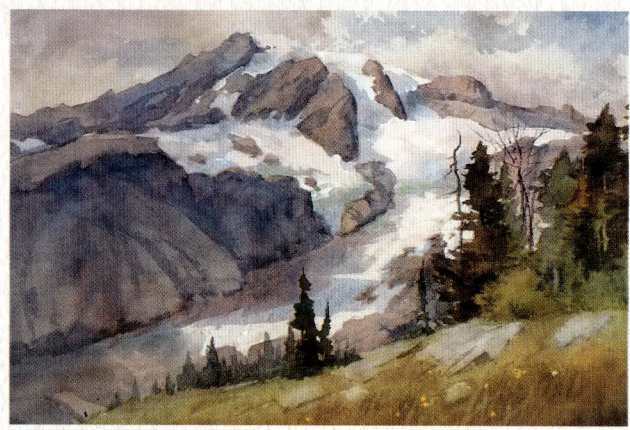

Glacier's Path

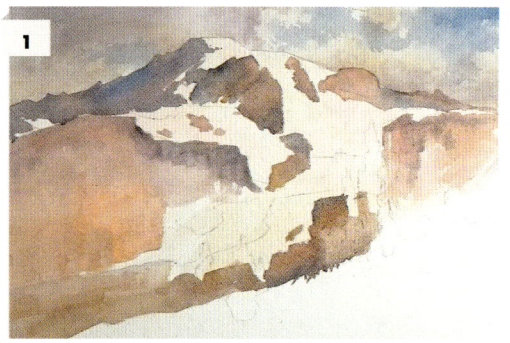

STEP 1 – DESIGNING CLIFFS IN ABSTRACT SHAPES

Add a wash over the entire painting with a very light value of raw sienna to warm up the white areas. Using yellow-orange paint with touches of pink, paint the orange cliffs that receive sunlight, working around the white areas that will become the snow patches. Carefully design and build the entire mountain with abstract shapes, ending with a pleasing, structured form. Allow to dry.

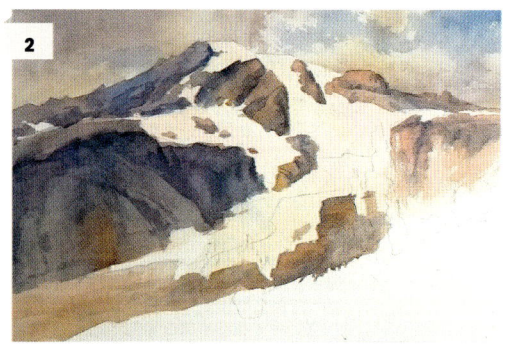

STEP 2 – CREATING ATMOSPHERIC PERSPECTIVE

Portray the mountain in the distance by using a blue tone to indicate atmospheric perspective for the cliffs not receiving sunlight. Make the closer cliff darker than the background to bring it forward. On dry paper, subdivide the cliffs with subtle crevices. Crevices give dimension to mountains. While real mountains have numerous crevices, focus on a few key ones to add dimension. Avoid "train-track" type parallel lines, as they will appear too manufactured.

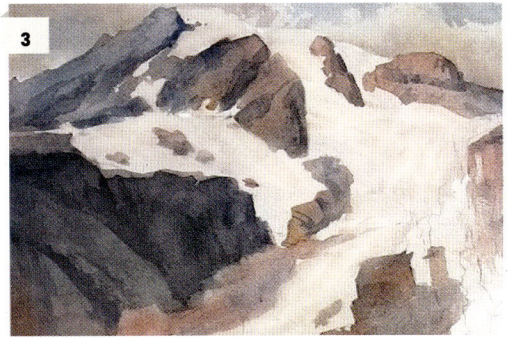

STEP 3 - PAINTING NATURAL, WEATHERED SNOW

Add a dirty brown tint to the snow to create a weathered look. Over time, snow collects pollutants as they settle on the snow. Pure white snow on mountains can appear artificial.

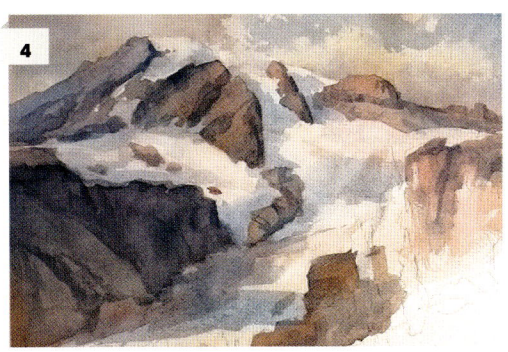

STEP 4 - GROUNDING THE SNOW WITH SHADOWS

Add cast shadows projected from the cliffs and a few irregular mounds and slopes over the white snow to ground them in the scene. Bare white paper can make snow patches appear unfinished.

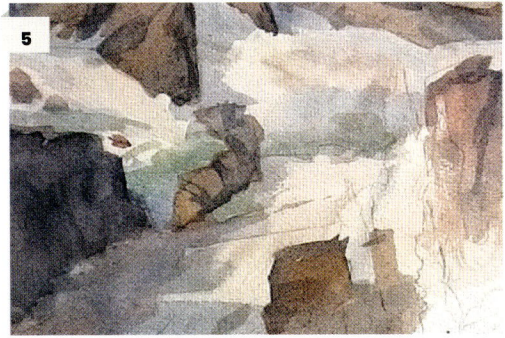

STEP 5 - PAINTING THE GLACIER

Mix a vibrant turquoise-green color for the glacier and place it where the snow drops vertically. This will be a striking focal point.

> **TIP**
>
> Position the mountain peak close to the top and off-center to achieve a dynamic, unbalanced composition.

Coastal Rocks

Rocky coastlines offer an opportunity to create angular, melodic leading lines that guide the wandering eye through a composition. Here, the sunbeams add a spectacular visual touch. I often look for ways to paint scenes that feel out of the ordinary—images that stand out and stay with the viewer. The white water is created using dry brushing (see Brushstrokes), but it's important to use restraint—too much can overwhelm a composition. Keep this lighter value mostly away from the foreground. Rocks beneath the water add visual magic, subtly inviting the viewer to mentally wade into the scene, as if stepping into the shallows of the beach.

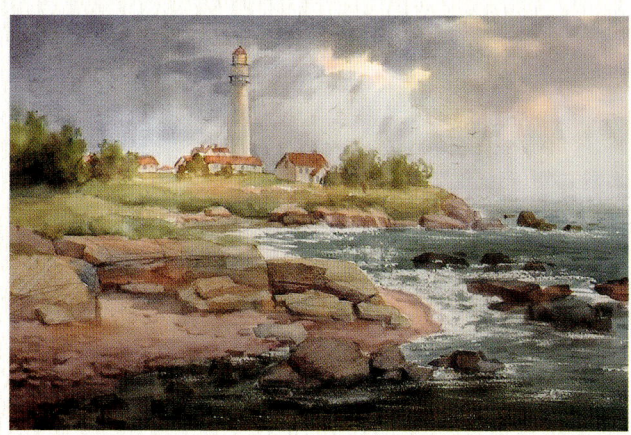

Pigeon Point Lighthouse

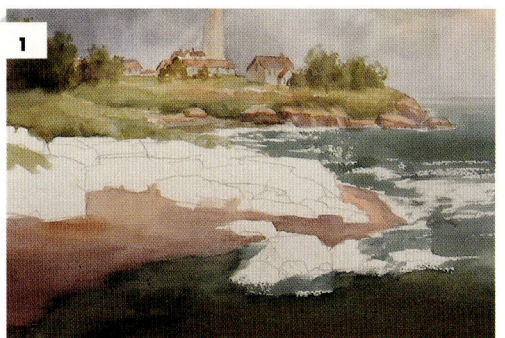

STEP 1 - CREATING A MASS OF ROCKS

Paint in the beach sand, leaving the general shape of rocks blank. At this stage, do not think of the rocks as individual boulders, but as a single large mass that includes all the rocks in one unit.

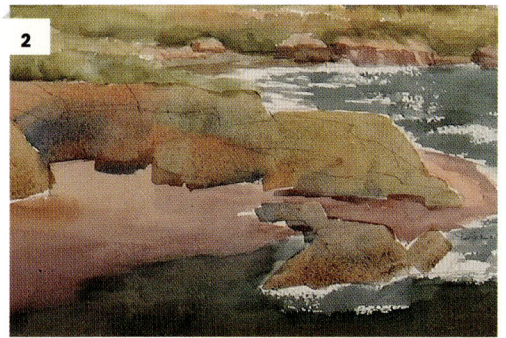

STEP 2 - CREATING HIGHLIGHTS, THE FIRST WASH

Prepare three separate pools of color on your palette: Payne's gray, raw sienna, and permanent rose. Without mixing them, load your brush with all three colors by pushing it forward, as if shoveling snow (see Mixing Paints). This method lets the colors blend naturally, creating smooth transitions once applied to the paper. If the result appears too garish, gently soften the effect by mingling in a touch of Payne's gray. Each subtle shift in hue should remain visible to maintain richness and variety.

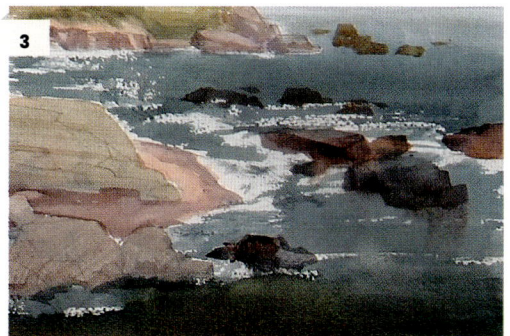

STEP 3 – PAINTING THE WET ROCKS

Wet rocks are the darkest objects in landscapes. Add the dark rocks in the ocean area. Avoid going so dark that they turn black. You should still see color shifts.

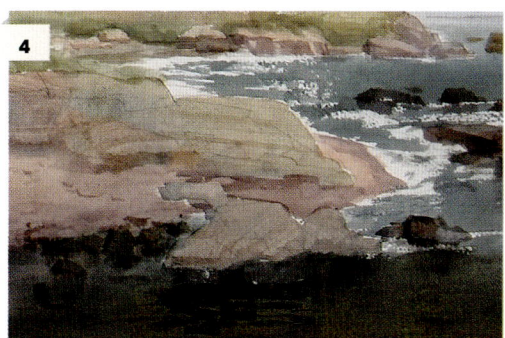

STEP 4 – ADDING REFLECTIONS

Add reflections by dragging your brush downward in a vertical motion while subtly wiggling it from side to side. At the bottom third, tap the brush to indicate rippling water.

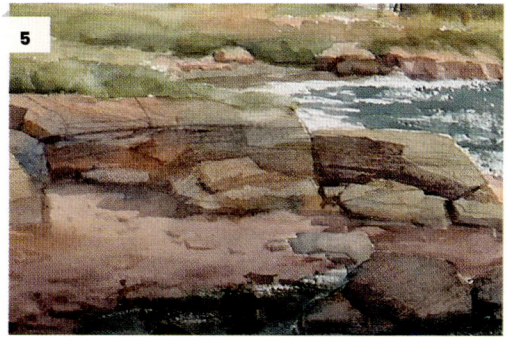

STEP 5 – RENDERING SHADOWS AND CREVICES

Darken the sides of the rocks to enhance their three-dimensional form, ensuring the top and side planes are not split evenly. Add small accents in areas where no light reaches. Finish by adding thin cracks with the smallest rigger brush for added detail. These move the eye nicely over the rocks.

TIP

When painting rocks in a group, be mindful of their sizes and shapes to avoid unintentional clones.

Flat Rocks in Grass

The goal of this composition is to give the viewer a high vantage point from atop a hill, overlooking the vast expanse of the lake beyond. The white rocks act as a platform for the viewer to stand on. Dry brushing adds texture to their surfaces, while grass spilling over the edges and surrounding bushes helps to nestle them naturally into the field. Viewers are rewarded for overlooking the lake when they see the distant snow-capped mountain.

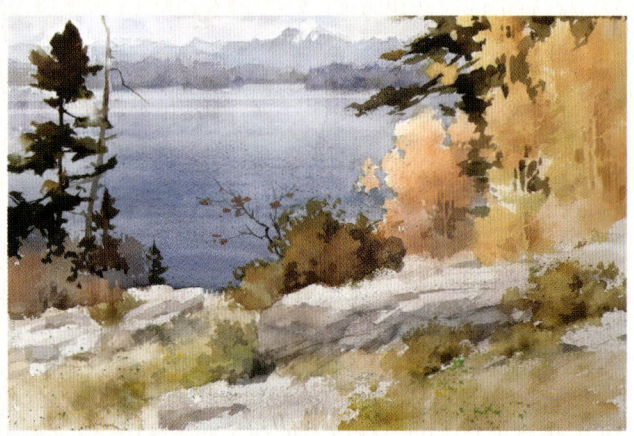

Overlooking Jenny's Lake, Grand Teton National Park

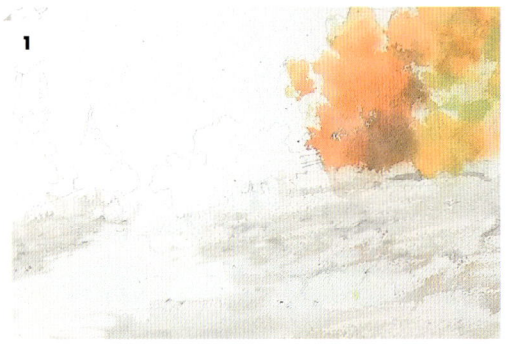

STEP 1 – DRY-BRUSHING TEXTURE

The rocks will be primarily white. For texture, sparingly dry-brush a light-valued gray-brown mixture over their tops, allowing the broken areas of the white to show through. Vary the grays from warm to cool to avoid uniformity.

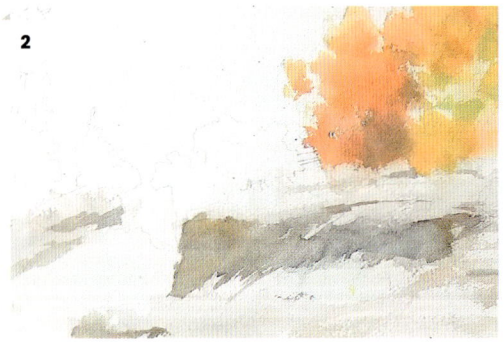

STEP 2 – GIVING THE ROCKS FORM

On the sides of the rocks, paint an interplay of warm and cool colors—grays and oranges—to give the rocks more colorful interest. Use the chisel edge of a bright brush and negative-paint the rocks to reserve the white jagged section for the upcoming grass against the main rock. Only the closest rock will show a few grass blades.

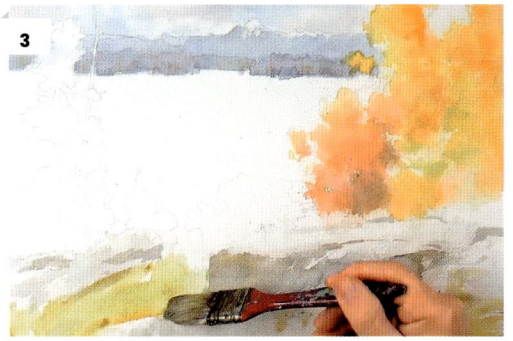

STEP 3 - INTEGRATING ROCKS AND GRASS

While the base of the rocks is still wet, introduce the grass. Solid green grass can feel monotonous, so leaning toward golden raw sienna adds warmth and variety. You can make all the grass golden or mix in some green for spice. Let the grass blend softly into the sides of the rocks to create the illusion of many grass blades hugging the rocks, helping them sit naturally within the scene.

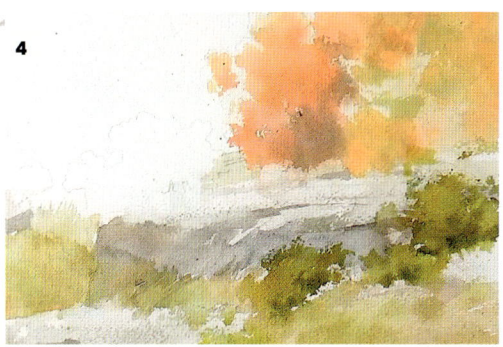

STEP 4 –ADDING BUSHES

Bushes are useful to offset symmetrical rocks and monotonous grass. Use the same dry-brush technique as you would for trees—jab upward to break up the paint to form natural-looking leaf clusters.

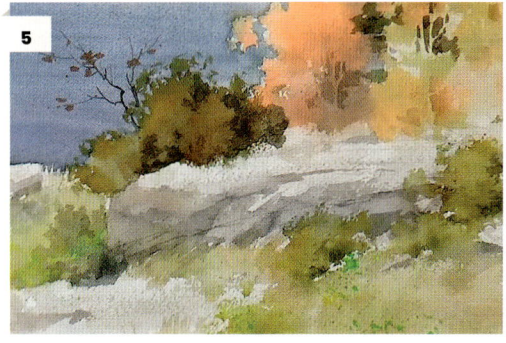

STEP 5 – ADDING WEEDS AND WILD FLOWERS

Splatter weeds or wildflowers randomly throughout the scene to add interesting texture and color variation (see Tricks of the Trade: Splattering). Keep them to a minimum. Less is more! You can use gouache or pastels for these additions.

TIP

Load a slight variation of color on your brush every time you return to the palette.

Cliffs

These rocky cliffs come alive with a symphony of shifting colors, showcasing watercolor's unmatched versatility. Warm hues dance against cool tones in the shadowed planes, creating a captivating interplay. As an artist, your role is to entertain by embracing abstract shapes and imaginative designs, with exaggerated color rather than replicating the symmetry and the dull colors found in reality. The dry-brush effect produces lovely white foam patterns.

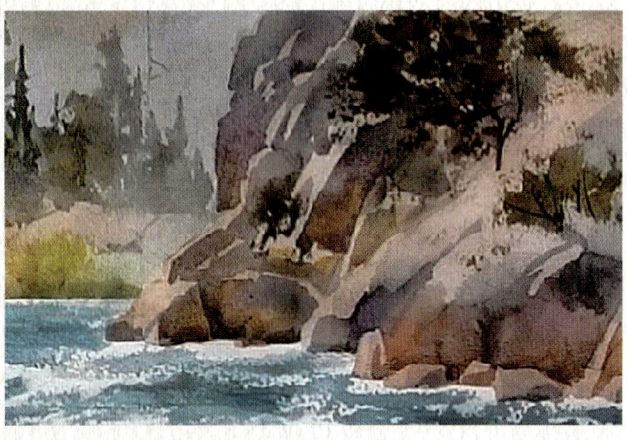

Jagged Edges, Liquid Grace

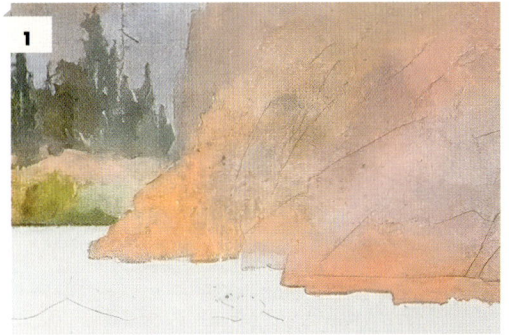

STEP 1 – CREATING HIGHLIGHTS

Prepare three distinct puddles on your palette: Payne's gray, permanent rose, and raw sienna. Keep the colors pure by rinsing your brush thoroughly between dips. When blocking in rocks or cliffs, make a habit of varying the colors roughly every 1.5in (4cm). Keep the values close together and the subtle color shifts should remain visible from about 8ft (2.5m) away. You can choose to lean the palette toward warmer tones or more neutral grays, depending on the desired mood.

STEP 2 – DEFINING SHADOWS

For the shadowed sides of the cliff divisions, combine Payne's gray, ultramarine blue, raw sienna, and a touch of permanent rose. Keep the mix subdued while allowing each hue to retain its identity. Let the colors blend softly on the paper, with an emphasis on cool tones. Use varied abstract shapes and avoid repetitive or parallel lines—variety in size is key. These designs add visual interest, capturing the rugged character of the cliffs through subtle color shifts.

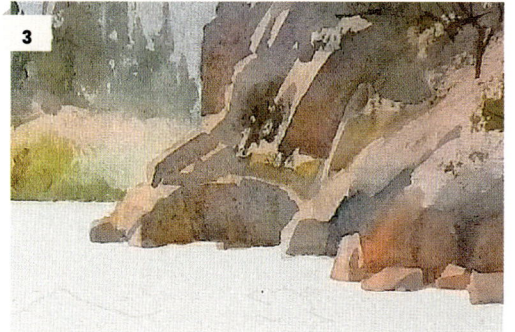

STEP 3 - CAPTURING REFLECTED LIGHT

Add warm reflected light while the paint is still wet at the bottom, where the shadow meets the highlights, to create smooth gradient planes. This technique, known as reflected light, enhances depth and adds a subtle glow, suggesting light bouncing off nearby sunlit surfaces.

TIP

To depict a natural, organic look to rocks in a group or cliffs, insert grass and bushes.

PRINCIPLES OF PAINTING MOUNTAINS

- Place the tallest peak just off-center to avoid an obvious symmetrical placement.

- Avoid over-simplifying ridges—mountains often have intricate, detailed contours.

- Avoid soft edges, including in snow patches, to maintain crispness and realism.

- Reduce the number of crevices to keep the composition uncluttered.

- To emphasize the mountain's majesty, give it as much space as possible and bring the peak close to the top edge without crowding the remaining space (see Composition: Stage 1).

- Small trees determine the scale contrast, making large mountains appear even larger.

- Avoid fluffy white clouds whose value competes with the white snow.

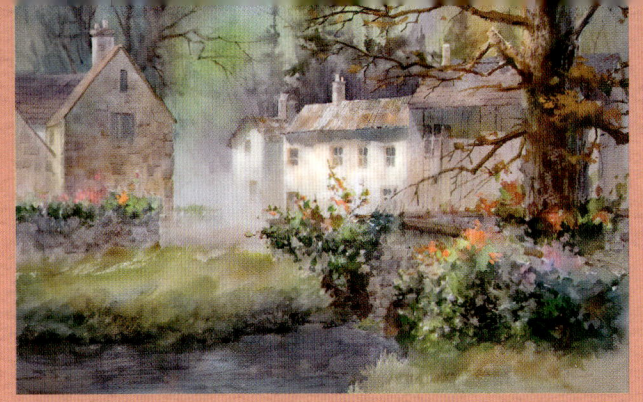

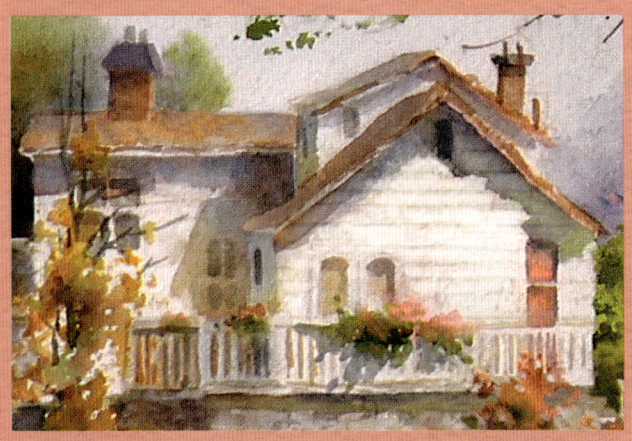

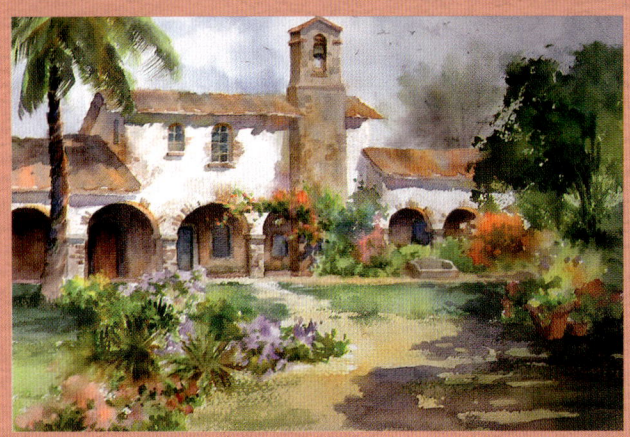

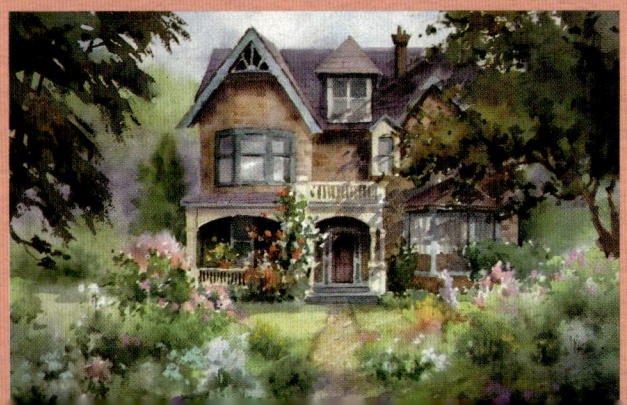

CHAPTER SIX:
Architecture

You will find that watercolor is the superior medium for painting architecture, outshining all others in handling the hard edges of man-made structures. In this chapter, you will learn how to represent different types of walls and roofs. At first, buildings may appear stiff and rigid, but you will discover how to give them personality—turning each one into a charming storybook character. By softening their edges, adding playful details, and nestling buildings among flowers, trees, and other natural elements, your architecture will feel alive, and fully part of the landscape.

Architectural Structures

Buildings make a popular subject for paintings, offering endless possibilities for artistic expression. The collection of buildings in this painting presents an opportunity to paint a range of architectural structures: a stone wall, a wooden wall, and a tin roof. In this chapter, you will learn there's no need to paint every brick, stone, or roof shingle. A few well-placed hints of texture will suffice, and the mind's vision will fill in the rest.

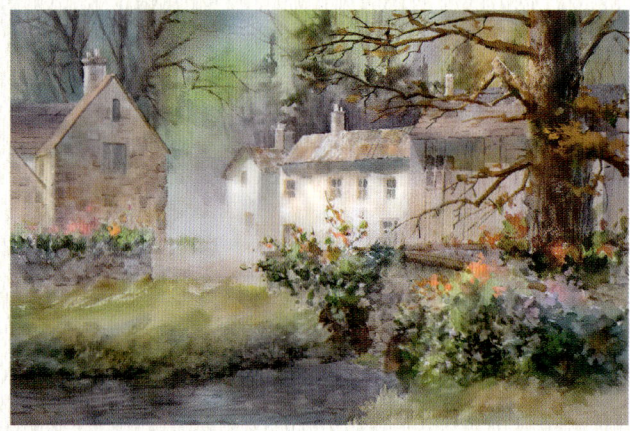

A Village Lost in the Breath of Mist

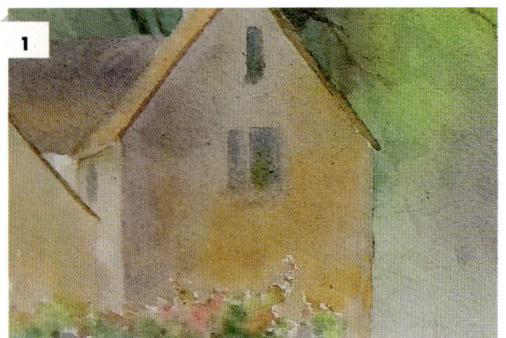

STEP 1 – ENRICHING WALL COLORS

Start by painting the average flat value of the wall, while introducing slight variations with random touches of violet. These subtle shifts create an appealing gradient and prevent the look of a freshly painted surface, instead suggesting aging.

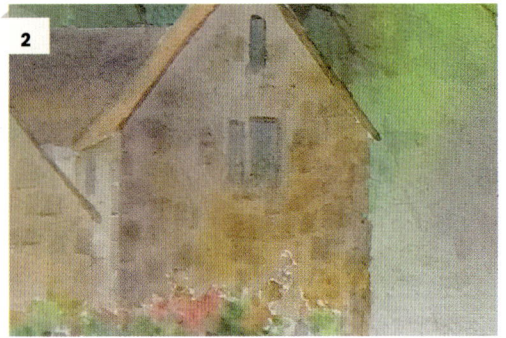

STEP 2 – ADDING DETAIL

Begin placing the stones at the wall's edge, grouping them in clusters. Leave solid gaps between the clusters, as this creates a non-repetitive contrast. Allow some stones to protrude along the edge. Stop adding stones once the arrangement starts to look spotty. Trust that the mind's vision will complete the visual suggestion.

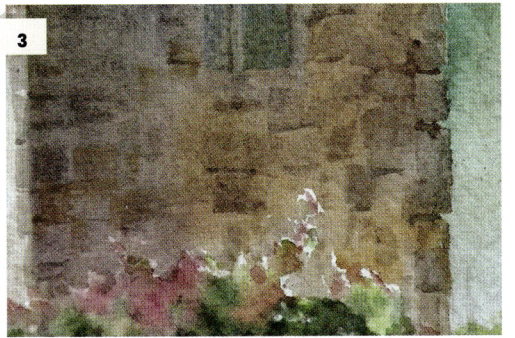

STEP 3 – CAPTURING PROTRUDING STONES

Add shadows beneath some stones while leaving others without shadows. This will give the impression that some stones are protruding.

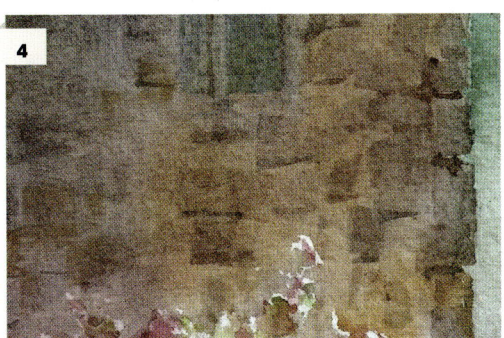

STEP 4 – CREATING A MELODIC LINE

Create a melodic line at the edge of the wall—that is, a line that is irregular, or broken, with no obvious repetition. The protruding stones will contribute more interest than a straight line.

TIP

Windows are symmetrical shapes. To disguise them, blur parts and keep their color values close to those of the wall. Adding stones or bricks next to windows can help break up the rectangular symmetry.

Wooden Wall

Wooden walls offer fascinating textures, especially when multiple colors are combined. The natural grain and weathered cracks suggest aging and character, enriching the narrative in architectural scenes.

STEP 1 – LAYING A FIRST WASH

Paint a warm, muted orange wash over the area, varying the colors with touches of blue and violet.

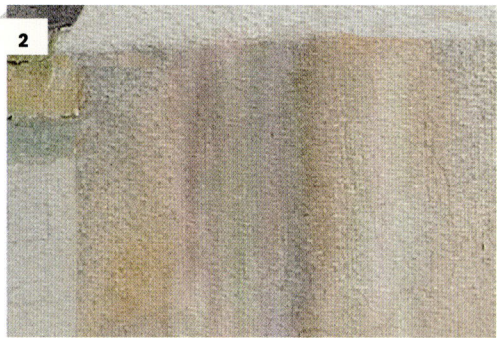

STEP 2 – LIFTING OUT BOARDS

While the paint is still wet, use a thirsty brush to lift paint and lighten a few boards (see Tricks of the Trade: Lightening Value with a Thirsty Brush). This prevents a flat, uniform look and creates fresh value shifts—this is where real wood has no say.

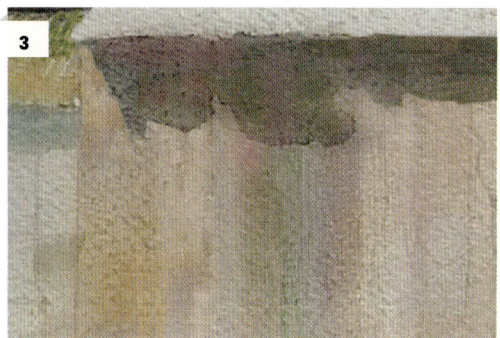

STEP 3 – CASTING SHADOW

Add cast shadows using a melodic, irregular line. Echo the surrounding colors.

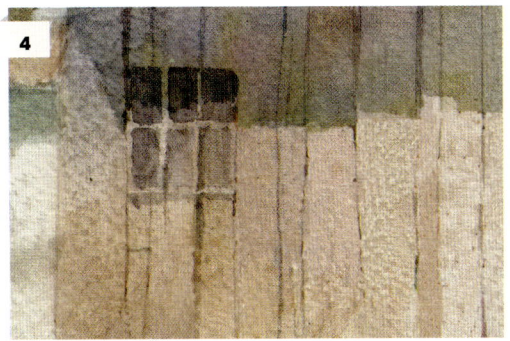

STEP 4 – ADDING THE BOARD CRACKS

Add cracks between the boards, varying their widths and lengths. They don't need to be perfectly vertical. While real boards are usually uniform in size, introducing irregularity enhances the visual narrative, adding charm and character. Differing board widths may not be realistic, but avoiding clones improves artistic appeal.

TIP

To ensure shadows feel they belong and convey transparency, include see-through elements such as board cracks, bricks, stones, and water or rust stains.

CLAPBOARD

Treat the clapboard like a white stucco wall (see Stucco Wall), but suggest horizontal lines with soft shadows to hint at the separate boards. Avoid too many repetitive straight lines by letting some segments fade out or vanish—the mind will naturally fill in the gaps.

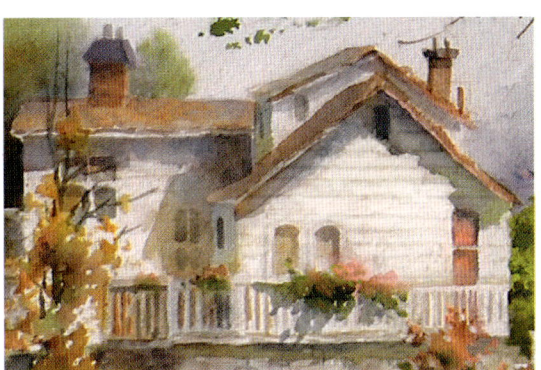

Tin Roof

Tin roofs are one of my favorites to add to barns and wooden shacks. The bare metal reflects the blue sky, achieving color harmony, while patches of rust add character and suggest decades of weathering.

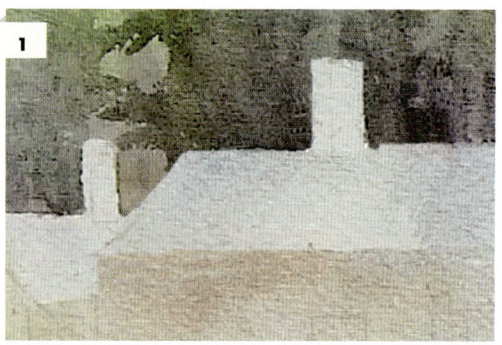

STEP 1 - STARTING WITH THE SKY COLOR

Start with a light wash of a blue gray over the whole roof area.

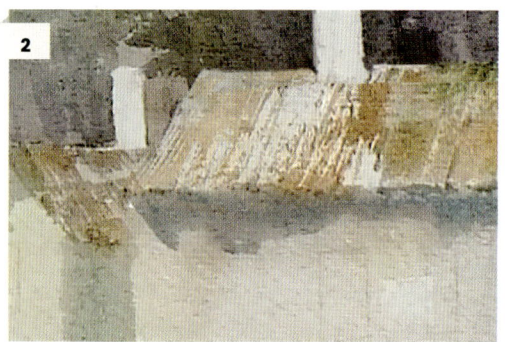

STEP 2 - DEPICTING RUST

Use burnt sienna straight from the tube for the rust. Rake in the rust streaks with a fan brush to mimic the natural grooves of the tin roof. Include more concentrated rust in some areas, for contrast. In general, contrasting two halves of a shape makes it more appealing. Add a touch of green mold as a color echo to enhance harmony.

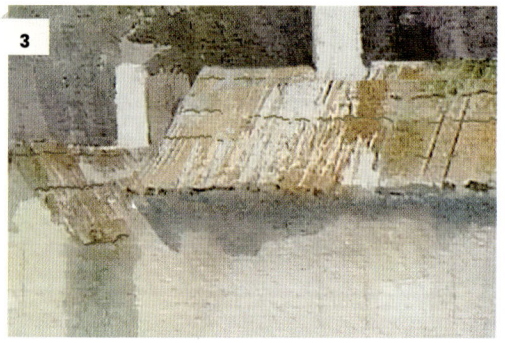

STEP 3 - CREATING TIN SHEETS

Indicate the separate tin sheets using irregular, interrupted shadow lines. Dark accents along the horizontal edge of the roof accentuate the overhang.

Clay Tile Roof

Tile roofs are common and often appear on houses. Their warm terra-cotta color makes them visually appealing. Adding some shadows to the rows of tiles makes them quite believable.

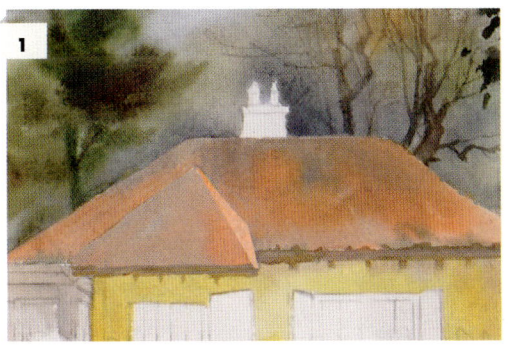

STEP 1 – LAYING A FIRST WASH

Wet parts of the roof to achieve lighter spots, creating a gradient plane. Paint the roof broadly, then add touches of violet and green for variety and to show aging.

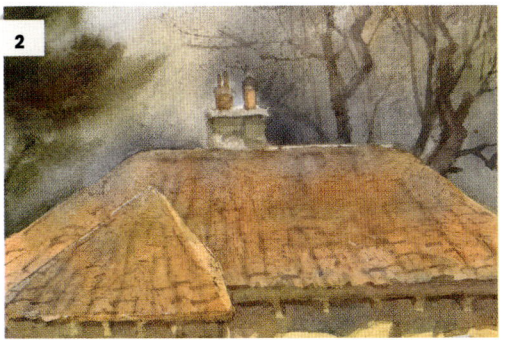

STEP 2 – SUGGESTING TILES

Suggest the edges of the tile shadows using thin, broken lines. Interrupting the lines will slow down the eye, allowing viewers to mentally fill in the gaps. Define some edges at the front while gradually tapering off as the roof recedes. The contrast between busy areas and solid edges makes the forms more interesting to look at, avoiding the monotony of a roof covered in uniform texture.

Stucco Wall

San Juan Capistrano Mission, a historic Spanish site in California, often inspires artists to paint its charming angles and arches. In this piece, I adjusted the path to lead toward the steeple and enriched the scene with flowers. The palm tree in the top left was subdued to keep focus on the building's arches. White walls feel more natural with ambient dirt, especially where rainwater collects. Rather than painting every stone or roof tile, suggesting a few defines their presence, while color shifts add interest.

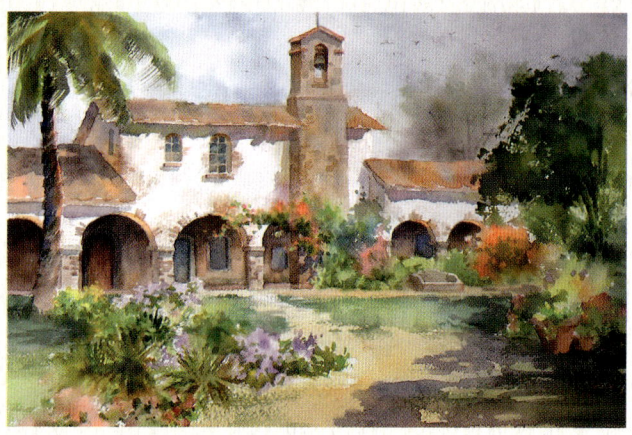

San Juan Capistrano Mission, California.

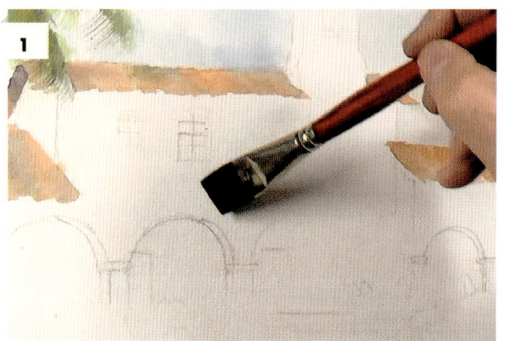

STEP 1 – PREPARING THE WALL

Spot-wet the wall with clear water, leaving a few random dry areas. Those areas will give the appearance that paint has peeled off. Add warmth to the entire wall with raw sienna.

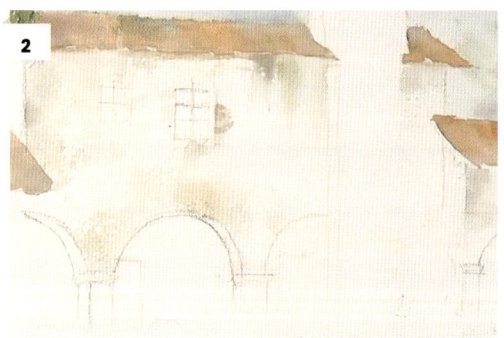

STEP 2 – AGING THE WALL

Use the flat side of your brush to randomly tap a loose mix of burnt sienna and Payne's gray for dirt stains, creating a weathered look. There should be more white wall than stains. Add green drips under the eaves for mold, tying in nearby foliage for color harmony.

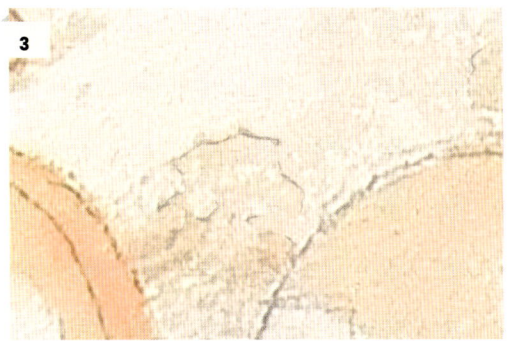

STEP 3 – RENDERING THE PEELING PAINT

To suggest peeling paint, hold your brush completely parallel to the paper and gently dry-brush a slightly darker color in various directions. Follow up with a few thin lines to indicate shadows beneath the lifted areas.

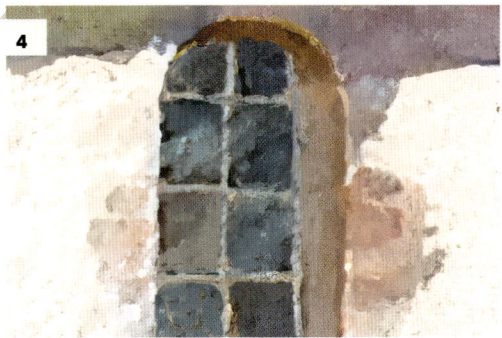

STEP 4 – OFFSETTING SYMMETRY

To break the window's symmetry, expose some bricks beneath the broken plaster for character and interest.

ENRICHING SHADOWS

Real shadows on white walls are a uniform, lifeless blue. In your paintings, you can dramatically enrich them by bouncing multiple colors borrowed from surrounding elements. In this example, they start out cool under the eaves and gradually become warmer, resulting in a colorful gradient plane.

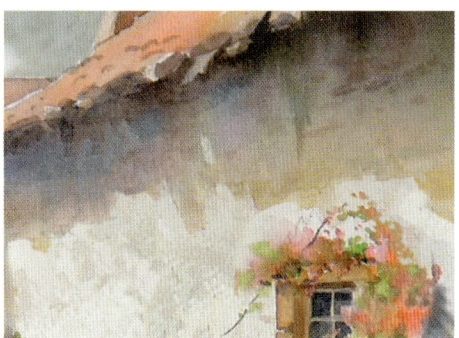

Brick Wall

Victorian houses are excellent subjects to paint due to their unique angles and intricate details. Brick walls are visually appealing, especially with their warm orange tones. In this composition, the plants creeping over the porch soften the otherwise rigid structure. Cast shadows across the walls create a pleasing, grounded effect. While you may never see a violet roof in reality, in this story book it adds a narrative personality.

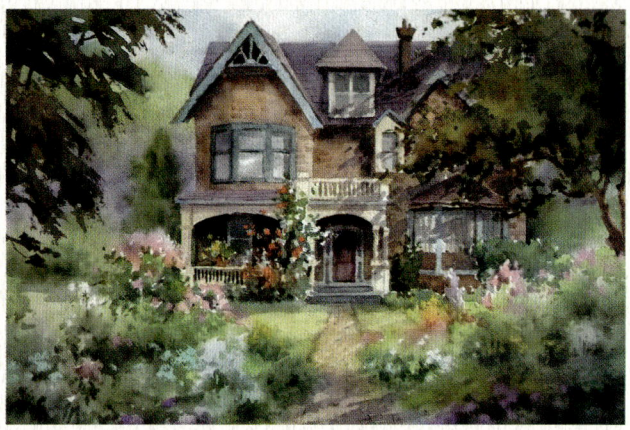

The Garden's Gentle Gateway

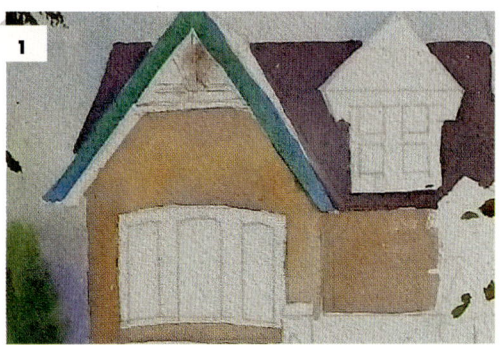

STEP 1 – AGING THE WALL

Paint the main wall in a muted orange color with random touches of violet. These act as a catalyst, aging the wall and giving it a more natural, weathered appearance.

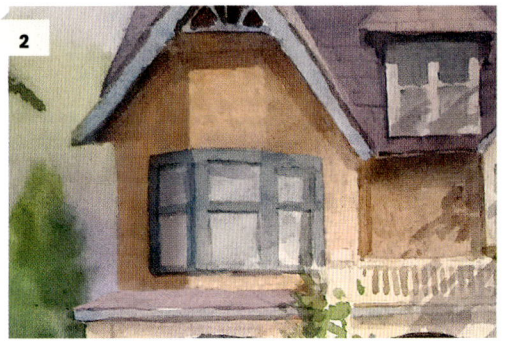

STEP 2 – CREATING THE PLANES

Glaze over your first wash to define the shadow sides of the planes with a grayed-down blue mixture. The original orange hue should still dominate, but a darker version of it.

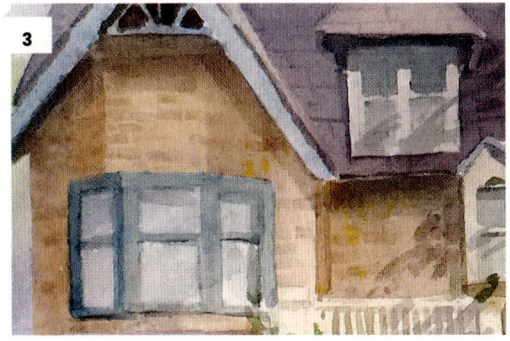

STEP 3 - ADDING THE BRICKS

Make the bricks larger than life so viewers can easily identify them from a distance. Ignore the literal size of bricks. Leave some areas blank—filling every space will make the wall look overly busy and repetitive. Let the mind's vision fill in the rest. Artistic appeal should always take priority over realism.

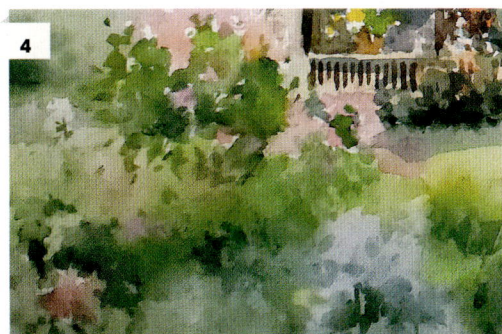

STEP 4 – DIRECTING FOCUS

Simplify the flower beds by reducing dark indentations. Keeping the foreground out of focus with the application of the wet-on-wet approach (see Wet-on-Wet) will direct more attention to the house. The bottom portion of the painting will become conceptual, mimicking human peripheral vision.

FLORAL DETAILS

Adding flowers around houses elevates a street scene, infusing it with life and vibrancy. I enjoy incorporating floral details to make scenes like this even more captivating. You can strategically place them to slow down the visual pace of rigid straight lines.

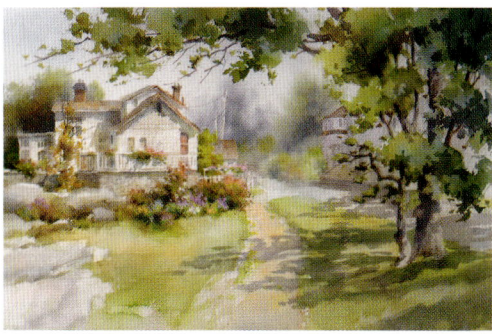

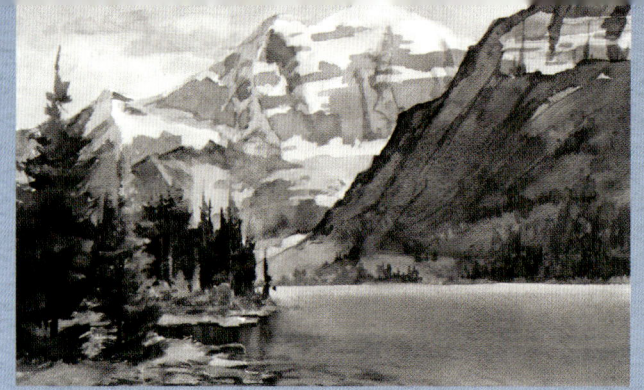

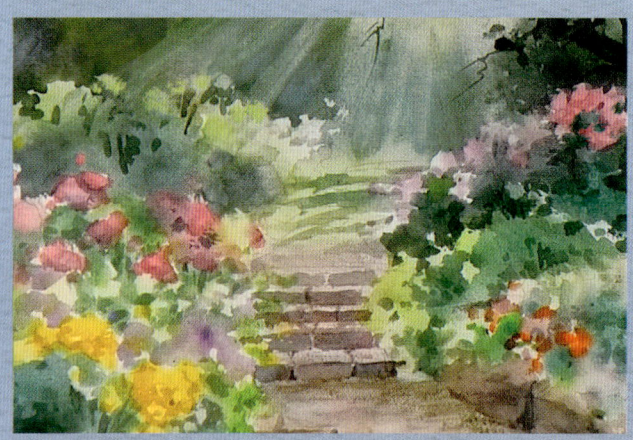

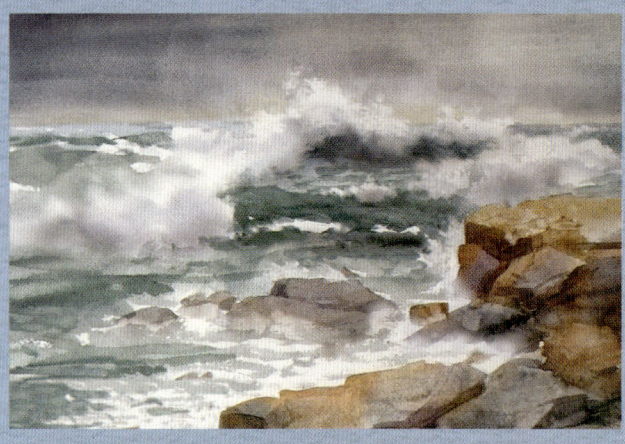

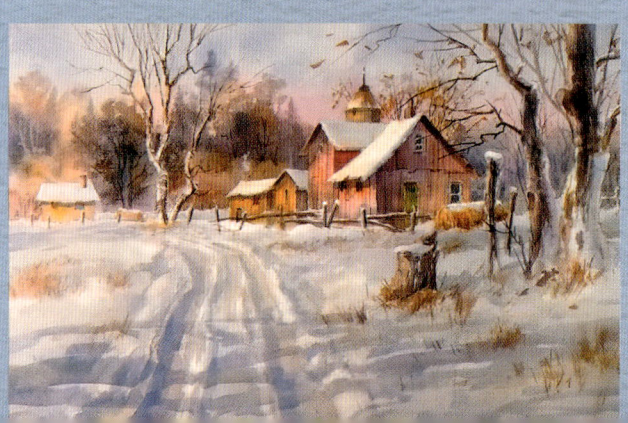

CHAPTER SEVEN

Composition

Composition is the backbone of any painting—the make-or-break element that determines its success. It can be a long and complex subject, but this chapter provides a simple, practical road map to help you design successful works. You will gain freedom from strict photo dependence while still learning how to use photos as helpful tools. Learn to maximize your canvas by assigning each plane the right amount of space to get the most visual impact. Guiding the viewer's eye to move effortlessly across a painting is an essential priority. Consider this chapter your aspirin for composition headaches.

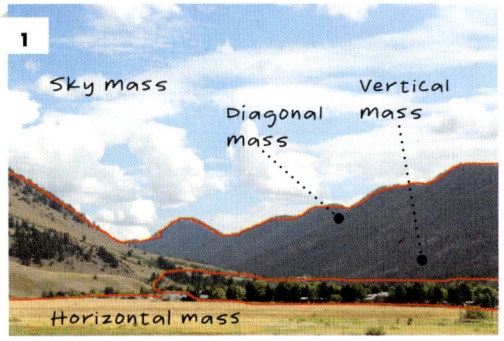

1

Sky mass

Diagonal mass

Vertical mass

Horizontal mass

Composition in Seven Stages

There is much to say on the subject of composition. In painting, we work within a confined space, unlike the infinite expanse of the real world. This requires us to thoughtfully crop and arrange elements to fit cohesively within the painting's rectangle. You will also want to express three-dimensional images from the real world and represent them on a two-dimensional canvas, tricking your viewers into momentarily believing in a convincing landscape. In order to achieve all of this, it helps to follow a basic, seven-stage formula.

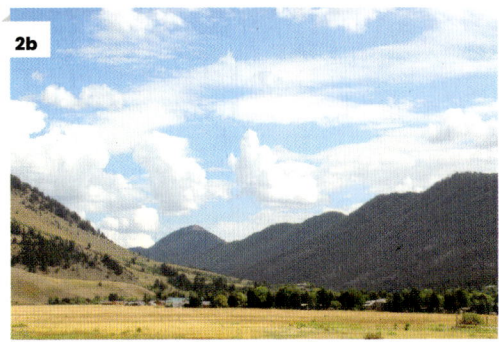

2a

2b

1: Assign Size Masses

STEP 1 – DIVIDE THE SCENE INTO MASSES

Every scene will contain three or four main masses: the sky; a vertical mass (trees and cliffs); a horizontal mass (flat terrain or bodies of water); and a diagonal mass (when mountains or hills are present).

STEP 2 – SELECT A DOMINANT MASS

After identifying the masses, choose the one with the greatest visual richness and refreshing information to be the main mass, ensuring it occupies the largest area. The next step is to trim away significant portions of the other competing masses, leaving just enough to serve as supporting subordinate planes (see opposite).

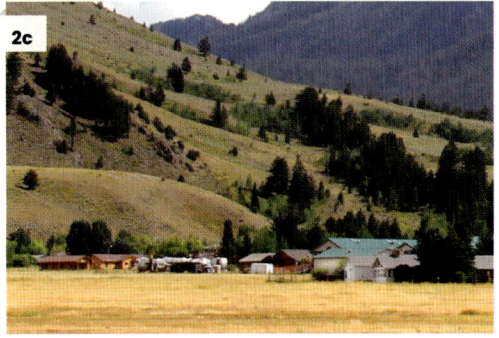

2c

STEP 3 – ASSIGN VALUES PER MASS

As you establish a dominant mass, also assign a dominant value to each. In 90 percent of typical sunny or overcast scenes, this approach works well.

- Mid–light value: The sky is usually the lightest value in a painting.

- Mid–value: The horizontal mass (ground or water).

- Mid–dark value: This is usually the diagonal mass, unless lightened from atmospheric perspective.

- Dark value: The vertical mass (trees or buildings) is usually the darkest value in a painting.

Exceptions to the 90 percent include low sun positions that illuminate trees while casting shadows on the ground, as well as nocturne scenes, which dramatically shift the value structure. (See also, Values Are Your Guitar Strings.) The list excludes accents—small touches of black or near-black used to suggest indentations in shapes.

In some cases, a mountain or hill—typically diagonal masses—may be absent, often due to tall trees, or their mid–dark value is lost due to atmospheric perspective. In such situations, you can reassign the mid–dark value usually reserved for that plane to the vertical mass such as trees or a cliff, shifting the dark value up one scale to mid–dark. This adjustment fills the entire painting with lighter values where color sings. Since color saturation diminishes as values darken, it's best to avoid pushing too far into dark values unless necessary, as hues become harder to distinguish from a distance.

In the first option (image 2a), the composition gives priority of size to the horizontal mass. But too many square inches of repetitive information in the field will make that composition feel monotonous and reduce visual interest. The prairie could work if animals were grazing to fill the large empty space or if a river were added.

Similarly, the skyscape (image 2b) takes up two-thirds of the space. But it is still not interesting enough to merit designation as the largest mass. It could be more appealing with a vibrant sunset instead of a plain blue sky with repetitive clouds, which lacks interest. Alternatively, you could enhance the composition by combining it with a second photo that features a more striking sky, such as sunbeams breaking through dark clouds. Using more than one photo opens up valuable references, enriching your options and solving many compositional challenges.

The final composition (image 2c), with the hill and trees as the dominant mass, has the strongest visual impact. By reducing the size of the sky and field, this is where viewers will linger the longest.

To strengthen your paintings, use four distinct gray markers to create simple thumbnails that map out the overall value range of each major mass (see below). To maintain unity, keep the values of your landscape symbols together, avoiding dramatic shifts—only slightly lightening for highlights or darkening for shadows. Reference values don't need to be fixed—the sun's position at different times of the day can rearrange the entire value structure. Try alternating the value-to-mass relationships to explore different compositional outcomes. Squint your eyes to assess whether you see the three or four distinct values.

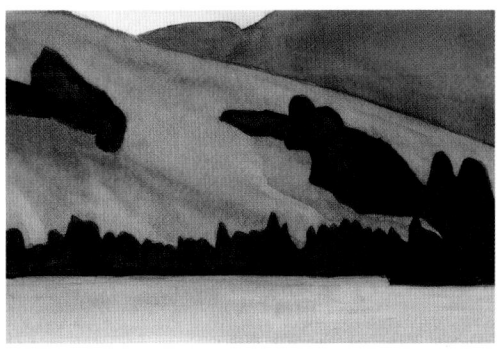

2: Values Are Your Guitar Strings

As you paint, visualize everything as it would appear in a black-and-white photo to ensure a strong value structure. Many art instructors reference a value scale of 10 distinct values, but it's nearly impossible to mix the exact grays on this scale. To simplify, I merge these into four grays, plus white and black, making for a more easily recognizable value scheme. Just as six guitar strings produce various music scales, values are your tools for determining how dark or light shapes will be.

COMMON VALUE RANGE

White: Sunlit snow, water foam, and clouds

Mid-light: Overall sky

Mid: Ground, including rivers and lakes

Mid-dark: Diagonal mass and trees

Dark: Trees, only use when needed

Black: Used for accents where no light reaches. Never use black for overall shapes during daylight.

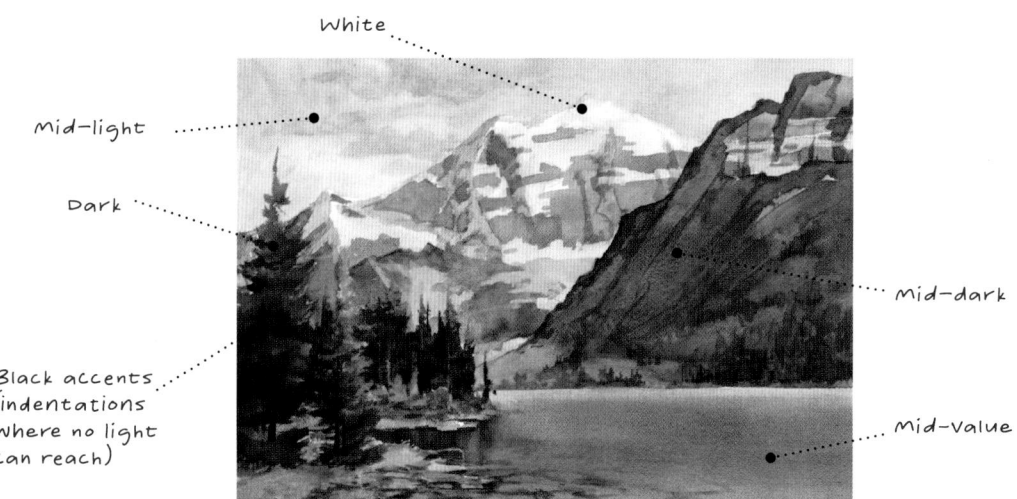

White

Mid-light

Dark

Black accents (indentations where no light can reach)

Mid-dark

Mid-value

Because there are two mountains that are slanted masses, I assigned a mid-value to the more distant one and a mid-dark value to the closer one. The evergreen trees took on a dark value.

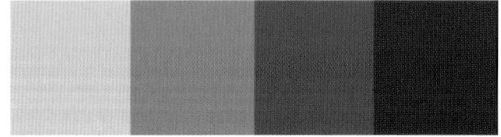

For your main shapes, refer to this simple four-value scale. Avoid using the darkest value unless necessary. Squinting while comparing colors is helpful for making an accurate judgment.

Simplified Three-Value Scale

This motif requires only a three-mass/value plan. Without a slanted plane to take the mid-dark value, the trees will inherit it. Reserve dark values for use only after the other three have been assigned. Use this simple three-value range in most of your landscapes.

Sky: Mid-light

Horizontal/Grass field: Mid

Vertical/Trees: Dark

If your painting reads well in grayscale, you're on the right path. Your composition will be stronger when your colors align with the correct grays on the value scale. However, maintaining the intended value requires skill, as it's easy to shift unintentionally. Keep in mind that watercolor dries up to 20 or 25 percent lighter than initially applied. To simplify this process, focus on just three or four distinct intermediary gray values—since white and black are naturally easy to recognize.

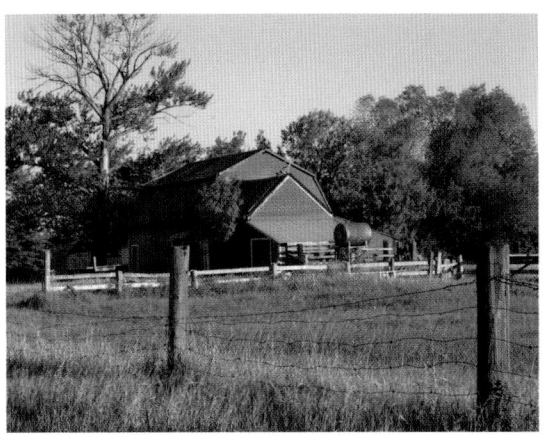

3: Place the Focal Area

The focal area is the most developed, attractive section that stands out in the composition. To decide on the focal area, visualize a tic-tac-toe grid over your paper. The four intersections where the lines meet are the common areas of the focal area, which can be the size of a dessert plate on a 12 x 16in (30 x 40cm) surface. There is leeway for adjustment.

The top-right is the best location for the focal point. This spot aligns with the natural left-to-right reading flow, guiding the viewer's eye smoothly similar to how you read. The top-left is the second-best option, the bottom-right comes in third, and the bottom-left is the least preferred.

The higher locations leave space in the bottom two-thirds of the canvas to design a compelling visual path that leads to the focal area.

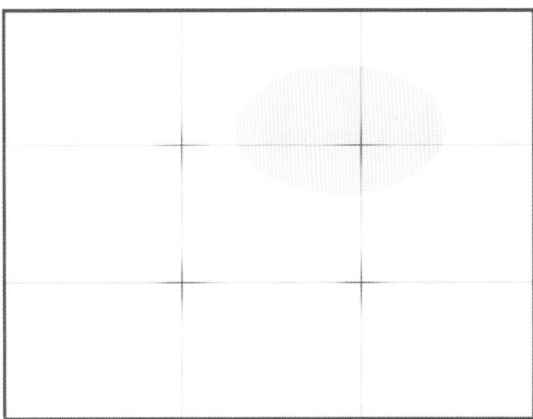

TIP

Form a square with four fingers to make a window. Move it around. If every section has a color shift, your painting is entertaining.

4: Create a Visual Path

After selecting the focal area, design a visual path to guide viewers toward it. Visual paths are powerful compositional tools that guide a viewer's eye from the foreground into the deeper parts of the painting. Design gentle, slow-moving leading lines to allow viewers extra time to explore the painting. They should never feel rushed. They will start out exploring the entire foreground, eventually making their way toward the focal area and beyond.
Visual paths can originate from the bottom—the most common approach—and, when it suits the composition, from the top, using clouds and sky openings to guide the eye. The most effective lead-in elements will form an implied "S" movement.

USEFUL PATHS:

Streams and rivers

Trails and walkways

Shorelines and coastlines

Roads

Cast shadows

Bushes and flowers

Connect-the-dots flowers or bushes

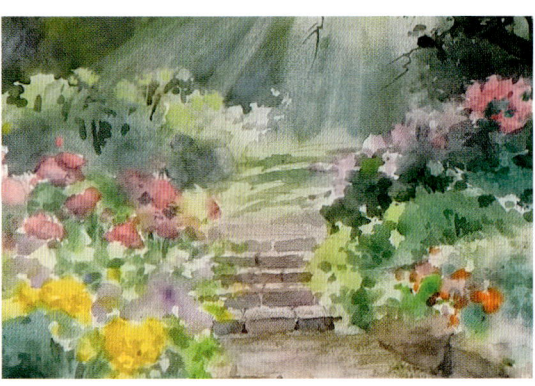

Walkway

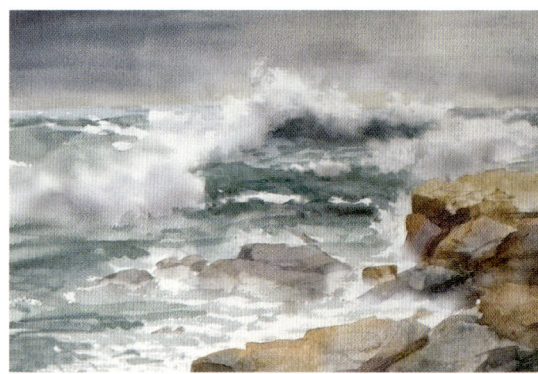

Coastline

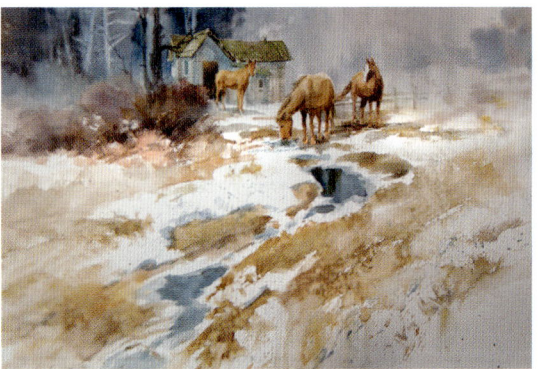

Stream

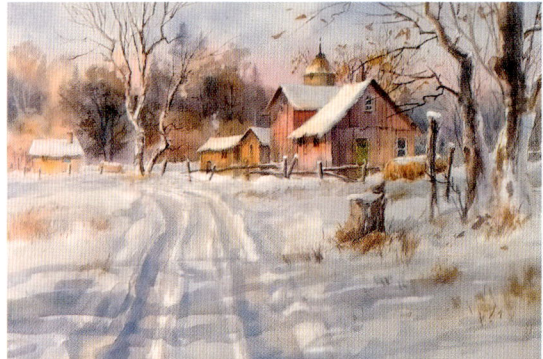

Roads and trails

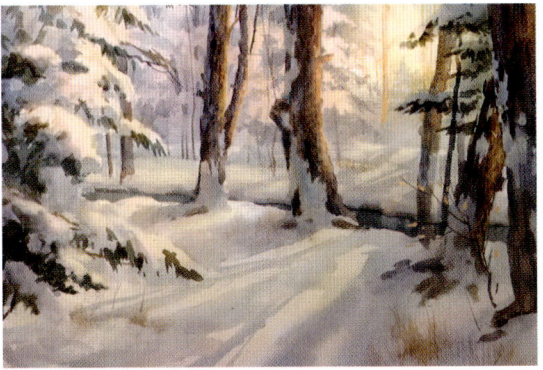

Cast shadows

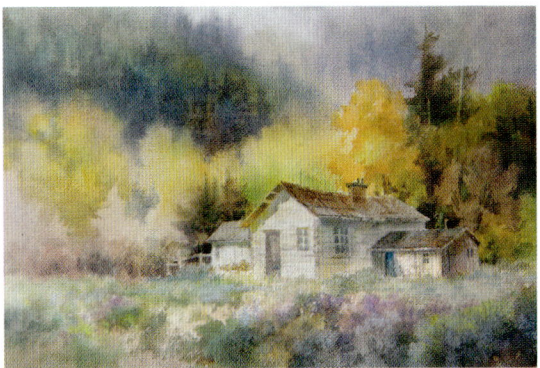

Using a "connect-the-dots" pattern of bushes and wildflowers draws the eye toward the house.

5: Render Three-Dimensional Shapes

Landscape photos often lack clear three-dimensional forms, especially when shot on overcast days. To avoid a flat, "pasted-on" appearance, intentionally add backside shading to your landscape shapes and light on the opposite side to overcome the inherent two-dimensional aspect. Even if three-dimensional forms aren't obvious in photos or nature, shape them as three-dimensional to avoid a two-dimensional look. Nature doesn't require exact rendering to appear three-dimensional, but you'll need to adjust your approach to create that effect in your painting.

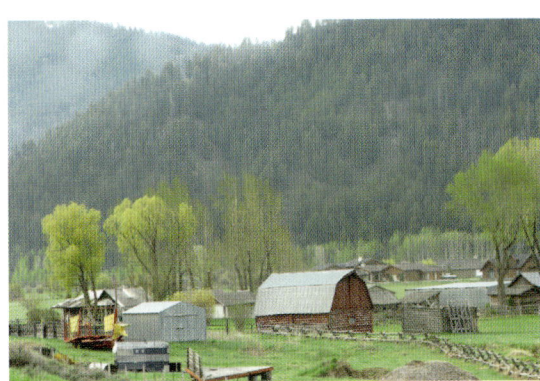

An example of how trees can lack volume and appear flat. Similarly, even if the barn is placed at a three-quarter position, it receives equal light on both facades, with no clear light direction. It's best to differentiate the front and side with shading.

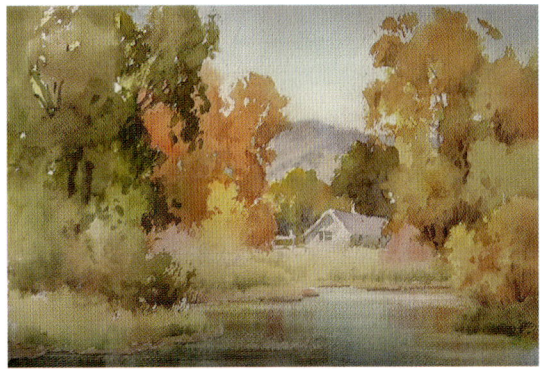

The trees are rendered as round forms by emphasizing a darker side. Avoid crossing the one-third to two-thirds ratio when shading.

6: Design Pleasing Contour Lines

When viewers admire your artwork, they subconsciously "read" contour lines while processing the visual information to make sense of forms. They prefer a gradual, smooth flow instead of a rapid or repetitive visual pace, which evokes discomfort. Artists deliberately slow down and alter these lines by restructuring shapes with more appealing contours.

LINES TO AVOID:

Straight line: Riverbanks, roads

Curved line: Symmetrical trees (tops and sides), rivers and streams, clouds, roads

Bumpy line: Tops of grouped trees

Zigzag line: Evergreens

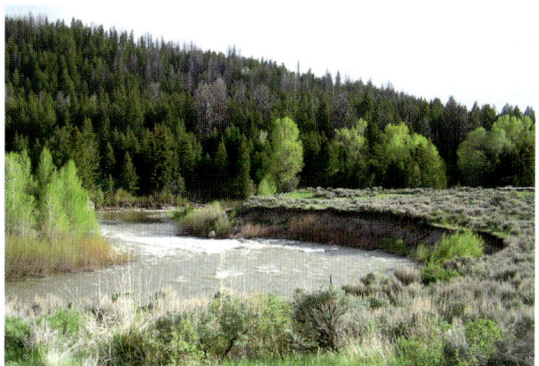

In this reference photo, the straight line of the riverbank is too "fast" paced.

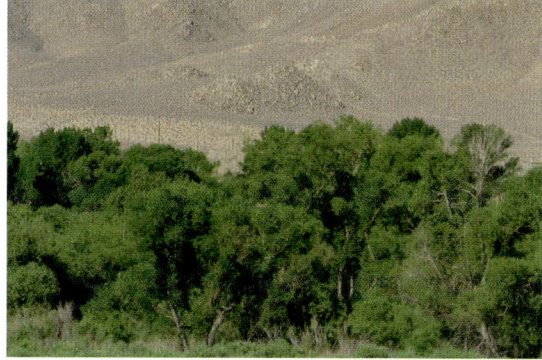

Here, the bumpy line of the seamless treetops is "monotonous."

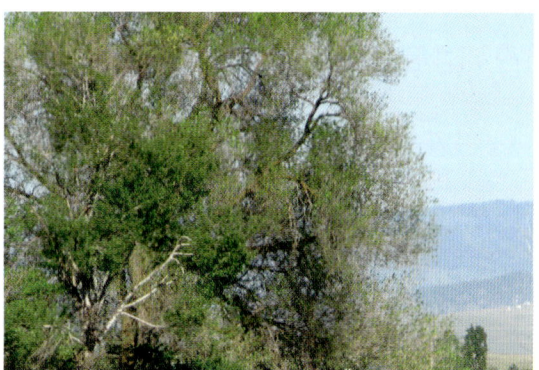

The curved line of this tree is "fast" paced.

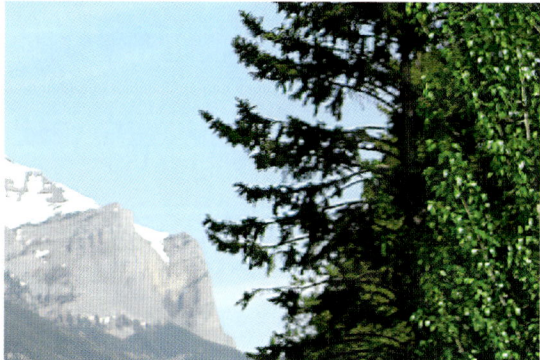

The zigzag of the boughs is "repetitive."

Modified Lines:

You can modify fast and monotonous lines in several ways by using the following substitutes—they can be applied everywhere.

Interrupted line: Runs, then stops or slows down, only to pick up pace again

Melodic line: Resembles the path of an irregular staircase

Pendulum line: Sways back and forth in a rocking motion

Graceful line: Resembles the path of a rollercoaster

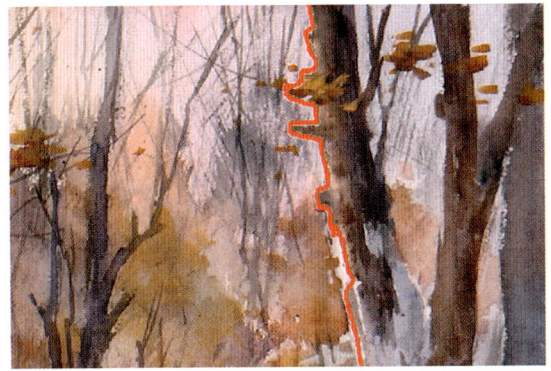

Interrupt fast-paced contour lines with a melodic line exploiting protrusions as speed bumps.

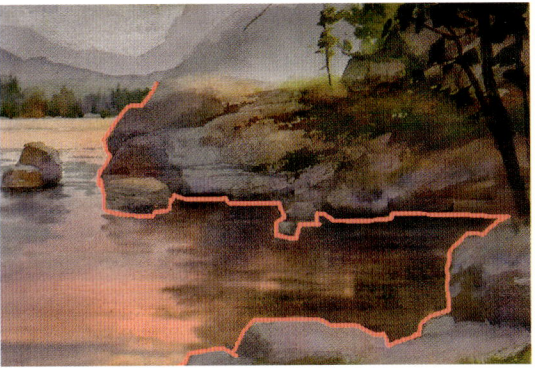

Here, there is a melodic line along the edge of the water.

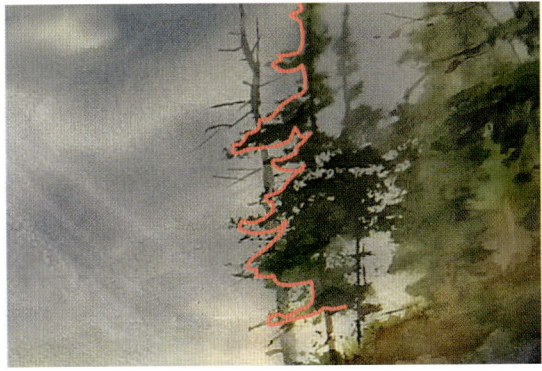

Reduce evergreen boughs and render them to form a pendulum line.

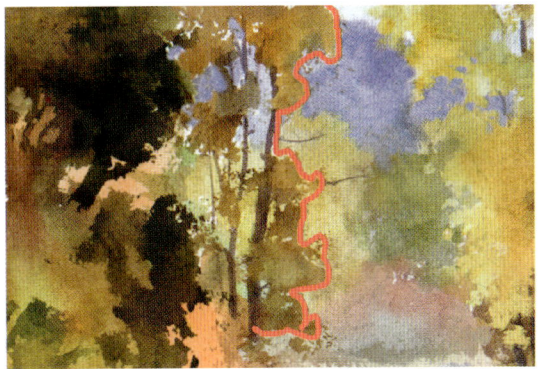

A graceful line can appear on the side of a tree or on the top of a group of trees.

7: Apply Color Variegation as Gradient Planes

Nature can outperform you in macro scale, but when working on smaller surfaces like a full or quarter sheet of watercolor paper, everything becomes much smaller. You, the artist, have the upper hand in breaking up the dull, symmetrical, and monochromatic color shapes of nature. Think of yourself as a performer, focusing on entertaining your viewers rather than trying simply to depict reality. I encourage you to seize the opportunity to design gradient planes with color variation in as many ways as possible—from small stones to large cliffs. Aim for subtle shifts in color approximately every 1.5in (4cm) to keep things visually engaging. One of my secret ingredients, now shared with you, is adding violets and pinks to areas you wouldn't typically see in nature. This book provides plenty of examples.

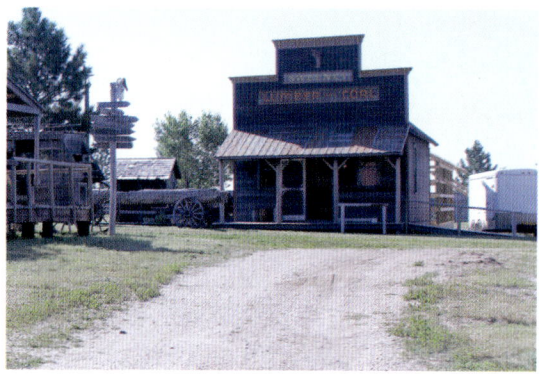

In this photo, the sky, road, and grass are dull and monochromatic.

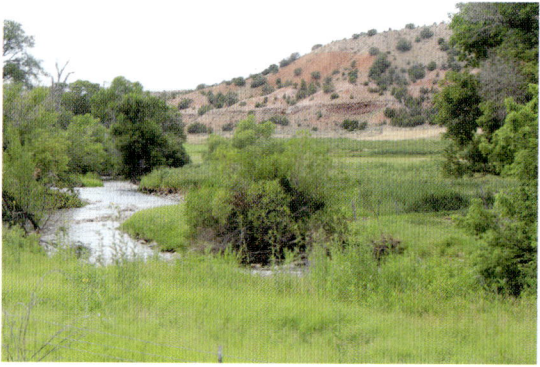

This image has no variety in greens whatsoever.

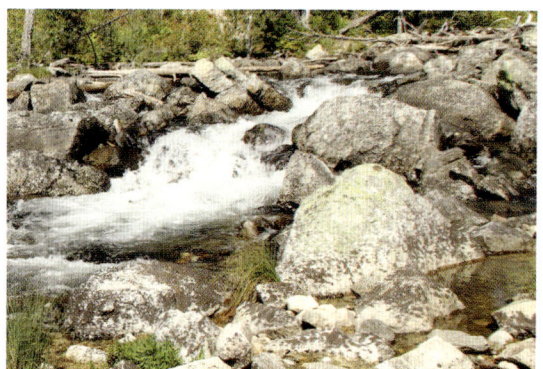

Almost all of these rocks are identical in tone and color.

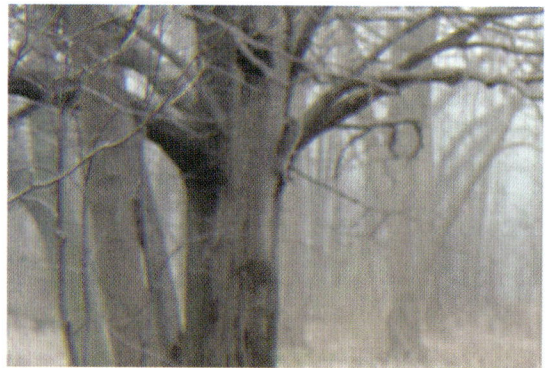

Totally monochromatic! Resist the temptation of painting what you see!

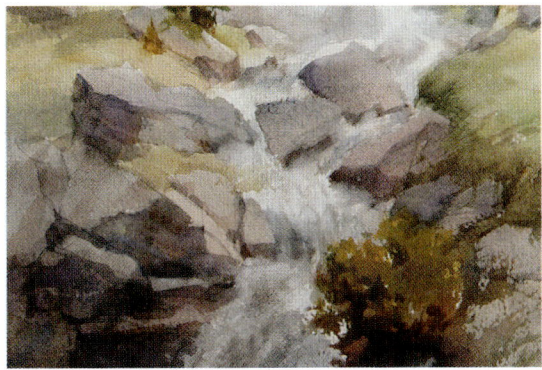

Rocks: Adding pink and violet, the latter better on the dark side, will make them more colorful.

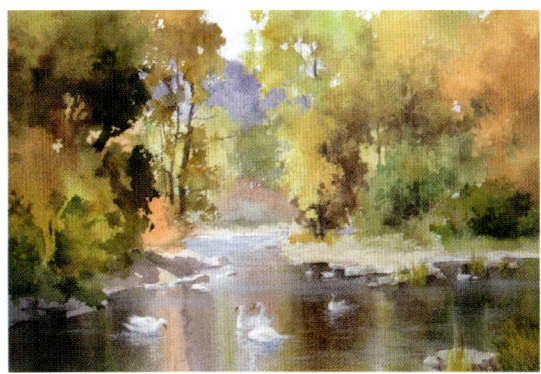

Seasons: Shifting summer scenes to early fall allows for dramatic, nuanced colors.

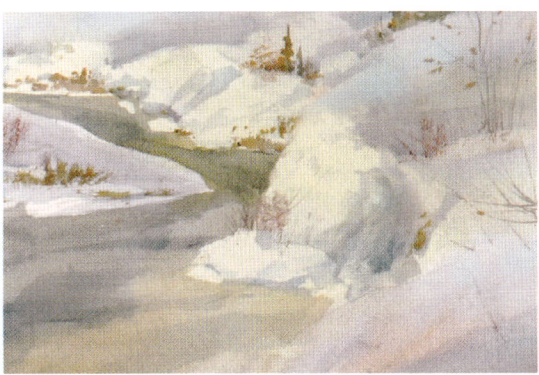

Snow: Shadows in nature are dull. Liven them up with pinks, oranges, and violets.

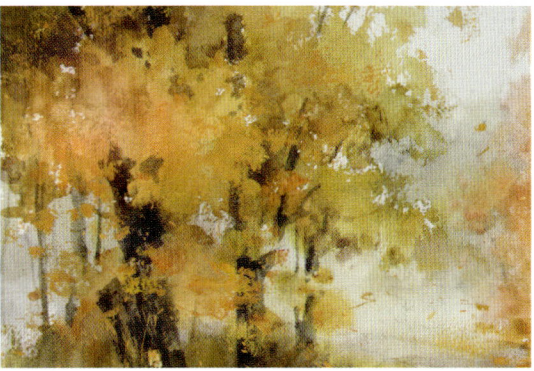

Autumn foliage: Devise ways to add oranges and pinks for warmth.

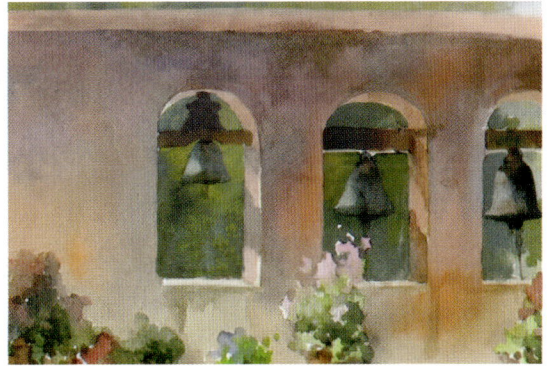

Facades: The wall has a gradient plane transitioning from light to dark and vibrant warm to cool colors.

TIP

When variegating, to avoid competing hues, ensure that only one hue dominates, allowing the others to support and enhance it without overpowering the composition.

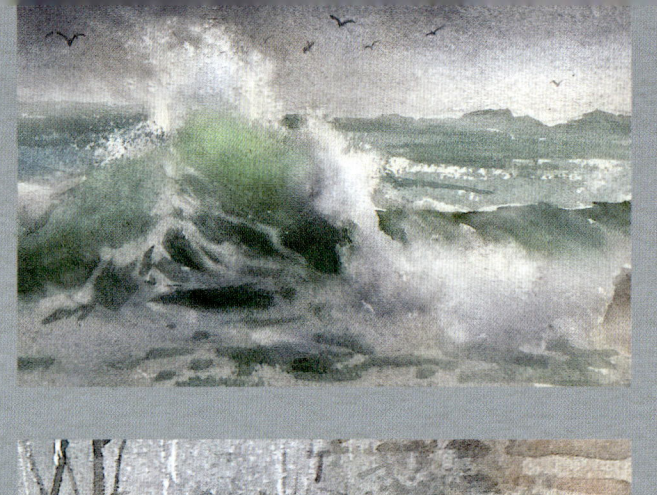

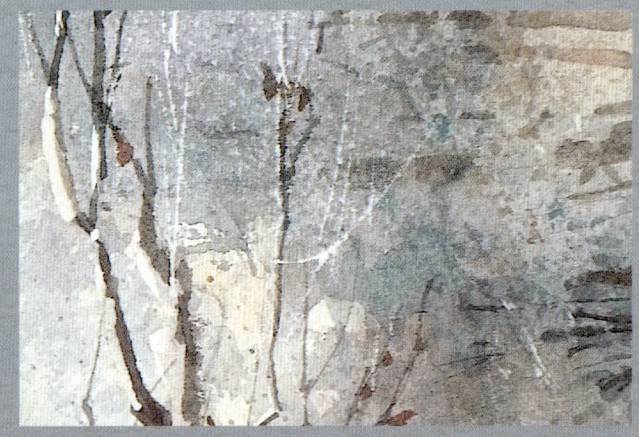

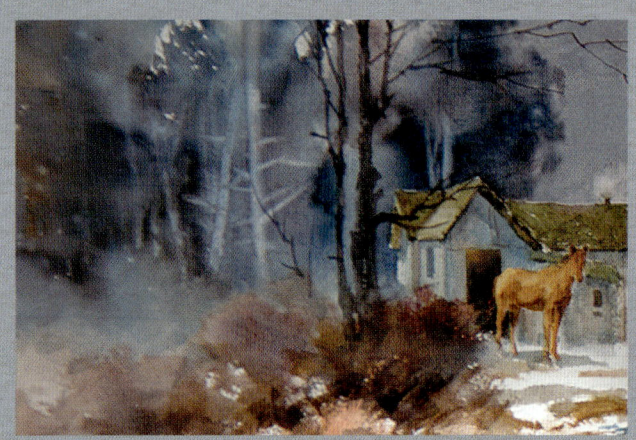

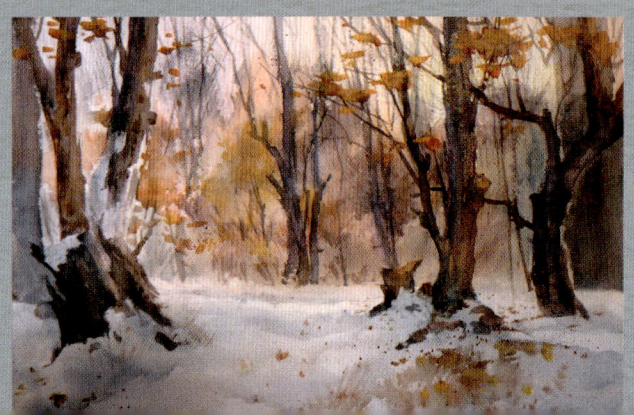

CHAPTER EIGHT:

Tricks of the Trade

This section is where you will explore techniques rarely seen in other mediums. Here, experimentation is encouraged—embrace fun, spontaneous, and even unpredictable reactions of pigment using simple tools easily found around the house. Some of these effects are especially useful for creating vignettes, adding a unique twist to your paintings that is sure to capture the attention of admirers. These playful discoveries will expand your creative toolbox and inspire new directions in your work.

Tricks of the Trade

Watercolor is a fun and show-off medium for demonstrations because, unlike other mediums, it allows for creative effects using household items and unconventional materials. On the following pages, you will find useful techniques for achieving a wide range of effects.

SCORING THE PAPER

If you want to regain the white of the paper, you can do so by scoring the paper with sharp objects and sandpaper.

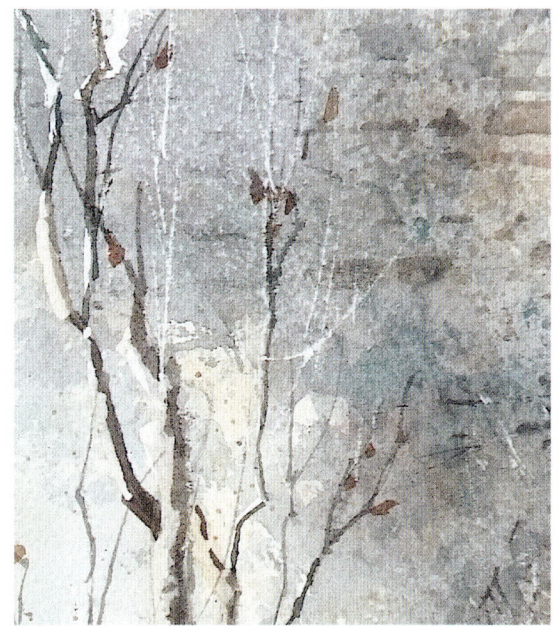

CREATING ICE CRYSTALS

To produce ice-coated branches, scrape out thin white lines using the tip of a precision knife.

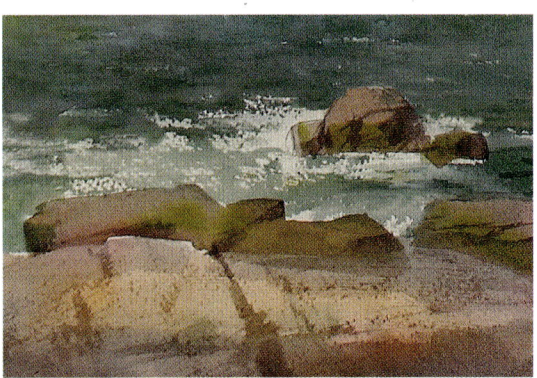

CREATING SEA SPUMES

Scrape out sea spumes using the blade of a precision knife or coarse sandpaper.

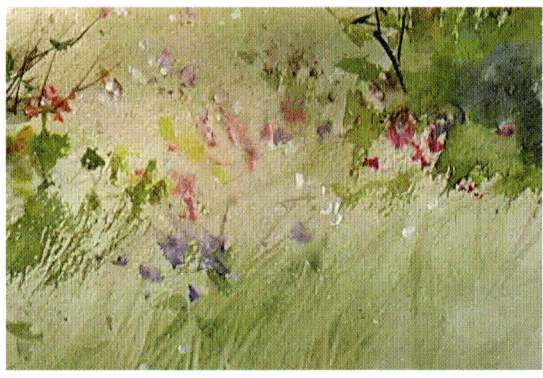

PULLING OUT GRASS BLADES

Using a jackknife, you can score the paper to pull out grass blades. Wait until the sheen is gone, and while the paper is still damp, push in the tip of the blade and lightly scrape out the paint. Clean the blade with a paper towel between strokes.

USING A CREDIT CARD
TO CREATE TEXTURE

Use a credit card or palette knife to scrape out texture on rocks and bark on trees. A credit card may be too big and cumbersome for some areas. You can cut it up into different sizes to have more control in smaller areas. This only works well on cold-pressed paper.

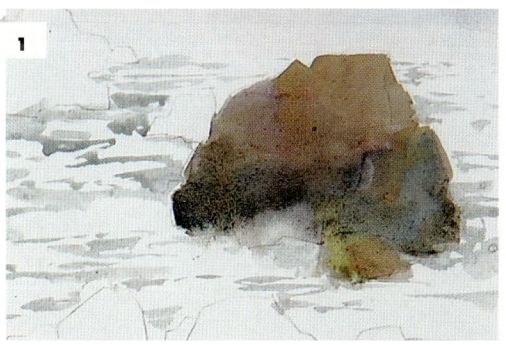

STEP 1 – DAMPENING THE PAPER

This technique must be carried out while the paper is moist but not soaked.

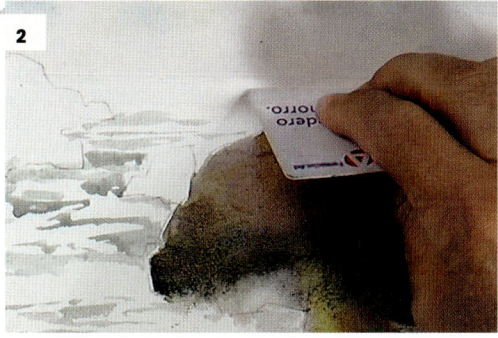

STEP 2 – USING THE CARD

Slightly bend the card for stronger support. As soon as the glisten fades, use the edge of the card to scrape in different directions, starting from beyond the contour of the shape. This adds intricate textures.

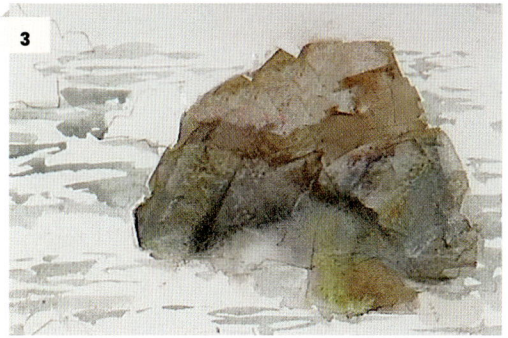

STEP 3 – SCULPTING THE FORMS

To achieve different planes, vary the pressure while scraping. After each stroke, wipe off excess paint from the card to avoid spreading runny pigment as it collects. If the paint dries before you can scrape, simply rewet the area and try again, but the results won't be as good.

USING SANDPAPER TO CREATE SHIMMERS AND WATER SPRAY

Experiment with different grades of coarseness to achieve a range of effects. Note that sandpaper will damage the surface of the paper, and you will not be able to paint on top of it.

RUBBER MASKING FLUID

Watercolor masking fluid is a liquid applied to paper to block areas from receiving paint. It dries to a rubbery, waterproof film, preserving the white of the paper for highlights or fine details. Once the painting is complete, the masking fluid can be removed using a masking fluid eraser, revealing the untouched paper underneath.

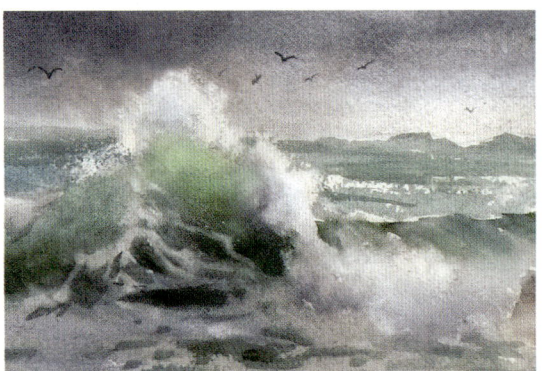

BEFORE

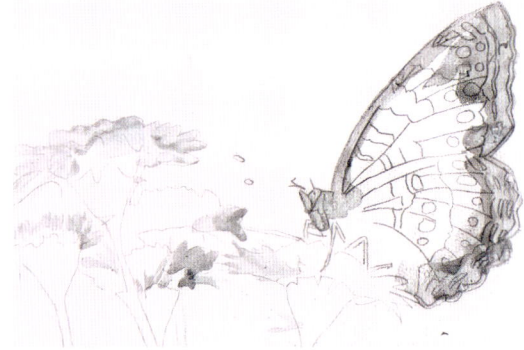

Use a tinted version of the fluid. Dip your brush in soapy water before applying masking fluid to prevent the rubber from sticking to the bristles.

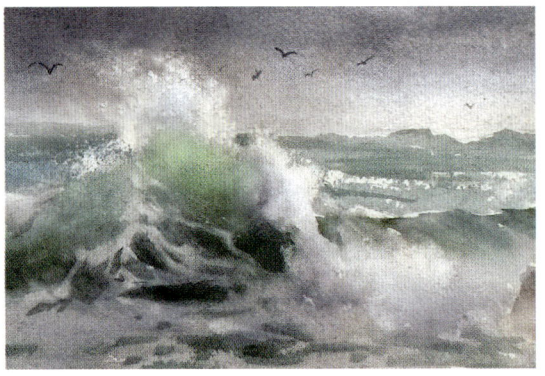

AFTER

Medium-coarse sandpaper created the fine droplets in the spray.

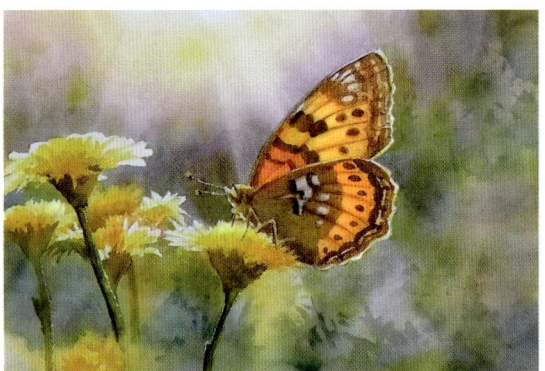

Masking fluid was applied to this painting.

BLOTTING WITH PAPER TOWEL

This very absorbent material removes quite a bit of paint while still wet. You can create interesting snow-covered bushes and cumulus clouds.

LIGHTENING VALUE WITH A THIRSTY BRUSH

Achieving the exact value when mixing paint on your palette can be challenging. If your wet paint appears too dark, use a paper towel to absorb excess water from your brush and turn it into a mop. It's not what you put on the paper; it's what you leave on. A thirsty brush can also lift out thin lines from dry paint by scrubbing gently—an effective way to suggest lighter tree branches.

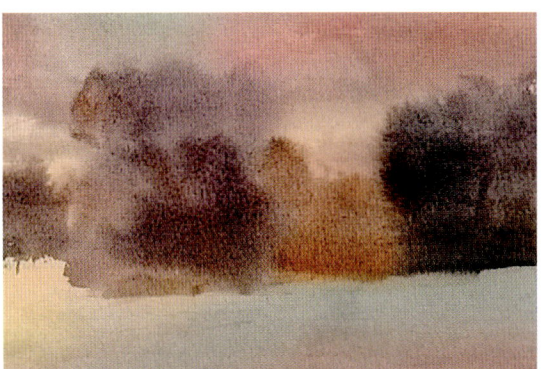

BEFORE

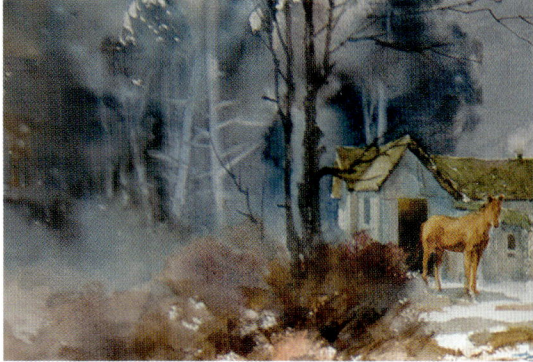

In this painting, the light-colored tree trunks were created by lifting paint with a thirsty brush while still damp. If the paint dries, rewet and scrub out.

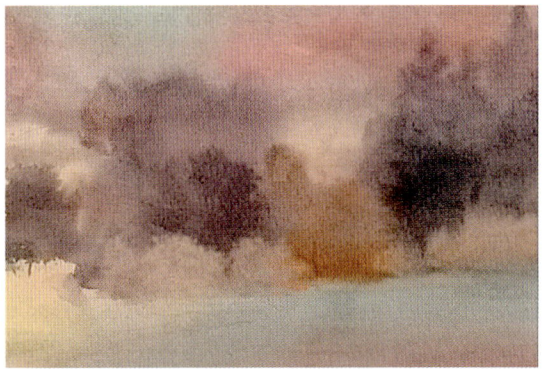

AFTER

SPLATTERING

Splattering can produce delightful unpredictable effects and is simple to apply. It is ideal for creating vignettes, leaves on the ground, footprints in snow, weeds, and flowers in fields.

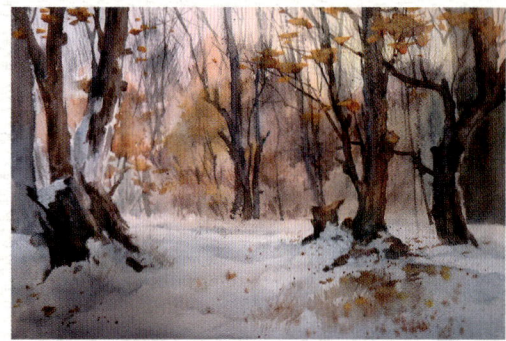

Splattered leaves on the ground, on damp paper.

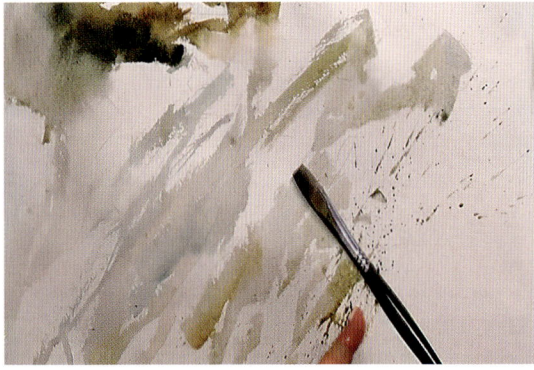

SPLATTERING TEXTURE

Tap your brush against your index finger, giving the splatter a direction by moving your hand up and down. Ensure randomness of the forms.

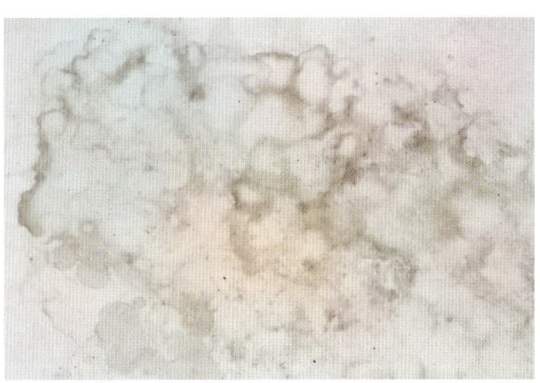

LARGER DROPLETS

While the paint still has a sheen, tap your brush with force against your index finger to send water droplets to the paper. This will separate the paint in blossoms, resulting in interesting effects.

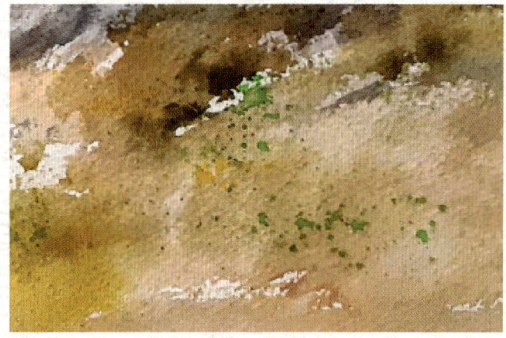

Splattered weeds on the ground.

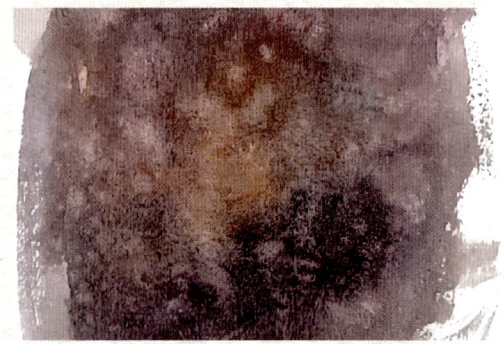

An interesting background for still lifes and portraits.

SALT

Salt crystallizes as it absorbs moisture, pushing pigment aside and leaving behind interesting blooming patterns. Timing is critical when using salt in watercolor. The paper should be damp—not soaking wet. Sprinkle the salt just before the surface loses its sheen. Experiment by sprinkling different amounts.

The effect is ideal for:

Wildflowers

Falling snow in the background

Distant butterflies

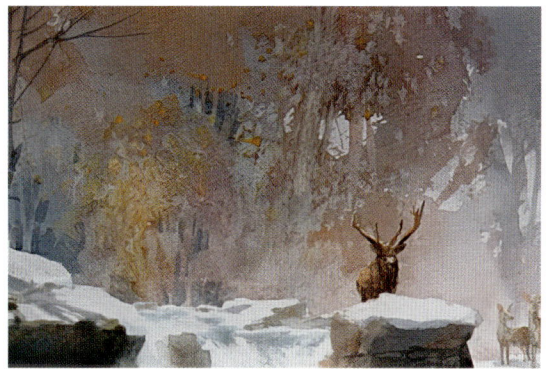

Close up of applied salt

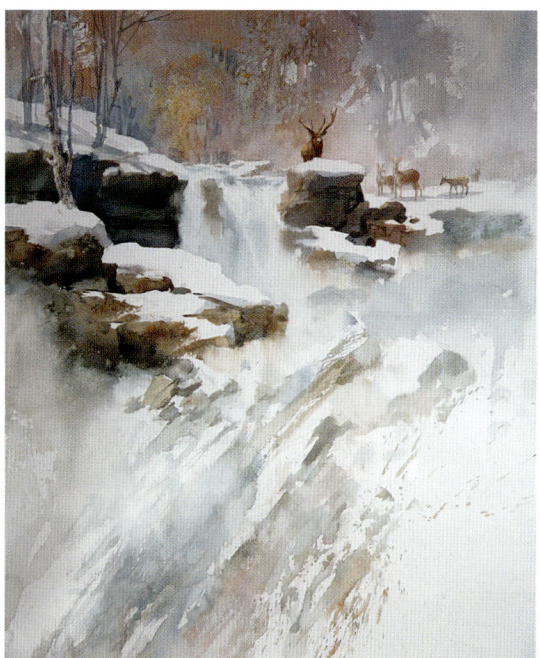

APPLYING SALT

Salt and splattering were combined to create texture in this vignette.

SPONGEWORK

Sea sponges have large crater-type holes that drop paint to form foliage clusters. They can be used to render foliage in a simple way. They also work well for winter frosted and cherry blossom trees.

FOLIAGE

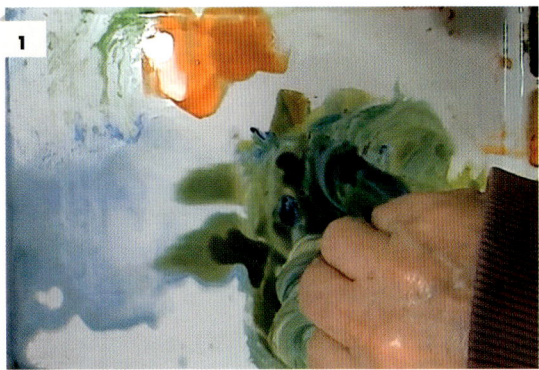

STEP 1 – PREPARING THE MIXTURE

Dip your sponge in a mixture of green that also has a bit of burnt sienna alongside for variety.

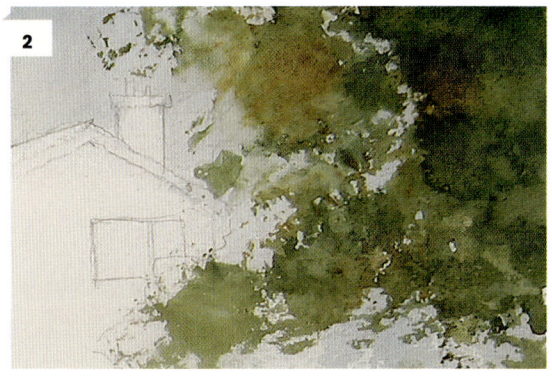

STEP 2 – CREATING HIGHLIGHTS

Stipple while squeezing and slightly releasing the sponge, allowing the holes to vary in size. If the sponge is too wet, tap it on a paper towel to remove excess moisture. Rotate the sponge in different directions to avoid a repetitive stipple effect. Indicate isolated clusters detached from the main tree.

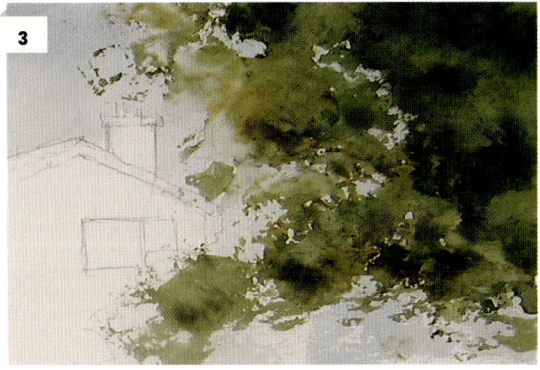

STEP 3 – ADDING THE DARKS

Repeat the same process as in Step 2 to tap in some dark areas under the highlights.

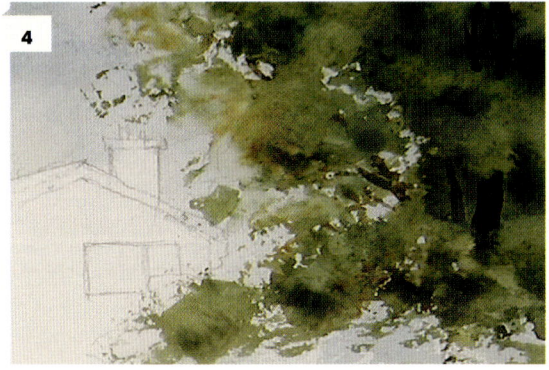

STEP 4 – ADDING BRANCHES

Place the tree trunks and branches in the dark areas. Skip the highlights.

FROSTED WINTER TREES

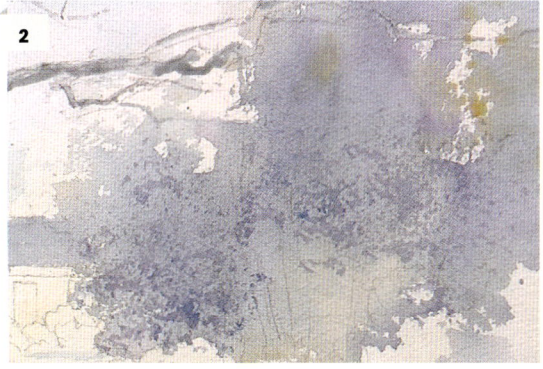

STEP 1 – CREATING HIGHLIGHTS

Paint the solid form first with a brush, leaving a few sky gaps. Add warm colors at the base to represent reflected light from the sunlit snow on the ground.

STEP 2 – STIPPLING

Stipple in the foliage indentations, avoiding equal amounts of darks and light. Apply more stippling at the bottom and gradually reduce as you approach the top for contrast. Be careful not to go too dark, as this represents snow and should maintain a light, soft appearance.

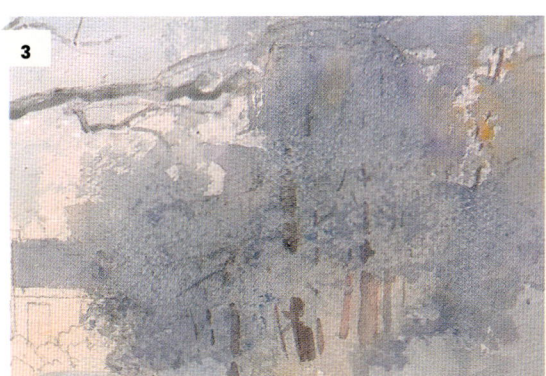

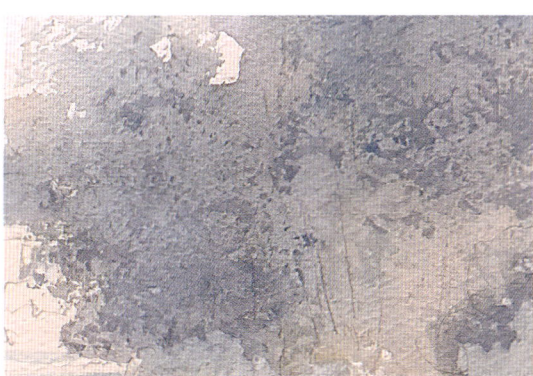

STEP 3 – ADDING BRANCHES

Add the tree trunks and branches in the darker areas of the painting.

Close-up of negative-painting the indentations.

CREATING A CRACKLED BACKGROUND

A crackled background can be more interesting than a flat one, even with variations of color. Experiment with plastic sandwich wrap, newspaper, paper towel, and bread to produce different effects

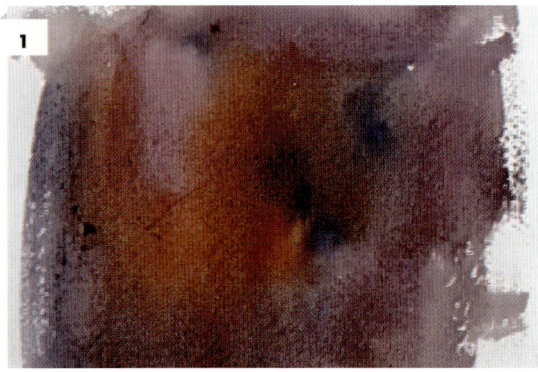

STEP 1 – LAYING A FIRST WASH

Paint the background, leaving it quite wet.

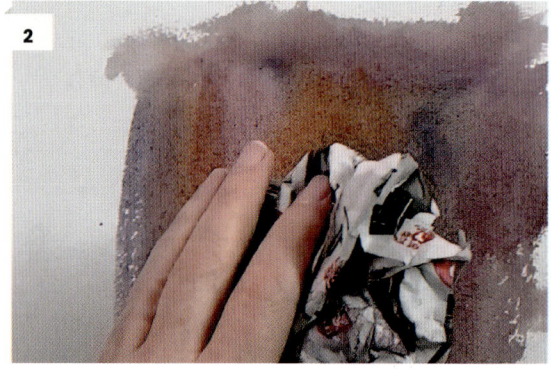

STEP 2 – CREATING TEXTURE

Dab at the wet paint using a crumpled piece of newspaper.

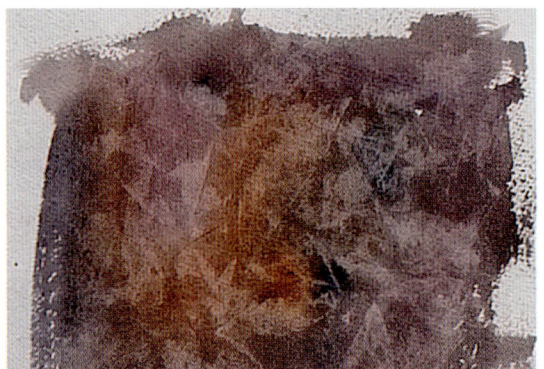

FINAL RESULT

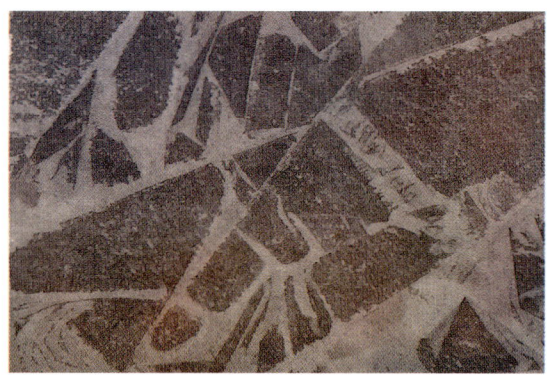

CRACKLING BACKGROUND

Explore using sandwich wrap to create this interesting background. Crumple the plastic sheet and apply while the paint is still very wet. Place a heavy book on top of it and allow the paint to dry overnight.

USING OPAQUE MEDIUMS

Opaque pastel mediums and watercolors work seamlessly together. PanPastels blend so well that their application is nearly undetectable compared to watercolor. Stick pastels can be rubbed into the paper's grooves with a finger or applied loosely for texture, such as in water foam. Gouache is an opaque version of watercolor and is very popular for adding to transparent watercolors where being a purist is too challenging.

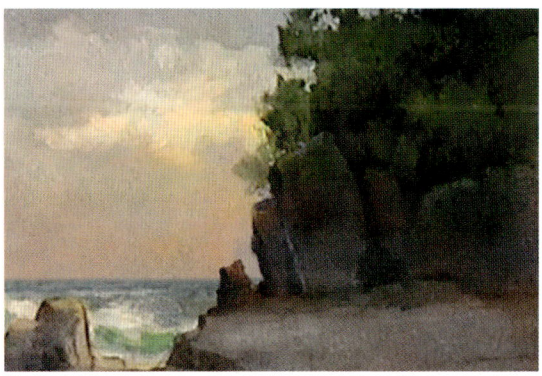

ENCHANCING COLOR: BEFORE

In this painting, the rocks are a dull monochromatic gray, typically seen in nature.

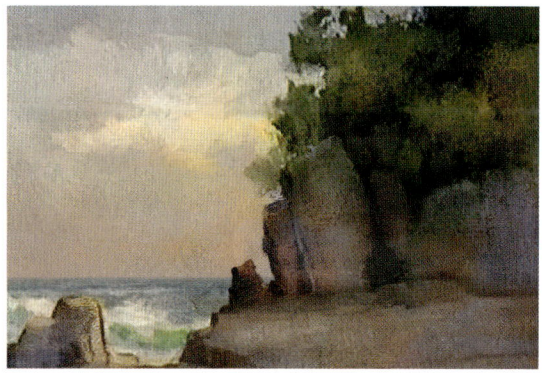

ENCHANCING COLOR: AFTER

Purple, orange, and blue were added to the rocks using pastels, to create more enhanced hues. The foliage now features warmer tones.

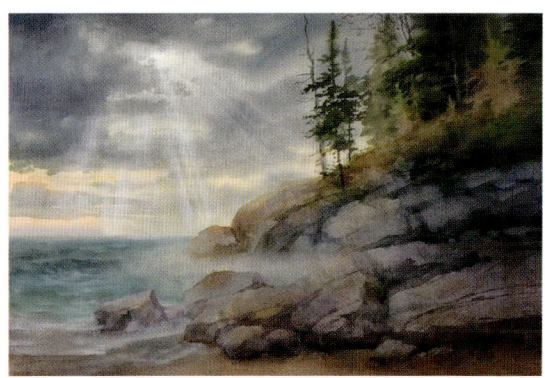

SUNBEAMS

The sunbeams were accomplished with PanPastel's titanium white. They gradually get wider the farther they are from the sun. Each ray, and the space between them, should vary in width. The sky should still be visible behind the veil of light. The beams should radiate out from the center of the sun.

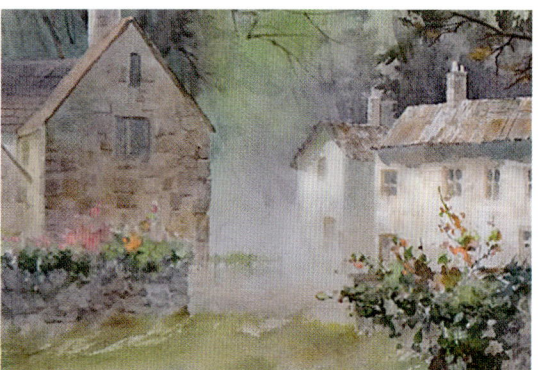

CREATING FOG

In this painting, the fog was added using white PanPastel, applied in a circular motion.

MAKING CORRECTIONS

Watercolor is notorious for being a somewhat rebellious medium. You will want to have an undo button. Watercolor paper is made from compressed cotton. Sizing is added to watercolor paper to slow down absorption, allowing the paint to sit on the surface longer. This gives artists more control over blending and layering. Contrary to all competing mediums, the pigment stains the paper, posing a challenge to remove unwanted paint. Some manufacturers use honey as a binding agent, which tends to stubbornly adhere to the paper, making it difficult to spray off and regain the white surface.

GARDEN SPRAY BOTTLE

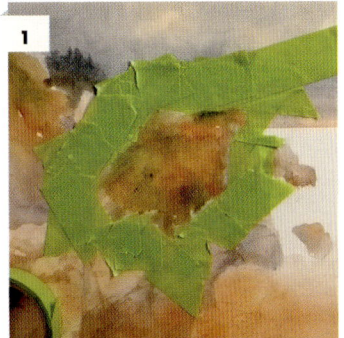

This technique can be used to remove a specific area where a defined edge is necessary. Protect the surrounding areas with painter's tape.

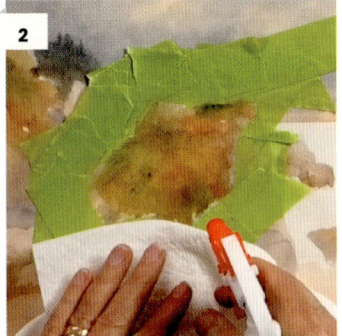

Spray off as much as you can with the jet stream of a garden water bottle. Adjust the nozzle for maximum stream.

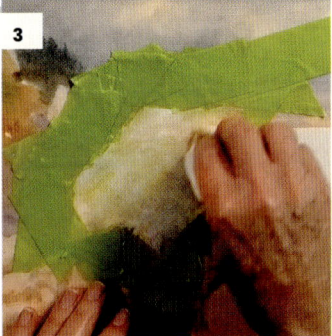

If the pigment is non-staining, extra cleaning may not be required. It's often unnecessary to fully regain the white paper if the goal is to introduce a similar color.

SPONGE ERASER

If spraying the paint with clear water fails to remove enough pigment, in order to prevent that underlayer from influencing the upcoming layer, use a magic sponge eraser. Start with a light touch increasing the pressure as necessary. But if small rolls begin to form, you're stripping cotton fibers and damaging the paper. Clear them away carefully. At this stage, some sizing will be lost, so you'll need to do a "skin craft," applying an off-white stick pastel (same color as the paper) to a fully dry surface to repair the paper. First, sweep off some of the dust to minimize pastel mixing with the watercolor. This will give you an amazingly cooperative surface to paint on again.

SANDPAPER

In case the paint is so stubborn that the sponge eraser still doesn't remove enough pigment, use fine sandpaper to gently sand the area back to white. Follow up with a stick pastel, as described in the sponge eraser caption.

BACKRUNS

Backruns, or blooming, occur when excess water unintentionally seeps into moist pigment, often due to an overly wet brush. The water pushes the pigment aside, creating a lighter, irregular shape that may seem out of place. To correct this, quickly flood more pigment to the puddle. Avoid blotting with paper towel, as this can worsen the effect. However, backruns can be a blessing rather than a curse if intentionally created for special effects in backgrounds, such as in still lifes or portraits.

FILLING IN A DRY SPOT

During the painting process, you may accidentally leave a small area of white paper exposed. Adding paint directly to this spot can cause it to bleed into the surrounding areas, darkening the existing layers unintentionally. These spots need to be darkened and blend naturally into the surrounding tones.

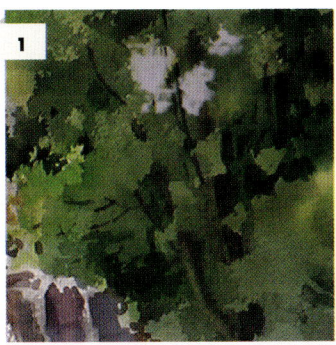

STEP 1 – PREPARING THE AREA

Wet all the green area around the white spots. Leave the bare areas bone dry. Give it two minutes for the water to seep in.

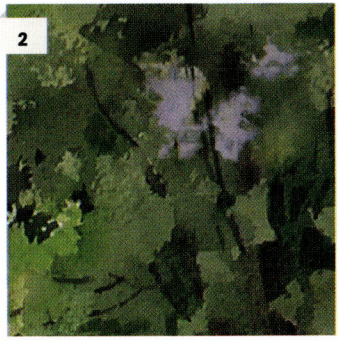

STEP 2 – FILLING IN THE SPOT

Add a darker version of the background color directly into the dry spots. Allow the rest to dilute in the green area—make sure this area is quite wet so the value doesn't darken. If necessary, use a thirsty brush to gently remove any excess violet paint from the tree foliage. The added paint should blend seamlessly, making the correction almost unnoticeable.

Glossary

Abstract shape Asymmetric shape with two distinctly different halves when split down the middle.

Accent The darkest spot, placed where no light reaches.

Atmospheric perspective When accumulated sky molecules form a veil that lightens, cools, and desaturates colors.

Background The farthest visible plane in a scene.

Backrun Excess water on a wet surface that spreads the pigment unevenly, diluting the paint in a spot.

Bleed Paint spreads on wet paper, creating soft, blurry edges.

Bloom Irregular pattern or hard edge, sometimes with a "cauliflower" aspect as a result of a backrun.

Clones Visually similar shapes.

Clusters, foliage Groups of leaves expressed in clumps.

Color The product of intermixing more than two primary hues.

Color harmony The unified sharing of a mother hue throughout a painting.

Color variegation Distinct transitional shifts of color.

Desaturate To reduce a color's intensity by adding its opposite hue (aka graying it down).

Diffused edge Subtle contour boundary with some blurry, fuzzy areas.

Discordant color A standout color not repeated elsewhere in a painting.

Dry brush A technique using streaks or grainy marks to break up paint. With a small amount of water added, used to create irregular clusters that represent foliage. Works better on rough paper.

Echo a hue/color Repeating a hue from within the painting, referring to the color wheel, to unify disconnected colors.

Edges Describes the contour of a shape. Edges can be very diffused, soft, hard, or a mixture of both (lost and found).

Focal area The most developed, attractive section that stands out in a composition.

Focal point A smaller "bull's eye" point placed within the focal area.

Foreground The horizontal section usually occupying the bottom third of a painting.

Gouache An opaque watercolor, useful for touch-ups.

Glaze A translucent layer applied over dry paint to alter its hue or darken it.

Graceful line A smooth, flowing contour resembling a rollercoaster track.

Gradient plane A gradual transition between light, dark, warm, and cool tones in all of their combinations within a plane and/or a shape.

Gray down To reduce a color's intensity by mixing in its opposite hue or white.

Hard edge A sharp, well-defined contour boundary without fuzziness.

Highlight The brightest area where light strikes a shape.

Hue The term used to identify the 12 established variations of color on the color wheel. It refers to one of the primaries—yellow, blue, red—or the mixture of only two together (not three).

Interrupted line Speed bumps to slow down or fracture an otherwise straight line.

Leading line Where contours or shapes direct the viewer's gaze to the focal area and through the painting.

Mass A group of elements combined as one unit, such as a field with rocks and a stream with similar value range. (A plane can be considered a mass.)

Melodic line An irregular, staircase-like edge without obvious repetition—for example, where rocks meet grass or water.

Mid-dark value The darkest gray tone with a discernable hue, typically assigned to vertical shapes like trees or cliffs.

Mid–light value The lightest value that reads as a gray in a black-and-white conversion. Generally assigned to skies and sunlit areas.

Mid-value A tone between mid-light and mid-dark. Colors appear the richest in this tone. Common for ground planes.

Middle ground The plane immediately beyond the foreground, typically featuring vertical elements such as trees or cliffs.

Mind's vision A conceptual reference to the viewers' imagination and participation in the scene. The mind wanders much like when reading a book.

Negative-paint To add shadows and accents by sculpting into positive shapes with a darker value.

Negative space Empty areas surrounding filled shapes, such as air gaps between branches.

Pendulum line A curving visual path that sways the viewer's gaze, often resembling cradling forms.

Periphery An area, usually along the far edges and foreground, where definition is lost; it should not compete with the focus of the center.

Plane Either the foreground, middle ground, or background of an area.

Pointer A subtle element directing attention to the focal area (grass blades or tree branches).

Positive shape Solid elements (rock shapes and tree shapes), as opposed to surrounding negative space.

Reflected light A warm glow added to the base of an object to create the gradient plane.

Rest area A dedicated section, simplified with minimal detail, that provides relief from surrounding busy areas.

Rhythm Where objects and lines subtly point in a similar direction.

Simplify To remove unnecessary details for clarity and impact, resulting in a visual poetic version.

Soft edge A blurred contour boundary where pigment spreads into wet areas. A tool used to convey recession or movement.

Splatter Random paint spots for added texture.

Spot-wet To spread clear water randomly, leaving dry areas and wet areas, resulting in a delightful contrast of edges.

Staining pigment Paint that strongly binds to the paper.

Symbol A shape that represents a literal element (a substitution, not factual realism).

Thirsty brush A damp brush used to lift paint to lighten a value.

Three-dimensional Referring to height, width, and depth; often abbreviated to 3D.

Underpainting A general, light, first glaze, preparing the surface for additional layers.

Value The relative lightness or darkness of an area in grayscale.

Variegate colors Gradual color shifts within a single shape, such as a rock transitioning from gray to orange.

Visual pace The speed at which the viewer's eye follows a contour.

Visual path A compositional element guiding viewers from the foreground to the depth.

Wet-on-wet A technique that involves applying moist paint to damp paper, allowing it to spread or bleed softly. The result is fuzzy edges.

About the Author

Since 2011, Johannes Vloothuis has taught live online art workshops with Artists Network USA (artistsnetwork.com), a premier name in fine art education and publisher of major art magazines including *Watercolor Artist*. His articles have appeared in most leading art magazines found in bookstores.

Jo has traveled extensively throughout national parks in the United States and Canada in his motorhome, completing hundreds of plein-air paintings and thousands of in-studio works. He received the top national watercolor award from the Mexican Watercolor Museum and also won a major award on faso.com, a website hosting over 75,000 artists, many of them professionals.

To find out more about Johannes: improvemypaintings.com

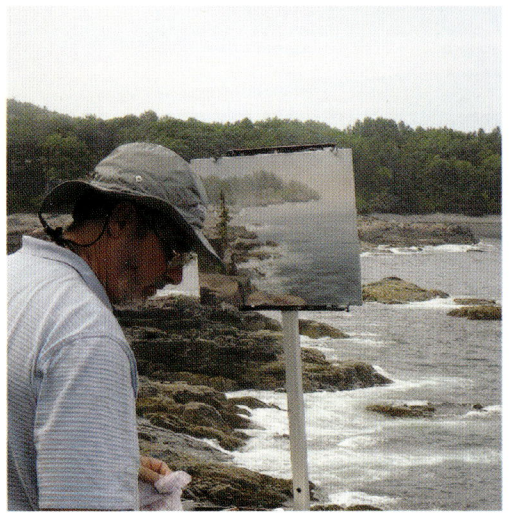

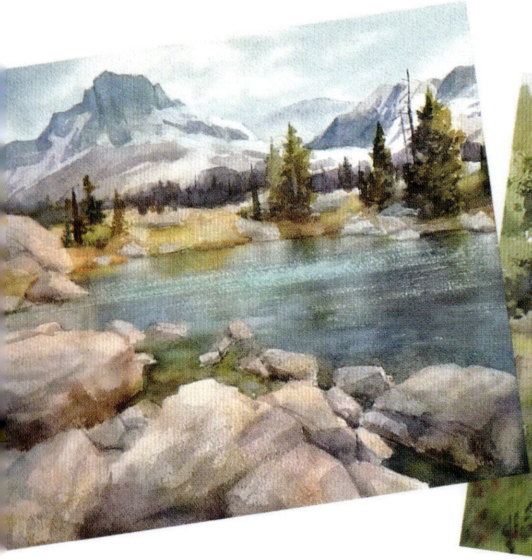

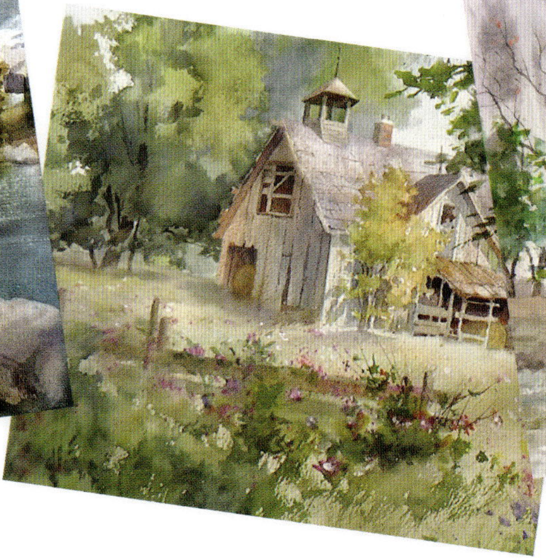

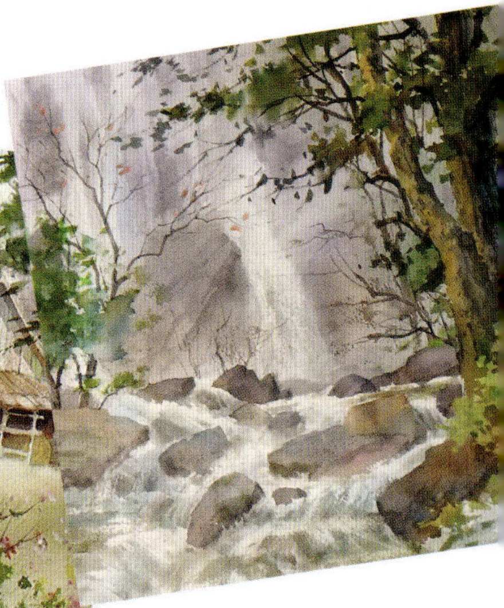

Index

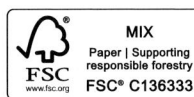

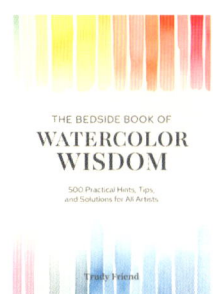
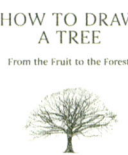
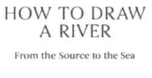
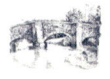
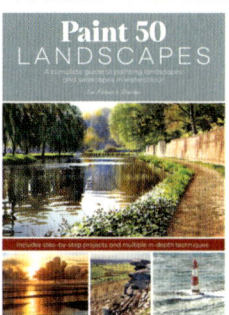

Join watercolor artist Johannes Vloothuis on an inspirational journey through the essentials of landscape painting.

With over 50 step-by-step examples, learn how to paint everything from rugged cliffs to dramatic skies, following clear visuals and practical guidance.

Discover how to create depth and realism, while picking up clever techniques for adding variety and interest to your scenes.

Whether you're a beginner or building on your skills, this guide provides the tools to bring your landscapes to life.

MORE BOOKS YOU'LL LOVE

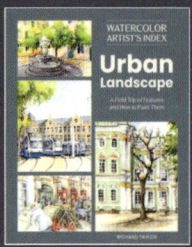

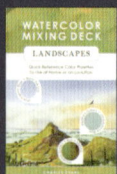

DAVID & CHARLES

ISBN-13: 9781446316191

UK £16.99
US $24.99

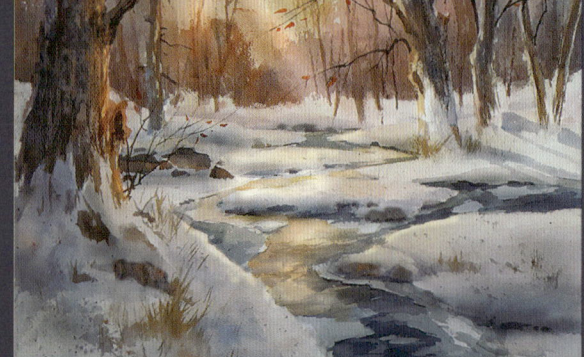

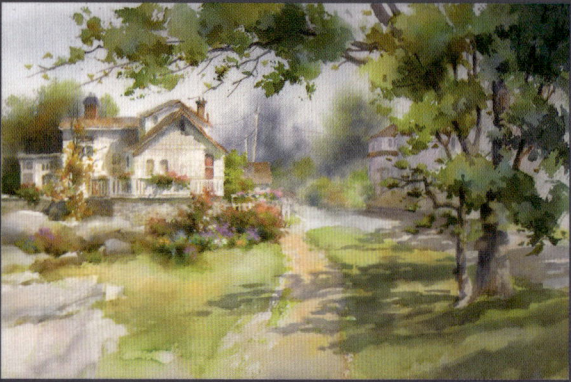

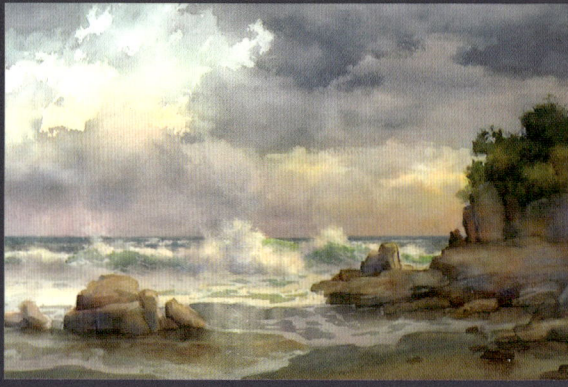

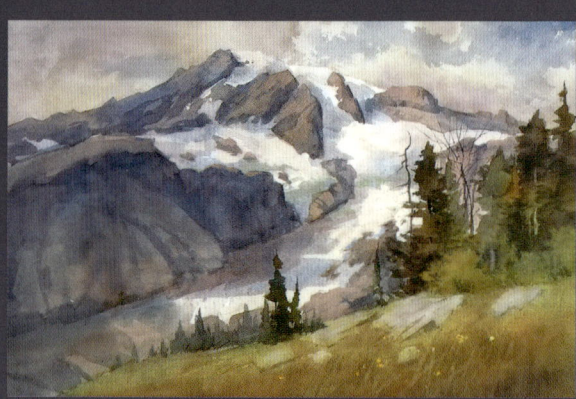